RETHEORISING STATELESSNESS

Studies in Global Justice and Human Rights
Series Editor: Thom Brooks

Immigration Justice
Peter W. Higgins

Rwanda and the Moral Obligation of Humanitarian Intervention
Joshua J. Kassner

Health Inequalities and Global Injustice
Patti Tamara Lenard and
Christine Straehle

The Morality of Peacekeeping
Daniel H. Levine

Institutions in Global Distributive Justice
Andras Miklos

Community and Human Rights
Oche Onazi

Retheorising Statelessness
Kelly Staples

www.euppublishing.com/series/sgjhr

RETHEORISING STATELESSNESS

A Background Theory of Membership in World Politics

Kelly Staples

EDINBURGH
University Press

Edinburgh University Press Ltd
22 George Square, Edinburgh EH8 9LF
www.euppublishing.com

Typeset in 11/13 Palatino Light by
Servis Filmsetting Ltd, Stockport, Cheshire, and
printed and bound in Great Britain by
CPI Group (UK) Ltd, Croydon CR0 4YY

A CIP record for this book is available from the British Library

ISBN 978 0 7486 4277 9 (hardback)
ISBN 978 0 7486 6906 6 (webready PDF)
ISBN 978 0 7486 6908 0 (epub)
ISBN 978 0 7486 6907 3 (Amazon ebook)

CONTENTS

ACKNOWLEDGEMENTS

Much of the initial research for this book was undertaken while I was a PhD student in politics at the University of Manchester, supported by a studentship from the Economic and Social Research Council (ESRC), whose support I gratefully acknowledge. Without the clarity and insight and unswerving academic, practical and emotional support of my supervisor, Véronique Pin-Fat, neither the PhD nor the book would have been finished. I have also benefitted greatly in the last eight years from the support of friends and colleagues at Manchester, Kingston University and the University of Leicester. In particular, I would like to thank John Davis and Mike Roberts for their encouragement and support and Terry Sullivan for his kindness and wise words. Laura Brace and Mark Phythian also deserve special mention for their support for me and for this project, as does Ricardo Blaug, who first interested me in political theory a decade ago.

Parts of the argument here have been subjected to the critical scrutiny of anonymous peer reviewers for *Millennium: Journal of International Studies* and *Contemporary Political Theory* and by participants in forums, including the political theory forum at the University of Westminster, the 2008 Workshops in Political Theory in Manchester and the 2006 European Consortium for Political Research (ECPR) joint sessions of workshops in Nicosia. Gideon Calder was helpful as a sounding board for my ideas about Rorty, while Brad Blitz encouraged me in my quest to take a theoretical look at statelessness. Two anonymous reviewers for Edinburgh University Press and Nicola Ramsey, Senior Commissioning Editor for the Press, also deserve thanks for their work in support of this project, as does the series editor, Thom Brooks. Although it might go without saying, I should acknowledge that all remaining flaws in the book are my own.

This book was written and researched at homes and libraries in Leeds, London, Manchester and Sheffield, with the support of my friends and family. Special mention is reserved for Jim Chappelow. The book is dedicated to him and to our unborn son or daughter, whose imminent arrival has been both a source of happiness and a valuable motivation!

INTRODUCTION

There are thought to be around 12 million stateless persons – that is, at its most basic, persons not considered as nationals by any state in the world – and this 'is a cautious estimate based on a conservative and legalistic understanding of statelessness' (Equal Rights Trust 2010: 3). Little – even of their origin or place of residence – is known about at least half of these stateless persons, given that only 'a minority of countries have procedures in place for the identification, registration and documentation of stateless persons, which facilitates gathering precise data' (UNHCR 2010: 29). The office of the United Nations High Commissioner for Refugees, mandated with the identification, protection and prevention of statelessness, has information on approximately 6.6 million stateless persons in sixty-one countries of the overall total of approximately 12 million (UNHCR 2010: 7). Of these, just under 209,000 were being assisted by UNHCR at the end of 2009 (Ibid. Table 3). When broken down by region, the UNHCR data shows that statelessness is a problem which affects all parts of the world. Nevertheless, South-East Asia, with some 4.3 million identified stateless persons (UNHCR 2011: 113), is very disproportionately affected. Slowly but surely, interest in statelessness is growing among governments, international agencies and NGOs. Between 2010 and 2011, the budget for UNHCR's Global Statelessness programme was increased from 38.5 million US dollars to 63 million US dollars (UNHCR 2011a: 45).

Statelessness today 'disproportionately affects racial and ethnic minorities' (Open Society Justice Initiative 2004: 4), who have been 'the principal victims' (Ibid. p. 16). Most so-called *de facto* stateless persons (those without an effective nationality) are 'the victims of state repression [. . . and] state discrimination' (Weissbrodt and Collins 2006: 263). For reasons that will soon become clear, I avoid

1

using categories that rest on strong foundational assumptions about nationality in this book. The often-used categories of '*de jure*' and '*de facto*' stateless persons are therefore addressed only where their critical examination helps in developing the book's theories of membership and statelessness.

The book, therefore, also avoids using terms like 'nationality', which, though contested, have very precise legal meanings. I tend to agree with one of the earliest experts on statelessness, that 'no accurate definition of nationality can be given' (Weis 1944: 3), and yet, it is a term which carries with it much baggage. Neither will the phrase 'citizenship' do, as, for the political theorist in particular, this calls to mind discourses of rights, duties and identity, which would obscure, rather than clarify, one of the principal aims of this book – namely, to explore the 'system of mutual recognition within which individuality comes to be of value' (Frost 1996: 141) in world politics today. By referring throughout to 'membership', rather than nationality or citizenship, I aim merely to offer one possible interpretation of the relationship between inclusion and exclusion and, hence, the way that individuality is constituted and constrained within international relations. The focus is international, partly because of the growth, within what is now called 'International Political Theory', of discussions about how we might understand the political and social mediation of the relationship between the individual and the world. A further reason is the extent to which 'statelessness is a global phenomenon with causes that lie both outside the state and within it' (Blitz and Lynch 2009: 95). One of the anticipated contributions of this book is an improvement in our understanding of the individual implications of the inter-state relationships which are embodied in today's laws, practices and institutions. The book, therefore, explores Weis's claim that 'membership of a certain State can only have a meaning if the existence of other States is presupposed' (Weis 1944: 4).

Given the disproportionate impact on national minorities, the book also focuses, in particular, on collective statelessness, exploring, at the same time, the individual implications of collective denials of membership. As a work of international political theory, the book is concerned, therefore, with the relationship between statelessness and 'social and political tensions', which often involve situations where a 'state has not yet learned to live with or tolerate its minorities' (UNHCR 1995: 67):

> Many minorities live in a precarious legal situation because, even though they may be entitled under law to citizenship in the State in which they live, they are often denied or deprived of that right and may in fact exist in a situation of statelessness. While many conditions give rise to the creation of statelessness, including protracted refugee situations and State succession, most stateless persons today are members of minority groups. (UN Human Rights Council 2008, cited by Equal Rights Trust 2010: 28)

Without pre-empting the discussion of membership, its international dimensions and individual implications, it is still worth noting that statelessness is problematic in part because possessing a nationality 'is essential for full participation in society and a prerequisite for the enjoyment of the full range of human rights' (UNHCR 2011b). However, the particular risks of being stateless do not, in and of themselves, explain why statelessness is so central to this book. The book looks at statelessness for two related reasons: first, because it is an obvious situation of exclusion and vulnerability; and second, because it has interesting implications for theorising world politics. The continued existence of statelessness seems to be unambiguous evidence of the 'reassertion of state sovereignty at the expense of human rights and the protection of human dignity' (Blitz and Lynch 2009: 100). Statelessness therefore presents the theorist of international politics with a 'hard case' for at least two reasons. First, statelessness has long been recognised (insofar as it has been theorised) as constituted by the basic tension between sovereignty norms and human rights norms. Second, enormous difficulties have been encountered in attempts to establish and extend the international protection of stateless persons. While international theorists have engaged consistently with questions of membership, rights and protection, there has been a tendency to refer only briefly to their limits in statelessness and also to side-step consistent and thorough-going ethical consideration of those limits. This book bridges existing empirical and legal accounts of statelessness and existing theoretical accounts of membership, rights and protection. An adequate theory of statelessness will, in the end, have to clarify its relationship to the wider discourse of international political theory that addresses the supposed tension between sovereignty and human rights and address the practical implications for the recognition of those who are stateless today.

I will begin here by describing in broad strokes the political conditions of statelessness, showing 'why statelessness?' for a theory of
membership in world politics. At an obvious level, most can agree that
a theory of membership in world politics will be limited to the extent
that it continues to exclude any (or, at least, any sizeable) number of
people (Walzer 1986: 231). The goal of most international theory is
to challenge unjustifiable exclusions that negatively affect individual
persons. There has, nevertheless (and, perhaps, surprisingly), been
relatively little direct attention to statelessness within the emerging
field of international political theory. This is a shame, both for stateless persons and their advocates and for the comprehensiveness of the
debates as a whole. It also means that I must start with what is still
the best account of the inextricable and tense relationship between
statelessness, sovereignty and human rights, namely, Hannah Arendt's
account of 'The Decline of the Nation-State and the End of the Rights
of Man' (1973). In it, she writes:

> The conception of human rights, based upon the assumed exist-
> ence of a human being as such, broke down at the very moment
> when those who professed to believe in it were for the first time
> confronted with people who had indeed lost all other qualities
> and specific relationships – except that they were still human. The
> world found nothing sacred in the abstract nakedness of being
> human. And in view of political conditions, it is hard to say how
> the concepts of man upon which human rights are based – that
> he is created in the image of God (in the American formula), or
> that he is the representative of mankind, or that he harbors within
> himself the sacred demands of natural law (in the French formula)
> – could have helped to find a solution to the problem. (Arendt
> 1973: 299–300)

Here, Arendt famously demonstrates the underlying difficulties of the
attempt to reconcile meaningful individual rights with a state system
premised on sovereignty, showing that individual status derives from
a place in the world. Indeed, there have historically been very few
exceptions. Brown points us to pirates and diplomats as the two major
categories of person recognised historically 'as legal personalities in
their own right' (Brown 2002: 115). While diplomats 'are representative of their state, pirates are deemed to have no state' (Ibid. p. 115),

and yet, as Arendt relates, it has proved extraordinarily difficult to recognise pirates and others with no state. A key task of this book is to explore the continuing difficulties of recognising people as persons in their own right and the related challenges of creating recognisable legal identities for those without a state. As Arendt had it, being stateless deprives individuals 'not only of protection, but also of all clearly established, officially recognized identity' (Arendt 1973: 287). Indeed, as the book will demonstrate quite clearly, what we call statelessness 'strips the citizen of his status in the national and international political community' (United States Supreme Court 1958: 101).

Arendt's theory is valuable in setting out a critique of the supposedly immediate value of the so-called 'rights of man'. She shows just how problematic it is to maintain that these are (or should be) independent of human plurality; 'valid and real even if only a single human being existed on earth' (Arendt 1973: 297–8). Plurality is not only a reality, but also inextricable from our identities as individuals. Following in Arendt's pessimistic footsteps, Giorgio Agamben has famously posited the conception of 'bare life', in which power is 'confronted only by pure life without any means of mediation' (Agamben 1998: 171). In this book, I want to argue that there is theoretical and practical potential for a more guardedly optimistic political response to statelessness. To theorists like Honneth, 'the most fundamental sort of personal degradation' (Honneth 1996: 132) is not the lack of political rights, but the negation of self-confidence, which is the ordinary result of an absence of love. Close personal relationships can be vital sources of confidence and esteem, with both recognition theories and empirical research suggesting that a significant degree of confidence and esteem are generally necessary to sustain and nurture 'a political identity of struggle and opposition' (Forst 2007: 222). Some evidence of relational subjectivity seems possible in the absence of the mediation of political institutions, and it would seem that Agamben and his followers can rightly be seen to conflate legal status and subjectivity (Malkki 1996: 358), with unnecessarily bleak consequences for our understanding of both membership and statelessness.

Nothing in the preceding argument is intended to undermine the clear importance of the denial of rights-respect, which does typically bring with it 'a loss of [. . .] the ability to relate to oneself as a legally equal interaction partner with all fellow humans' (Honneth 1996: 134). These difficulties are compounded by the displacement, often characteristic of statelessness, which tends to break down networks of 'voluntary exchange and mutual support' (Smith 2004: 43). In the United Kingdom, it has been well-noted that the government's policy of enforced dispersal of asylum seekers not only took away their freedom to choose where they settled, but also removed them 'from kinship and other social networks as well as community organizations that are known to be crucial in the early stages of settlement' (Bloch and Schuster 2005: 493). Similarly, the treatment of stateless persons negates not only their political and legal status, but also tests to the limit their self-confidence and self-esteem. Again, Arendt's work is instructive here. The stateless person is no doubt 'left with those qualities which usually become articulate only in the sphere of private life [. . . and] can be adequately dealt with only by the unpredictable hazards of friendship and sympathy, or by the great and incalculable grace of love' (Arendt 1973: 301). While this situation seems ethically intolerable, it does not imply that we yield to the intent of those who denationalise and, hence, exclude the stateless. It is almost impossible to overestimate the present importance of state membership. It is also highly undesirable to overestimate the minor benefits that stateless persons might derive from family and friendship networks. Nevertheless, as theorists such as Bhabha (2002), Douzinas (2007), Malkki (1996) and Rancière (2004) remind us, it is our task to identify and extend the language and possibility of contestation. To too quickly accept the stateless as 'bare life' is to succumb to the unending logic of sovereign exception, to the 'ontological trap' (Rancière 2004: 302) which has long inhibited theoretical progress.

This book strives throughout to avoid the tempting, but self-defeating conclusion that people are not people if they are excluded from the wide-ranging benefits of belonging to some or other state. It is an attempt to reject the claim that the stateless are necessarily 'denied the fundamental human capacity to act' (Krause 2008: 335). As such, it is to be read alongside other works which reclaim the 'signifier of the human', using it to dismiss the supposed 'difference between those who are qualified to participate in politics and those who are not' (Schaap 2011: 3). On this understanding, the term human is 'the opening of an interval for political subjectivization' (Rancière 2004: 304).

The book acknowledges the continuing impact that states have on the relationship between the universal and the particular (Brown 2002: 245), that is, between 'humanity' and sovereignty. Indeed, it argues that this apparent opposition is today contingent on states and the state system. It also recognises, and takes as a starting point, the persistent vulnerabilities of those on the outside of the state-based relationships, which sustain the contingent antagonism between 'human' and citizen. Using theory to rethink the relationship between universal and particular, between 'human' and citizen, this book outlines a space in which we might come to recognise the depoliticised, but already human, stateless person.

As we will see, it is not as easy as pointing to the way in which 'the major international human rights instruments [. . .] erode the importance' of citizenship, 'in the interest of doing away altogether with boundaries between privileged and non-privileged' (Cahn 2002, cited by Weissbrodt and Collins 2006: 249). The continuing existence and deprivation of statelessness demonstrates the continuing importance of being recognised as a member. We therefore encounter the paradox that 'while international human rights law enshrines a right to nationality, that right can only be provided through an exercise of state sovereignty' (Equal Rights Trust 2010: 31). This tension is explored in significant depth in the book as a whole. Part of the overall finding is that human rights discourse is limited by its need to hold on to the fiction that the importance of citizenship (or membership) has been eroded. The reliance of the idea of human rights on this assumption inevitably constrains its ability to constructively theorise the value of membership. On the other hand, assuming too much about the value of membership can significantly undermine the scope for theorising its individual implications. This apparent impasse is the starting point of Chapter 1, which also explores the practical tension between the scope and limits of membership, that is, between the value of membership and the vulnerability of statelessness. Both are constituted in clear ways by existing practices of recognition. The task of the theorist, as I see it, is to try, as far as is possible, to avoid reproducing the kind of exclusions which currently affect the world's 12 million stateless persons.

Chapter 1 outlines the broad approach taken in the book as a whole. This approach is influenced by the constitutive theory of Mervyn Frost, with its focus on the 'system of mutual recognition within which individuality comes to be of value' (Frost 1996: 141). While there are key areas of disagreement between my approach and his, I share his interest in making 'explicit the moral dimension that is already implicit in the simultaneous acceptance of the state and sovereignty norms [. . .]

on the one hand, and the rights-related norms on the other hand' (Ibid. p. 141). The chapter aims to explore the relationship between inclusion and exclusion in world politics by highlighting the connection between the value of membership and the vulnerability of statelessness. It sets out the beginnings of my argument that there is no 'settled' (Ibid. p. 106) moral dimension implicit in the practices which constitute individuality today, as well as my claim that it is nevertheless possible to critically theorise these practices and narratives.

Chapter 2 focuses on the political theory of Michael Walzer. It addresses the way that he conceives of the relationship between difference and universality, the ethical implications which he thinks follows and the overall contribution of his theory for understanding membership in world politics today. It argues, in the end, that Walzer's theory overestimates the potential for reconciling the state with the demands of universality. The chapter also shows how the underlying assumptions of Walzer's theory prevent him from fully grasping the extent to which membership is already constituted by international meanings. I argue that these meanings can be used as a basis for constructing encounters between members and 'strangers' which challenge local dynamics of exclusion and might help us reconceive of the ethics of denials of membership.

Chapter 3 considers the scope of Richard Rorty's arguments about the inclusive potential of what I have called 'the kindness of strangers'. It finds that what Cochran has called Rorty's 'quasi-foundationalism' can be helpful for thinking about membership in a way which avoids the tensions which often plague attempts to theorise it (Cochran 1999: 170). Its primary advantages are its flexibility and rigorous acknowledgement of fallibility. I argue, in this chapter, that, even so, Rorty's work is hampered by its inability to engage with the actual relationships which constitute and constrain personhood in today's world. In particular, the chapter points to the wider implications of the untheorised conditions of Rorty's liberalism. It argues, in the end, that Rorty is insufficiently attentive to the relationship between the value of membership and the vulnerability of exclusion.

Having argued that Walzer's theory is constrained by his implicit commitment to the state and that Rorty's theory is limited by his unwillingness to engage with its political conditions, I argue, in Chapter 4, that O'Neill's work has real potential for critical, constructive engagement with the institutions on which individuality is contingent today. O'Neill strives not to begin with any fixed assumptions about the scope of ethical justification; neither community (as Walzer has it), nor vocabulary (as Rorty has it) are held to limit our ability to communicate with strangers and, hence, to address the relationship between inclusion and exclusion. Indeed, O'Neill argues that we might be required to address others. I argue that we have no grounds for articulating such a strong requirement. Even so, I argue, in this chapter, that communicability is a plausible goal for the discussion of membership in the light of its international dimensions, outlined in Chapter 5.

Chapter 5 continues to develop my interest in the individual implications of existing practices of recognition, focusing in particular on the international dimensions which might facilitate new encounters and justifications. The relationship between recognition and individual personality is mediated by domestic and international meanings and practices. Chapter 5 focuses on a few aspects of the latter, including the mutual interest of states in exclusion and in the regulation of the inter-state movement of persons. It aims to show how this and other state-based relations of recognition both constitute and constrain vital attributes of individuality and their recognition by relevant actors. I argue, on that basis, that there are more-or-less universal implications of international practices of recognition, although these are not universally distributed. International society, therefore, has its own inclusionary and exclusionary effects. This lesson challenges the often-held assumption that international recognition is necessarily a mitigating factor in the exclusions sustained by the plurality of the state system. The often harmful impact of international practices on individual lives is demonstrated by Chapters 6 and 7, which explore two case studies of statelessness.

Chapters 6 and 7 offer brief critical overviews of statelessness in the context of the Eastern Democratic Republic of Congo and Burma.[1] Minority Rights Group International ranks these countries 7th and 5th, respectively, in its 2011 report on peoples under threat (Lattimer 2011: 234). Both countries are dangerous for minorities, and the chapters explore the domestic dynamics which constitute and constrain individual and minority recognition. And yet, as the earlier chapters will have demonstrated, it is equally important to explore the individual implications of international practices. Chapters 6 and 7 therefore draw out the practical problems which result from attempts to assert individual status without paying proper attention to the practices which sustain recognition. They show that it is probably misguided to attempt to determine where excluded minorities and individuals 'in fact' belong. On that basis, I argue that it is worth recognising statelessness for what it is, rather than rushing to invalidate it. Indeed, the long-standing tendency to ignore statelessness has been incredibly problematic in theory and in practice, as the book as a whole demonstrates.

In the concluding chapter of the book, I set out my approach to theorising statelessness. I argue that statelessness must be understood in the context of an international framework, which is often constitutive of injury. Today, 'the international machinery for the enactment and enforcement of universal rules' is more developed than it was in the early days of attention to statelessness, and yet, these developments have not resolved the crisis of nationality, as it was hoped they might (Weis 1944: 26). One implication of this finding is the need for those who interact with stateless persons to consider much more carefully the individual implications of international recognition. Statelessness has long been under-theorised. The objective of this book as a whole is to retheorise statelessness, bearing in mind Weis' claim that 'optimum suggestions are not likely to lead to practical results' and that we can therefore 'put forward only such minimum solutions as appear realisable under existing conditions' (Weis 1944: 22). A secondary task of the book, then, is to show how we might combine a degree of pragmatism with a meaningful and critical approach to the contemporary exclusions of statelessness.

Note

1 Following the usage of many, including the United Kingdom and NGOs such as Human Rights Watch, I refer to this country as Burma throughout the book, in spite of a name-change to Myanmar by the incumbent regime in 1989.

Chapter 1

MEMBERSHIP IN WORLD POLITICS

This chapter engages with the debate in political and international theory around the ostensible tension between citizenship rights and human rights, offering a contribution to understanding the relationship between self-determination, sovereignty and individual personality. The overall argument of the chapter is comprised of three main points, addressed in separate sections. First, I show that when it comes to theory, this 'tension' is, in some ways, less acute than has often been assumed. Second, I show that there is, nevertheless, a substantive practical tension. While the relationship between individuality and the state system is mutually constitutive, states nevertheless play a powerful role in mediating individual recognition. An understanding of this role is vital to any theoretical response to statelessness. The final part of the chapter sets out the basic framework for my response to statelessness and, hence, to the 'tension' between sovereignty and human rights. Key here is the assumption that we can conclude neither that the state or state system is 'fundamentally ethical' (Cochran 1999: 85), nor that they are 'essentially' unethical or inherently contradictory. It follows that there are insufficient grounds either to rationalise or deconstruct the state and its role in world politics. I will argue instead that a realistic goal for theory is to explore the roles that existing institutions and norms seem to play in enhancing recognition and to better understand the limits of those functions so that the injuries which result might be mitigated.

I CITIZENSHIP AND HUMAN RIGHTS: AN ESSENTIAL TENSION?

The painful realities of statelessness have often been seen as symptomatic of a basic tension between self-determination, sovereignty and citizenship, on the one hand, and individual human rights on the other. In a famous treatise on 'the end of the rights of man' (Arendt 1973), Hannah Arendt argued persuasively that the emergence of stateless-ness represented the victory of the nation over the promised equality of the modern state (Ibid. p. 275). The union of nation and state served also, in her view, to cast the stateless into a 'peculiar state of nature', which showed the hollowness of conceptions of the 'rights of man' (Ibid. pp. 299–302). This alleged tension between the particular and the universal is, furthermore, a central concern of international political theory. In recent years, significant advances in our understanding of this relationship have been made. This chapter deals, first, with post-Arendtian developments in the theory of the politics of human rights and then with the insights of 'International Political Theory' into the so-called communitarian/cosmopolitan debate. It argues that these developments, taken together, are vital to a more adequate theory of membership and, hence, of statelessness.

Most people with any knowledge of statelessness, or of political theory, will be familiar with Arendt's ground-breaking analysis of the weaknesses inherent in the theory and practice of human rights. For those who are not, and as a reminder, I will briefly outline her key claims here. In 'The Decline of the Nation-State and the End of the Rights of Man' (1973), Arendt accounts for the exclusionary effects of the wider implementation of the ideal of self-determination. The idea of the nation-state conflated nation and law, with the consequence that the protections of law became increasingly unequal, dependent on the distinction between citizens and aliens and between majority and minority. In the twentieth century, national minorities often faced exclusion from the protections of law, on the basis of their difference from the majority, that is, the nation. Arendt was, therefore, among the first to clearly articulate the paradox of self-determination and sovereignty, namely, the resulting discrimination and exclusion. Her experience of (and insight into) statelessness, furthermore, led her to chilling conclusions about the dark side of the nation-state. The dena-tionalisation and expulsion of, henceforth, stateless peoples created a sub-stratum of humanity. No other government proved willing to offer refuge (nor even countenance the presence of) stateless exiles, who 'threatened to increase their numbers indefinitely' (Ibid. p. 282). For to do otherwise, would likely have encouraged other nation-states to expel non-national minorities, which might, in turn, 'lead to the use of their country as a dumping-ground for the expelled refugees of the entire world' (Rubinstein 1936: 724). In the absence of a supra-state authority, self-determination and sovereignty were tied inextricably with exclusion. Statelessness was thus effectively equivalent to 'the total destruction of the individual's status in organized society' (United States Supreme Court 1958: 101). And yet, surely such persons would – at least – be able to claim those rights which they possessed, simply by virtue of being human. Perhaps the most piercing and far-reaching observation Arendt made was in respect of the hollow promise of the so-called 'rights of man'. While social contract theory attended to the value of the sovereign nation-state, Arendt understood that the complete organisation of humanity (Arendt 1973: 297) into a plurality of sovereign states necessarily diminished the promise of non-national forms of protection:

> When, as in the case of the minorities, an international body abrogated to itself a non-governmental authority, its failure was apparent even before its measures were fully realized; not only were the governments more or less opposed to this encroachment on their sovereignty, but the concerned nationalities themselves did not recognize a non-national guarantee. (Ibid. p. 292)

Arendt therefore traces a modern paradox: while modernity has exalted the idea of 'the rights of man', the development of the modern state has tended to undermine the idea's promise. For while such rights should be 'independent of human plurality' (Ibid. p. 298), it was clear in reality that 'a man who is nothing but a man has lost the very qualities which make it possible for other people to treat him as a fellow man' (Ibid. p. 300).

Even the most cursory survey of statelessness in the twenty-first century vindicates Arendt's analysis of the tension between the modern nation-state and the unmediated, universal protections promised in the rights of man and, later, by human rights. Chapter 5 picks this thread back up, demonstrating the regrettable reality that the aspirational universal right to 'recognition everywhere as a person before the law' (United Nations 1949: Article 6) is substantially thwarted by a range of recognition practices. Nevertheless, the present work is a constructive work. It seeks not only to understand the limits of membership and recognition, but also to theorise the potential for their expansion. The basic framework in which this effort is situated still requires elaboration. The first step in this task is to assess the importance of recent Arendtian scholarship for understanding the so-far intractable tension between the promise of universal recognition and the realities of the state system.

Unsurprisingly, Arendt's penetrating insights into modern rightlessness have been subject to the continued attention of political theorists. While many have developed her ideas, restating the dilemmas inherent in the modern rights-regime (notably, Agamben 1998), there is a growing body of work reclaiming the productive power of the idea of human rights. Much of this work disputes Arendt and Agamben's pessimism about the rigid tension between the political life of the citizen and the 'bare life' or 'unqualified, mere existence' (Arendt 1973: 301) of the outlaw. As I now aim to show, breaking open this dichotomy opens up ethical space for challenging the exclusion of modern states and the state system.

A voice which stands out in this discussion is that of Jacques Rancière. He and his followers have posited a means of escape from the 'ontological trap' constructed by Arendt (Rancière 2004: 302). Rancière charts the on-going problems of maintaining the artifice of human rights (Ibid. p. 298). Nevertheless, he is troubled by the way in which Arendt's account depoliticises rightlessness, by the way in which the theory itself closes down any possibility of politics and, hence, of inclusion. In his re-analysis, political predicates, such as man and citizen or freedom and equality, are 'open predicates: they open up a dispute about what they exactly entail and whom they concern in which cases' (Ibid. p. 303). In a move against depoliticisation, he recasts the situation of the excluded: 'These rights are theirs when they can do something with them to construct a dissensus against the denial of the rights they suffer' (Ibid. pp. 305–6). Qualified optimism is found, also, in recent works by Balibar (1994), Douzinas (2000; 2007) and Gearty (2007). For Balibar, too, concrete resistance to oppression and persecution is an operation in 'inventing rights' (Balibar 1994: 224). In the view of Douzinas, the term 'human rights' is a 'floating signifier' (2000: 255), and Gearty similarly holds that:

> It is precisely because of the space generated between theory and practice that human rights (or equivalent) ideas are so often deployed by the weak and the vulnerable: you say you are com-

mitted to human dignity ('human rights'/cieng) but look at how I am treated; you say yours is a 'democratic' society but who listens to me? (Gearty 2007: 10)

There are now several persuasive arguments which suggest that the act of claiming human rights can be political. The implication for Arendt's account of statelessness is that it is not necessarily a condition of total abjection. While political challenges to state power are subject to significant constraints, and while wholesale transcendence of the quandary Arendt identified seems as unlikely as ever, there is also evidence of previously rightless groups contesting – and claiming – political rights (see Nyers 2006).

Seyla Benhabib has also been concerned with what she believes might be a 'constitutive tension' (Benhabib 2004: 365). Her response is to demonstrate that cosmopolitan rights 'create a network of obligations and imbrications around sovereignty' (Ibid. pp. 66–7). I return to the detail of how this might be possible in Chapter 8. Here, I am concerned rather to demonstrate that there is some preliminary scope for finding a way out of the horns of the Arendtian dilemma. For Benhabib, the dilemma centres on the important question of 'how to create quasi-legally binding obligations through voluntary commitments and in the absence of an overwhelming sovereign power with the ultimate rights of enforcement' (Benhabib 2001: 369). Paradox may well be 'the organising principle of human rights' (Douzinas 2007: 8), but it is not a paradox that requires us to cede to despair. Indeed, the task of theory must be to work within the paradoxes of right, in order to better understand the political character of rights and rightlessness, of inclusion and exclusion.

In the discipline of international relations, the last twenty years have seen fresh interest in the development of a distinctive body of international political theory (IPT). A few important works have made important steps in setting aside (if not completely overcoming) the communitarian/cosmopolitan debate, which was previously seen to be central to the endeavour (see, for example, Brown 2002; Cochran 1999; Hutchings 1999; Walker 1993). Innovations here have made further useful recommendations about the way we might think productively about the relationship between political particularism and political universality. My focus here will be on Molly Cochran's helpful efforts to shed light on this relationship. So far, this chapter has provided some preliminary reasons for rejecting Arendt's pessimism about the rights of the man. In what follows, I aim to show the critical ethical importance of avoiding over-confidence in theorising the tension between citizenship and human rights. Cochran's insights help illustrate the problems with deriving strong claims for ethical judgment from weak foundations. As such, they help demonstrate the importance of leaving room for ethical negotiation (Cochran 1999: 118).

Cochran's critique of theorists, including Mervyn Frost, has parallels to the criticisms of Arendt's 'ontological trap'. It is now argued that Arendt's critique of the nation-state had the paradoxical effect of affirming its unchanging ontological status. Similarly, Cochran shows that in spite of moves to reject abstract foundations for ethical claims, many theorists have remained in thrall to the quest for certain knowledge. Broadly speaking, there are two problems with theory that derives 'strong claims for ethical judgment' from 'weak foundations' (Ibid. p. 118). First, the attempt to derive certain knowledge from historically situated, imperfect practices and institutions has the effect of constructing a 'house of cards'. Second, even the creation of such a deceptively robust structure can recreate unnecessary boundaries, shoring up what Cochran describes as an unhelpful 'structural opposition' (Ibid. p. 188). Cochran's theory has made important advances in the attempt to finally divest IPT of the foundations which have, as she shows, made the tension between universal and particular seem so intractable. Her work has therefore helped international theory move beyond the cosmopolitan/communitarian debate which had previously closed down innovation. Her account is valuable, in particular, because it shows that attempts to reconcile seemingly opposing norms (such as citizenship and human rights) can come unstuck if they lead to the recreation of artificially discrete concepts and categories.

Guided by Cochran, the theory outlined in this book represents a self-conscious attempt not only to eschew foundational assumptions about individual rights or the value of the state, but also to recognise the unavoidable contingency of normative standards. A key insight of post-Arendtian scholarship has been the idea that the character of citizenship does not necessarily oppose the inclusion of the rightless. Cochran has similarly called for theory to avoid ascribing necessary characteristics to our reinterpretations of concepts such as citizenship or human rights. This book takes these two acknowledgements of contingency as its point of departure in its attempt to side-step, rather than transcend, the alleged conflict between universal human rights and sovereignty claims, which has been set up as the 'root paradox at the heart of the territorially bounded state-centric international order' (Benhabib 2004: 69).

II MEMBERSHIP AND STATELESSNESS

So far, I have briefly outlined the constructive benefits of avoiding the pitfalls of ontological and epistemological traps, suggesting that recourse to essential and non-essential oppositions can close down possibilities for what Cochran calls 'the expansion of moral inclusion in international practice' (Cochran 1999: 273). This section should make it clear that I do not therefore intend to offer up an ungrounded critique of membership. While I am claiming that it is desirable to recognise the impermanence of the state system and to acknowledge, therefore, the limits to our ethical judgments in respect of its value, there is nothing to say that this starting point is incompatible with the desire to develop constructive ethical theories. The fact that the state is neither permanent and ahistorical, nor objectively valuable, does not make consideration of its present scope and limits any less important. In what follows, I will attempt, therefore, ahead of Chapter 5, to sketch out the principal ways in which the state and state system today generate relations of inclusion and exclusion.

In the early part of the twentieth century, statelessness came to prominence as an international issue. By the end of the Second World War, it was an issue on the agenda of the newly-formed United Nations, which quickly recognised its connection to nationality and the nation-state. In 1949, the UN Secretary General, Trygve Lie, published a thorough 'study of statelessness' (United Nations 1949). One of the major observations of the study was that statelessness 'is a phenomenon as old as the concept of nationality' (Ibid. p. 4). The distinction between nationals and aliens is generally more familiar than the opposition between nationality and statelessness. The latter represents the difference between the person in possession of a 'legal personality' (United Nations 1949: 11) and the person 'not considered as a national by any state under the operation of its law' (United Nations 1954: Article 1). While the international system is constituted by a plurality of states, the norm of legal personality means that, in effect, the exception to nationality is not foreignness, but statelessness. Chapter 5 will outline in more detail the ways in which the state system has come to administer foreignness. For now, I aim to demonstrate the durability of the opposition between nationality and statelessness, drawing out its implications for the practical tension between inclusion and exclusion in the contemporary world.

The 1949 UN study reported that 'the organization of the entire legal and economic life of the individual residing in a foreign country depends on his possession of a nationality' (Ibid. p. 9). The 1954 Convention Relating to the Status of Stateless Persons was an attempt to address the 'anomalous' situation (Ibid. p. 8) of individuals residing in a foreign country who did not possess a nationality. The problems associated with statelessness remain closely connected to the ways in which the lives of all individuals are organised around national identity (Ibid. p. 9). The passport and visa system and 'the regulations governing all aspects of social life' (Ibid. p. 9) have raised the stakes of statelessness, exacerbating the reluctance of states to host and admit persons without an identity, as well as persons whose identity is unclear. The refugee studies literature contains a wealth of research into this inclusion/exclusion nexus, and there is widespread agreement that state sovereignty continues to be reasserted 'at the expense of [. . .] the protection of human dignity' (Blitz and Lynch 2009: 100). And yet, the continuing practical value of sovereignty cannot be ignored. It is for this reason that there is talk of a practical 'tension' between citizenship and human rights.

This tension is illustrated by an unfortunate consequence of statelessness. States have long been extremely reluctant to receive stateless persons. There are at least three reasons for this. The 1949 UN study refers to the stateless person's unclear identity, uncertain legal status and the resulting difficulties of ensuring his or her departure (United Nations 1949: 15). Stateless persons cannot be 'repatriated to a country of origin' (Ibid. p. 15), due to the fact that even punitive decisions to denationalise citizens are 'valid', at the same time as being 'unlawful' (Weis 1979: 242). As I will now show, there are various trends which suggest that this tension has been mitigated. There are now various sources of international law which affirm – directly or indirectly – the unlawful character of denationalisation, where it would result in statelessness (for example, United Nations 1961; United Nations 1965; United Nations 1979; United Nations 1989). My interest, however, is in the political context and expressions of this trend. Two of the major political manifestations of the attempt to invalidate denationalisation are the construction of '*de facto*' statelessness and the continued expulsion and deportation of stateless persons.

Historically, denationalisation was unlawful, primarily because it imposed a burden on other states, although it is arguably now also unlawful under international human rights law. It remains 'valid', in the sense that it is 'the sovereign right and responsibility of each State to determine, through the operation of its national law, who are its citizens' (UNHCR 2004: viii). This 'validity' inevitably poses problems to other states, particularly states which border discriminatory regimes. It is for this reason that states, acting separately and together, have moved to make denationalisation more clearly unlawful. By doing so, they have made it possible, after all, to repatriate the denationalised person or persons to a country of origin. A key part of this endeavour has been the creation of an operational distinction between *de jure* and *de facto* stateless persons. Batchelor points to the desire of the framers of the 1954 Convention Relating to the Status of Stateless Persons to 'avoid abuse, overlap and potential conflicts between States' (Batchelor 1995: 248). The result has been a 'protection hierarchy [. . .] within this extremely vulnerable group' (Equal Rights Trust 2010a: xi).

Legally, '*de facto*' statelessness designates those 'persons who, having left the country of which they were nationals, no longer enjoy the protection and assistance of their national authorities' (United Nations 1949: 7). In simpler terms, it encompasses people who have been allowed entry to another state on the basis of their formal nationality and are later refused protection and assistance by their 'own' government. Predictably, states were wary, with the emergence of statelessness, of compounding its problems by allowing other states to take advantage of the rules which facilitate the 'in good faith' admittance of foreigners. *De jure* statelessness was therefore defined to the exclusion of people who should be understood as retaining the international political protection associated with the bond of nationality (Ibid. p. 7). The category distinction was constructed in spite of the acknowledgement of various observers, including the UN Secretary General, that although 'in law the status of stateless persons *de facto* differs appreciably from that of stateless persons *de jure*, in practice it is similar' (Ibid. p. 7).

The construction of separate categories of statelessness rested on an assumption about the enduring basic functions of nationality. On this basis, it was decided that only *de jure* stateless persons with no identifiable nationality whatsoever were in need of more substantive international protection. A leading expert on statelessness in the 1950s affirmed that when it comes to statelessness, the '"most crucial question" is one of protection' (Weis 1961, cited by Carol Batchelor 1995: 252). And yet, curiously, neither the 1954 Convention, nor the 1961 Convention on the Reduction of Statelessness, offer much in the way of such protection. The requirements for naturalisation, for example, are rather weak. Of the sixty-six states which are signatories of the 1954 Convention at the time of writing, it is only required that they 'facilitate the assimilation and naturalization of stateless persons' as far as possible (United Nations 1954: Article 32). Further protections are examined in Chapter 5.

The legal situation is clearly the result of an artificial construct, premised on a particular idea of nationality as a formal, operational concept, detached from the content of citizenship (which includes protection). This distinction was also used to exclude *de facto* stateless persons in possession of a formal nationality from the provisions of the 1954 Convention (Weissbrodt and Collins 2006: 252). It can clearly be seen as a counterbalance to the fact that otherwise, statelessness can afford the individual greater protection than his or her own strictly legal status (Walker 1981: 117). Walker suggests further that it might be ethically more desirable to accept the validity of denationalisations, even when these are the result of the basest discrimination (Ibid. p. 116). She recognises, thereby, that the 'snapping of the legal tie between the State and the citizen' (Ibid. p. 116) might often be the more humanitarian option. Yet, there have been few moves in this direction. As such, Arendt's analysis could not have been more prescient; she acknowledged that governments tend to fear that 'even the smallest positive gesture' might encourage countries to get rid of their unwanted people and that many might emigrate who would otherwise remain in their countries, 'even under serious disabilities' (Arendt 1973: 281).

By attempting to forge agreement on the unlawful status of denationalisations of non-residents, states implicitly affirmed the importance of formal nationality status. What mattered most to receiving states was the formal identity that enabled them to treat non-citizen residents as foreign. Whether or not this identity conferred assistance or protection was a secondary question. Insofar as nationality represents a functional bond in international relations, this relates to its allocation of final and fundamental responsibility for the residence of citizens. Chapter 5 will explore this relationship in more detail. This relationship and its necessity to inter-state relations clearly informed the chosen definition of statelessness, which informs the 1954 Convention, and excluded those in possession of a formal connection, which often amounted to 'legal fiction' (Weis 1979: 241). For better or worse, the assertion of sovereignty at the expense of human dignity is a well-integrated principle in the operation of world politics. The creation of a legal category of 'merely' *de facto* stateless persons can also be seen as helping to invalidate the denationalisation of non-resident nationals, making such actions more clearly unlawful.

The underlying distinction between operational nationality and the wider legal protection and status of citizenship continues to have important effects today when it comes to the deportation and repatriation of refugees and stateless persons. Even those who are stateless *de jure* are often 'smuggled' (Arendt 1973: 284) or pushed back in to their state of origin (Acharya et al. 2003). These kinds of actions represent clear attempts again to emphasise the 'unlawful' dimension of denationalisation and to demand that the state of origin take responsibility for those who would legally, but for discrimination, be their citizens. Similarly, states have often taken great pains to determine the 'real origin' (Arendt 1973: 277) of stateless persons, in an attempt to clarify their identity and verify their status. There is, however, little evidence that involuntary repatriations of this kind can guarantee any improvement in the legal status of those deported. As Chapter 6 will show, the repatriation of the Rohingya to their country of origin tended to exacerbate their effective rightlessness. Repatriations of this kind can hardly be considered any kind of real resolution to statelessness. Instead, they seem to represent an attempt to ignore or refuse to recognise it (Ibid. p. 281):

> Nonrecognition of statelessness always means repatriation, i.e. deportation to a country of origin, which either refuses to recognize the prospective repatriate as a citizen, or, on the contrary, urgently wants him back for punishment. (Ibid. p. 279)

There are those who argue that 'international human rights are here to stay in international relations' (Forsythe 2006: 252). Evidence of this trend can arguably be found in the increasing regularisation of the situation of foreigners or 'non-citizens' (OHCHR 2006). However, the legal position of stateless persons remains far inferior to that of regular non-citizens, particularly when it comes to political rights and the right to residence (Weissbrodt 2008). Nevertheless, UNHCR maintains that the basic human rights 'of stateless persons are, in principle, to be respected in the country of habitual residence' (UNHCR 1995: iv). And yet, stateless persons are often subjected to the extreme interference of 'prolonged and unwarranted punishment', including detention (Weissbrodt 2008: 99). This kind of treatment has been a longstanding feature of their treatment and the seemingly inevitable result of the difficulties of ensuring stateless persons' departure from a state of residence.

Of course, the fact that human rights are violated does not necessarily negate their existence. Post-Arendtian discussions of the idea of human rights make this clear. However, as I also suggested earlier in this chapter, the theorist concerned to build not on abstract foundations, but on existing social and political relations, cannot simply and straightforwardly affirm the existence of such rights. As the practice of membership exists today, there are significant practical obstacles in the way of the following so-called rights: the right to a nationality (United Nations 1948: Article 15) and the dependent rights to 'recognition everywhere as a person before the law' (Ibid. Article 6) and to leave and enter any country, including one's own (Ibid. Article 13). The most obvious obstacle in the way of these rights is state sovereignty. Sovereignty has been exercised in increasingly coercive ways by the developed states in the last decade. The concept and practice of sovereignty have also caused and exacerbated statelessness in less secure regions of the world. Whether or not these are inescapable obstacles are questions for this book as a whole. In what follows, I will briefly outline the two principal ethical proposals for dealing with statelessness, before analysing their implications for the practical tension between states' rights and individuals' rights.

Broadly speaking, the existing discussion about the ethics of statelessness has two main reference points. Some prefer to utilise the idea of universal human rights, while others emphasise the importance of a 'genuine and effective link' (Weissbrodt and Collins 2006: 276) between individuals and states. By focusing on the practical connections between persons and states, it seems that it may be possible to avoid becoming caught up in the myth that the rights of man exist in a meaningfully pre-political sense. However, as I noted in the first section of this chapter, there is a risk that this approach (following Arendt) accords unnecessary 'symbolic power' (Bourdieu 1990: 18) to the already too powerful sovereign state. The depoliticisation of the non-state realm can be observed in Arendt's pessimistic claim that 'a man who is nothing but a man has lost the very qualities which make it possible for other people to treat him as a fellow man' (Arendt 1973: 300). And yet, it is clear that there is a very real tension between states and the promise of individuality, and there is wide agreement that statelessness 'destroys for the individual the political existence that was centuries in the development' (US Supreme Court 1958: 101). Walker (1981) comes to the conclusion that statelessness itself must therefore be seen as a violation of human rights. It nevertheless remains unclear in her account how such extra-political rights are to be grounded.

Lawyers and others have tried to address the practical tension between sovereignty and individuality, without becoming engaged in the philosophical morass which threatens to overwhelm thinking about statelessness. This kind of analysis tends to avoid either assuming or concluding that there is an abstract 'right' to nationality, focusing instead on the empirical claim that everyone has genuine and effective links. These accounts tend to emphasise links such as birth, descent and residence (Hudson 1953: 12). Batchelor has argued that everyone has such links, with the majority of people 'having all of them in a single State' (Batchelor 1998: 168). This kind of analysis is very important, although it cannot help us think about how to mitigate states' power to refuse to recognise these links. There remain significant difficulties in accounting for how the 'genuine' links of stateless persons to given states might be made individually effective, and the history of such actions suggests that they can lead to a battle of sovereign wills (Rubinstein 1936: 723), which only renders the situation of the stateless person more precarious. Invocations of a person's 'real origin' have too often merely refused to recognise statelessness.

Given that neither human rights nor declarations of effective links engage particularly constructively with how the practical tension between states' rights and individuals' rights might be resolved, the final section of this chapter will set out the framework which will be used in an attempt to retheorise statelessness.

III RETHINKING MEMBERSHIP AND STATELESSNESS

So far, this chapter has attempted to outline the contours of a type of theorising which both rejects firm foundations and holds back from outlining contingent claims to certain ethical knowledge. It has also suggested that the existing discussion about the ethics of statelessness might benefit from this type of theorising. In this final section of the chapter, I will demonstrate more precisely how I think that political theory can help us think more constructively about how to understand statelessness or exclusion and, hence, membership or inclusion. I will first say something about why I intend to use the concept of membership.

Membership, in distinction to citizenship, is a generic term. While it implies belonging, it does not circumscribe the type of unit to which one might belong. It neither assumes the essential rationality of the state, nor forecloses the possibility of other political relationships. In distinction to human rights, it neither implies an abstract form of individual dignity, nor any concrete content to the realisation of dignity. Membership is – I hope – sufficiently broad a concept to allow for a fully contingent discussion of the possibilities for extending inclusion. Using membership is an attempt to avoid the ontological trap which, by assuming too much of the state, over-determines the possibilities (and impossibilities) of political and ethical life. It is also an attempt to remedy the epistemic commitments which continue to lead theorists to search for timeless wisdom about the path to individual self-determination. I do not, however, intend to suggest that membership is an entirely hollow concept. It clearly implies that intersubjective relations are constitutive of a range of political and social 'goods'. It further implies that political theory is an appropriate way of discussing the ethics of peoples' inclusion in these practices, even if it can never lead to certain knowledge of their value.

An ethics of membership worth its salt must attempt to critically engage with the political and social relations which facilitate and complicate individuals' ability to lead meaningful lives. Again, it should be assumed, going forward, that I intend no substantive content to the term 'meaningful'. Even without a thick account of what counts as a meaningful life, it is possible to identify contradictions which mean that certain goods are almost impossible for certain persons to access, in spite of their (contingent) necessity. Two brief examples may be helpful here. In Burma today, a whole range of social goods, including the right to marry, require the express permission of the state government. The same government has enacted laws which make marriage the prerequisite of certain entitlements, in relation to property and inheritance. The same government consistently denies permission to marry to the minority Rohingya people. In this way, marriage is the necessary, but impossible condition of a range of possibilities which are upheld as important and valuable. A further example of statelessness highlights the existence of international contradictions. States today retain the right to restrict a range of legal protections and provisions to citizens. Allied to this state right is the freedom to determine the criteria of citizenship. This practice, it has long been argued, has the effect of making citizenship the necessary, but impossible condition of a range of social goods. Even if we let go of our ontological and epistemological commitments to the state or to individual self-determination, we cannot avoid the conclusion that the lives of given individuals are seriously damaged by the practice of citizenship.

How, then, might we attempt to more constructively theorise the contemporary dynamics of inclusion and exclusion in world politics? The approach to be taken in this book is influenced by the constitutive theory of Mervyn Frost and the criticisms made by various theorists, including Molly Cochran, of Frost's 'developmental communitarianism' (Sutch 2006: 6) or 'secular Hegelianism' (Ibid. p. 6). Frost's attempt at reconstructing Hegelian ethical theory, without recourse to Hegel's foundations in a 'spirit of the age', offers up an extremely productive way of thinking about ethical issues in world politics. In what follows, I will outline the most important aspects of his constitutive theory, before turning to a brief analysis of his attempt to apply this broad theory to the practice of international relations by way of a background theory of individuality. Finally, I will raise a few pertinent questions about its empirical foundations, methods and scope – the answers to which will inform the framework for the next chapters.

Frost has outlined his theoretical method in various places (Frost 1986; 1996; 2002; 2009). Here I will outline, fairly briefly, the principal dimensions of his constitutive theory. This type of theory begins with the assumption that 'we are constituted as the actors we are within social practices' (Frost 2002: 112). Furthermore, 'we are all constituted as actors in any number of different practices', which each has different rules and each has an embedded ethics (Ibid. pp. 112–13). The plurality of social practices which constitute us as actors means that we frequently face 'particularly difficult' kinds of ethical dilemmas (Ibid. p. 113). As we saw earlier in the chapter, the tension between the ethics of citizenship and the ethics of human rights is often seen as constituting just such a dilemma. Frost is motivated in his international relations theory by the desire to provide some method by which participants in these two practices might overcome this apparent dilemma. In broad terms, he labels this endeavour 'ethical constructivism' (Ibid. p. 114).

Frost's constitutive theory offers a specific mode of ethical constructivism. The constitutive method has three main steps. First, it requires us (as participants in the practices whose ethics seem to give rise to dilemmas) to identify the settled norms of the practice as a whole. This method of argument relies on the assumption that there will be some 'common basis from which argument [. . .] might proceed' (Frost 1996: 77). This 'context of shared understandings' (Ibid. p. 78) represents, for Frost, a 'domain of discourse', which 'gives us a basis from which we might construct an argument towards a substantive normative theory' (Ibid. p. 75). Such a position assumes that 'when we reason about normative issues we do so from within a standpoint defined by specific institutions such as the state and the inter-state system' (Ibid. p. 141):

> Constitutive theory does not reason from the 'mid-air' position occupied by the contractualists [. . .] Rather it takes seriously the truth that when we reason about normative issues we do so from within a standpoint defined by specific institutions such as the state and the inter-state system. (Ibid. p. 141)

Within a given domain, we will tend to be able to identify a settled norm by the language actors use to justify their actions. If violation of the norm is generally undertaken covertly, this will be prima facie evidence 'that the norm in question is a settled one' (Ibid. p. 106). The second stage of Frost's constitutive method requires us to attempt the more difficult task of constructing a 'background theory' which will justify the settled norms in that domain (Ibid. p. 9). This stage rests on the assumption that coherence is achievable. In order to show just how it might be achieved, Frost uses a method first applied to jurisprudence by Ronald Dworkin. One of the primary advantages of this approach, we are told, is that it excludes the imposition of extraneous principles (Ibid. p. 94).

The method Frost proposes, following Dworkin (1981), requires the theorist (or other participant) to ask herself a range of questions in an attempt to construct the character of the practice (Frost 1996: 95). Frost believes that a satisfactory background theory can, once thoughtfully and interpretively constructed, lead us towards correct decisions on what action to take in 'hard cases'. Before further examining the coherence and feasibility of this theory, I will briefly describe his attempt to provide a background theory, which might provide us with answers to the hard cases which arise in the modern state domain of discourse.

Frost identifies a long list of norms which he claims are settled in the modern state domain of discourse. Included in this list are sovereignty norms and human rights norms (Ibid. pp. 106–12). To be clear, this points to an acknowledgement of a type of weak, empirical foundation. It says nothing about whether sovereignty or 'human rights' are inherently valuable concepts. I am going to accept here that there is sufficient evidence in international relations of established sovereignty norms and established human rights norms. The debates set out at the beginning of this chapter, and the dilemma in which stateless persons find themselves, provide compelling evidence of a practical tension. For now, I am going to leave aside the other norms Frost identifies, in order to focus on this long-standing tension.

Frost calls the background theory, which he offers as a way of reconciling these norms, 'the constitutive theory of individuality' (Ibid. p. 127). His primary influence in the development of this theory is Hegel, although he strives for a 'secular' Hegelianism (Sutch 2006: 6). This secular aspiration is intended to represent Frost's empirical foundations. The constitutive theory of individuality considers the major practices in which we are all constituted as individuals. He focuses on the family, civil society and the state, following Hegel, and also includes the society of sovereign states (Frost 1996: 143–55). For my purposes here, it is only important to highlight the broad approach to individuality that is taken. Frost outlines a 'system of mutual recognition within which individuality comes to be of value' (Ibid. p. 141). This approach claims that 'a person is constituted as a rights holder of a certain sort within the context of a specific social relationship' (Ibid. p. 138). It therefore avoids the intractable tension which results when rights are assumed to have *a priori* meaning and content. Frost is very clear that rights 'are not things which a person can be conceived as having outside of or prior to any and all social and political institutions. A Robinson Crusoe has no rights' (Ibid. p. 138). Given the centrality of actual practices to individuality, it is 'a commonplace' today that 'being deprived of citizenship rights [. . . is] a major threat to a person's sense of self' (Ibid. pp. 148–9). As the evidence of statelessness demonstrates, this is a sad truth of today's world.

Before outlining the use that will be made (in the remainder of the book) of Frost's constitutive framework, there are a few qualifications to be made to the theory. The amendments are the result of questions raised by Molly Cochran and Peter Sutch about the scope of Frost's theory. Both theorists raise important points, qualifying the judgments he makes. They broadly agree that the conclusions he reaches do not follow from his foundations and methods. Sutch follows Chris Brown in arguing that there is 'a dislocation between the starting point of his argument and its conclusion' (Sutch 2006: 129). Cochran's criticisms are very similar. However, neither Cochran nor Sutch are entirely critical of Frost's basic approach. Instead, they call our attention to the need to rethink the kind of ethics that result from weak foundations (Cochran 1999: 108). It is likely that a more contingent mode of constructivism will provide less 'aggressive' conclusions than those which Frost wants to provide (Sutch 2006: 136). It might, however, simultaneously allow for more critical and constructive engagement with the practical connections between my freedom and 'the unfreedom of others' (Cochran 1999: 110) and, hence, between the value of citizenship and its limits. While 'Hegelian theories of international relations have not received the attention they deserve' (Sutch 2006: 117), recent work integrating political sociology and political philosophy share the idea that we might, through internal critique, 'gain a clearer understanding of our rights and freedoms [. . . and of] the contradictory nature of the present' (Benhabib 2004: 143).

IV SUMMARY

The introduction to this book told of the continuing vulnerabilities and deprivations associated with being a stateless person and of the critical role statelessness has to play in understanding the ostensible tension between sovereignty norms and human rights norms. As I said there, statelessness has often been held up as embodying and exemplifying an apparent tension between, on the one hand, demands for individual dignity and, on the other hand, demands of collective sovereignty. From this starting point, critics have often, as we have seen, been split on whether to demand human rights. Constitutive theory both problematises and clarifies what is stake in this debate, revealing the close links between these ostensibly disparate bundles of rights, as well as the challenges of extending the political relationships which sustain recognition. Perhaps its major strength, as an approach, is its relational approach to individual status as it is recognised and identified by practices within the state and between states.

As Cochran has so convincingly argued (1999), the theorist who works in this way with weak foundations must be self-critical, conscious of the necessary contingency of his or her judgements and conclusions. As it is, she finds that in Frost's case, 'pre-agreed institutional frameworks' still over-determine his 'social critique and resulting ethics' (Cochran 1999: 106). Without recourse to Hegel's teleology (Ibid. p. 107), theories of recognition can aim only for contingent judgements. As such, I endeavour in this book to temper all analysis of the benefits of existing relationships with attention to their weaknesses, exclusions and inequalities and to the possible value of other subsets of social relations. Theory of this kind will be unsatisfying to some in its inability and unwillingness to 'reconcile' dignity and sovereignty and, hence, square the circle of inclusion and exclusion.

The approach that I will take in this book is substantially influenced by Frost's constitutive theory. It shares with it the idea that we are constituted as actors within a range of social practices with different rules and ethics. It also accepts that we can work constructively within the modern state domain of discourse and agrees with Frost that it is helpful to exclude contentious principles, as far as possible. However, it also differs in some important ways. My theory will be applied to the sovereignty norms and human rights norms, which are important parts of the practice of states today. These norms will not, however, be considered as 'settled' in the way that Frost thinks they are. Furthermore, insofar as my theory rejects the pursuit of certain judgment, it rejects also Frost's convictions that a satisfactory background theory can rationalise a practice or provide a basis for making 'correct' decisions. I leave to one side, for now, the task of constructing a more contingent, critical background theory. This will be the task of Chapter 5. The question of whether my approach has anything interesting to say about the hard case of statelessness will also have to wait until

Chapter 8. In the next four chapters, the task of the framework theory will be twofold. It will be used, first, to critically address the ostensible tension between individuality and the state system and, second, to help illuminate the connection between inclusion and exclusion in world politics.

Chapter 2

MICHAEL WALZER AND THE DENIAL
OF MEMBERSHIP

Michael Walzer has written much that is of direct interest to the questions addressed by this book. He has written extensively about the scope and limits of political theory, and his work is therefore helpful in thinking about the kind of background theory by which we can evaluate our present institutions. The chapter addresses this potential in three sections. The first section outlines and assesses Walzer's particular brand of reiterative universalism, focusing on the way that he views the relationship between individual and communal rights. The second section moves on to the question of how Walzer understands the ethical relationship between inclusion and exclusion. Here, I will take up the potential of his theory for understanding the possibility of inclusion. The final section of the chapter sets out my own view on the potential contribution of Walzer's theory to a suitable background theory of membership in world politics. I try, in the end, to imagine how something like a conception of reiterative universality (Walzer 1989: 514) might be employed to different effect and briefly outline the preliminaries of an alternative way of thinking about the relationship between inclusion and exclusion in world politics.

I THE ART OF SEPARATION

In this part of the chapter, I focus, in particular, upon Walzer's insights into the interpretive method, the necessity of empirical starting points and the possibility of reaching ethical judgements outside of the political arena of the state. Taken together, these aspects of his theory lead him to outline a version of 'reiterative universalism' (Walzer 1989: 514), which has interesting consequences for the way we understand the relationship between universality and particularism and, in particular, the right of the territorial state to exclude non-members.

The tension between universal rights and the arrangements of communal difference remains a key consideration for my attempt to construct a background theory which might illuminate the relationship between inclusion and exclusion in the world. Walzer is not convinced that there is a necessary tension. In Orend's words, he 'believes we both can and should have it both ways' (Orend 2000: 156). Walzer attempts, therefore, to outline a universalism which is respecting of difference. Though commonly referred to as a communitarian, it has often been noted that his position is rather more complex than that label implies.

Walzer's theory is avowedly interpretivist in its commitments to available starting points, as we see in his admission that 'I know very little about things as they really are, social construction apart' (Walzer 1993: 176). He has been particularly critical of cosmopolitan thinkers who are insufficiently attuned to the particularist implications of the universal values on which they rely (Walzer 1989: 518) and has argued strongly that political theorists must pay explicit attention to the political and social arrangements which have both informed and are informed by values such as autonomy and self-determination (Ibid. p. 518). In his view, 'thick' local meanings and the 'thin' shared meanings that we might distil from these are inextricably connected to the existing arrangements which safeguard diversity. In his view, then, existing arrangements are of considerable value to nations and their individual members. Before moving on to consideration of the latter (and, hence, the more properly universal implications of particularism), I will sketch out the communal value which Walzer sees as inherent in the current state system.

For Walzer, diversity is both an empirical fact of life and a valuable attribute of the world. Fact and value are intimately connected in his theoretical approach. It is, in his view, a fact that the world is 'a community of nations, not of humanity' (Walzer 1980: 226). Community is at the same time 'a feature of our lived reality, a source of our identity and self-understanding' (Walzer 2004: 49). In this phrase alone, we begin to see how fact and value interact. Community has both empirical and normative status. We see the latter very clearly when Walzer makes claims like, 'as individuals need a home, so rights require a location' (Walzer 1980: 228). This claim clearly represents Walzer's focus on the importance of the particularist implications of universal ideas, like 'rights'. However, this kind of claim is arguably informed by empirical reality, rather than abstract foundations.

Walzer's ostensibly empirical (and, hence, weak) foundation in community incorporates observable social meanings and the 'real processes' through which they are constructed (Walzer 1993: 177). While meanings can never be 'objectively true or right or necessary' (Ibid. p. 177), Walzer uses them as theoretical building blocks. Their relationship to the world is mutually constitutive; social meanings both inform and are informed by the world as it is. The concepts we use when talking about local or international justice are therefore implied by the world and have implications for the kind of claims we can make about it. Walzer therefore assumes that we have a constructive language with which to address difficult ethical questions and that this language and its use are necessarily constituted and constrained by existing institutional arrangements.

On the one hand, Walzer maintains that the world is 'not so organized that citizenship in it is much of a benefit – as stateless persons have learned over and over again' (Walzer 1970: 149). And yet, acknowledgement of this reality does not lead him to abandon the attempt to elaborate some form of universalism which might help mitigate the deprivations of statelessness. Indeed, he can be seen as a theorist in search of 'another universalism, a non standard variety, which encompasses and perhaps even helps to explain the appeal of moral particularism' (Walzer 1989: 509). This ambitious project encapsulates an important dimension of Walzer's political theory, namely, the attempt to demonstrate the universal value of pluralism and diversity.

As we have seen, Walzer's theory is of interest for understanding the relationship between (universal) individual rights and the diverse reality and value of the state system. To the extent that he offers a theory of universality, then, it is a theory based on the practical acknowledgement of diversity. Walzer's version of universality is defined by a 'particularist focus and [. . .] pluralizing tendency' (Walzer 1989: 513). It therefore builds on not a restrictive foundation of agency (Ibid. pp. 522–3), but begins instead with plurality. His, then, is a universalism which begins from the acknowledgement of diversity; it is additive and inductive '[. . . and] does not require an external standpoint or a universal perspective' (Ibid. p. 527). In his words:

Reiteration makes for difference. We will find, however, an overlapping plurality of sets, each of which bears a family resemblance
to the others. Hence we will know them (all) to be principles
of justice, and we may well be led, by the interactions of states
and peoples, say, to interpret them in ways that emphasize their
common features. But our interpretation can do no more than
suggest the differentiated commonalities of justice. (Ibid. p. 525)

The importance of social meanings and alternatives leaves Walzer very
sceptical about the desirability of a world state or, indeed, any form of
universal jurisdiction. His brand of universality, therefore, aims not at
the transcendence of diversity and alternatives, but at their preserva-
tion (Walzer 1982: 50). It acknowledges the particular social relationships through which we make others special to us and requires that
we recognise 'these repeated acts of moral specialization' as legitimate
(Walzer 1989: 531).

He uses the concept of reciprocity to show how diversity can be
constitutive of universality. He is not claiming that people and nations
naturally act according to a principle of reciprocity, but rather that it is
a narrow principle which does not presuppose thick common understandings or abstract foundations. It requires 'only a reiteration of
local self-understanding' (Walzer 1995: 289). Walzer's view is that the
acknowledgment of the diversity and particularity of social relationships might itself be an act of moral universalism, recognising what is
appealing in repeated and reiterated acts of moral specialisation. The
'universalism of reiteration' follows from recognising ourselves and
others as 'moral makers' (Walzer 1989: 532).

This sort of acknowledgement enables relevant actors to work
towards difficult decisions in situations where there can be no guidance
from social meanings. In such cases, we are required to look not to the
kind of meanings found in political arenas, but towards the possibility of constructing 'thin' moralities. It is 'thin' morality which provides
the kind of basic prohibitions – 'of murder, deception, betrayal, gross
cruelty' (Walzer 1985: 22) – found reiterated across a range of otherwise
diverse cultures. They are not abstract, but remain parochial concerns
– 'concerns, that is, of every human parish' (Ibid. p. 22). 'Thin' morality
is, by nature, intense (Walzer 1994: 6), distilling these key prohibitions
from much thicker moralities, characterised by 'qualification, compromise, complexity and disagreement' (Ibid. p. 6). Therefore, while

the rights recognised outside of nations have been minimal (Walzer 1980: 226), those which have possess a special strength. They are, in Walzer's terms, more-or-less universal (Walzer 1985: 16). However, the pathways to their implementation remain under-determined; such 'thin' judgements made can never amount to 'full-blooded universal doctrine' (Walzer 1994: 11).

We therefore have the outlines of a universalism which does not begin with the autonomous individual, but rather with the 'overlapping plurality' (Walzer 1989: 525) of existing social and political forms. Applied to the state system, the implications are consistent with Walzer's demand that we acknowledge the validity of limited and exclusive principles of justice (Ibid. p. 525). This requirement derives, in part, from the absence of any external standpoint for judging between different social and political models. It is also derived from Walzer's observation that individuals require community – we 'literally cannot live apart' (Walzer 1982: 64). Walzer's view on the importance of community clearly implies the reverse, namely the disadvantage of being excluded from community.

The centrality of plurality and particularism to Walzer's political theory means that he is careful to acknowledge that many (if not all) of the most valuable processes of meaning and inclusion rely on plurality, that is, on the separation of communities. When it comes to political theories of membership, then the centrality of the state to distribution makes it necessary to pay particular attention to the positive and negative effects of separation. Walzer is very clear about the risks of statelessness (Walzer 1970: 119, 147; Walzer 1982: 62) and therefore clearly accepts that the current system of world organisation helps explain exclusion, as well as inclusion. His constructivist approach also leads him to try to identify and understand how our existing practices might already enable us to counter some of the most serious cases of exclusion.

Chapter 1 discussed the fact that denationalisations have often been seen as simultaneously valid and unlawful. I suggested there that there are considerable risks in taking the simple decision to outlaw and invalidate the denial of membership. Walzer's account of membership is helpful for thinking about the relationship between inside and outside, inclusion and exclusion. Membership brings people into 'the circle of recognition' (Walzer 1982: 272) and also into 'patterns of relationship, networks of power, and communities of meaning' (Walzer 1990: 10).

This empowering function not only grounds self-respect (Walzer 1982: 278), but works, in turn, to ground the distribution of further goods within communities (Ibid. p. 32). Denial of membership, then, constitutes not only an exclusion from that community's networks of power (Ibid. p. 278), but also from international recognition. He is highly critical of states which deny membership to those otherwise entitled, acknowledging (rightly) that:

> The denial of membership is always the first of a long train of abuses. There is no way to break the train, so we must deny the rightfulness of the denial [. . .] it is only as members somewhere that men and women can hope to share in all the others social goods – security, wealth, honor, office, and power – that communal life makes possible. (Ibid. p. 62)

Chapter 1 also noted the tendency to merely ignore statelessness. Walzer wants us to recognise 'those men and women whose condition [statelessness] is' (Walzer 1970: 119) and is clearly aware of the moral difficulties which arise when considerations of order are not balanced by considerations of protection (Walzer 2004: xi).

He also makes some more specific assumptions about the value of existing arrangements. These are based, in part, on a liberal argument about the value of separation (Walzer 1984). Walzer alludes to one of the most common justifications for state sovereignty when he talks about the benefits of separation. He argues that by separating 'institutions, practices, relationships of different sorts', we can aim for a kind of 'institutional integrity', which will best preserve the social meanings central to identity (Ibid. p. 325). Separation is, on this view, a necessary condition of communal life (Walzer 1982: 62) and of the avoidance of conflict (Walzer 1997: 89). The availability of alternative practices and relationships also confers the possibility of refuge (Walzer 1980: 228), which is particularly important, given that outside intervention into communities is generally prohibited. Allowing external intervention into a community tends, in Walzer's view, to 'generate a real loss for the individual members' (Ibid. p. 228). In linking the fates of individual members so clearly to the arrangements which protect communities, Walzer commits himself to consideration of the relationship between individuality and particularism. He addresses this concern in two important ways. First, he attempts to show that communal rights are derived from individual rights. Second, he outlines a range of restrictions on the rights of communities to exclude individuals. In both cases, he utilises a specific conception of membership as a formalised mechanism for safeguarding the mutual constitution of individuality and community.

As we have seen, for Walzer, community is central to the distribution of social goods and the construction of our own personal identities (see Orend 2000: 59). He accepts the logic of social contract theory that collective rights 'came into existence for the sake of' individual rights (Walzer 1982: 43). The individual rights associated with membership in community thus imply that membership in some human community is 'the primary good' that we distribute to one another (Ibid. p. 31). On this view, the state owes something to its members as individual members, 'without reference to their collective or national identity' (Ibid. p. 43). This claim implies the existence of a normative limit on what states can do to their members. This limit is expressed as comprising two provisos on the specific state right to exclude. Before moving on to these provisos, I will first outline the contours of the state right to exclude.

Walzer remains committed to the state's right to control membership. He rejects the idea that we should propose denying to states 'as we deny to churches and political parties, the collective right of territorial jurisdiction' (Ibid. p. 43), arguing that any theory of justice must 'allow for the territorial state [. . .] recognizing the collective right of admission and refusal' (Ibid. p. 44). Nonetheless, Orend's analysis of Walzer's theory argues that he is now 'of the more defensible view that "there are minimalist versions" of distributive justice which limit what is permissible on the maximalist culturally relative front' (Orend 2000: 55):

> One of the most plausible of these minimalist versions involves universal rights claims, 'the minimal rights of all'. In particular those to membership in some human community, to 'security and welfare', and to whatever is defined as need within the community one is attached to. (Ibid. p. 55)

Therefore, while Walzer maintains that, as a general rule, the collective right of admission and refusal is a right which must be respected by other states, he is clear that denials of membership are often, ethically speaking, invalid. How are we to understand this validity/invalidity nexus? For Walzer, there are practical limits on the state's right to exclude. Given the importance of local meanings, this prohibition must weigh far more heavily on an individual or group's 'home' state. However, as we will see, it applies also to states of refuge in certain circumstances. In this way, the political alternatives and possibility of refuge conferred by a pluralist world order mean that denials of membership are not as all-excluding as they might otherwise be. In both cases, the restriction on states' rights is grounded in the relationship between individual rights and collective rights and in Walzer's conception of the socially constituted self.

Speaking generally about the vitality of attachments to the constitution of the self, he argues that alternatives are never easily available. To try to change this fact of the world would potentially destabilise the relationships which give our lives meaning (Walzer 1990: 21). Speaking directly about the relative merit of homes over sanctuaries, he argues that the ideal task of any future organisation with universal jurisdiction would be intervention 'against the states whose brutal policies had driven their own citizens into exile, and so enable them all to go home' (Walzer 1982: 50). He assumes here that going home is the precursor to struggles for inclusion, in which others will come to acknowledge our rights. In fact, there is solid evidence that this kind of assumption has undermined the real chances for autonomy of stateless persons. In Chapter 1, for example, I argued that the creation of an operational distinction between *de jure* and *de facto* statelessness has legitimised the return of stateless persons to states where there is no meaningful potential for inclusion. On that basis, it is important not to confuse 'home' with a degraded, but enforceable right of entry. The next section explores Walzer's analysis of the difference between access to territory and full membership. Before we get there, I should point out that the experience of statelessness suggests that there is no clear causal connection between access to territory and autonomy, even if the former is a condition of the latter. Access to territory may therefore be a necessary, but insufficient condition of meaningful individuality.

Walzer has much to say about the value of territory to persons and communities. It is not only 'a resource for the destitute and the hungry', but also 'protected living space, with borders and police, a resource for the persecuted and the stateless' (Ibid. p. 45). It is, for him, a 'vital human need'. Thus, 'it is a matter of thin morality' that we all have a human right to 'a place where we can make a life' (Ibid. p. 43). Given the vital importance of states in providing security and welfare, Walzer puts forward the strong claim that political justice always requires borders which match those of the state. It would not, therefore, be just for a majority to define justice to the exclusion of a resident minority. To do so would exclude them from precisely what is valuable about territory. Access to territory seems already to represent some form of inclusion, albeit a lesser form than is intended by 'membership'. It already implies certain limited individual rights. In this way, the principle of reciprocity or acknowledgement restricts us from making difference a deliberate vehicle for exclusion from the vital human need for access to territory (Orend 2000: 171). Put more simply, Walzer is clear that while reiteration is premised on exclusion, it is an approach intended to acknowledge the differentiation of inclusion, rather than to sanction the kind of exclusion which would undermine the appeal of pluralism. A form of reiteration which authorised statelessness would hardly be a 'moral act' (Walzer 1989: 527).

This analysis suggests a tension which we have already encountered. It appears that Walzer must be of the view that denials of membership, though ethically undesirable, are sometimes to be acknowledged as valid, in order both to recognise statelessness and to acknowledge communal rights. Thus, while sanctuaries are necessarily narrow approximations of home, they can provide access to vital goods. In some cases then, denials of membership are going to be at the same time valid and unlawful. While there is much of value that is protected by territorial separation and the state rights which enable and safeguard it, Walzer goes on to outline two ethical provisos. The first requires everyone to be a member somewhere, while the second requires membership to be a genuine good (Walzer 1995: 288). These serve as a way of mitigating and acknowledging states' rights of exclusion.

II THE VALUE OF MEMBERSHIP

As we have seen, Walzer is committed to the state's right in matters of inclusion and exclusion from its physical territory. He is also, however, interested in establishing the universal implications of particularism. This interest leads him to outline two provisos which impose constraints on this general right. They are both – in keeping with his reiterated universality – necessarily 'minimalist and universal' (Walzer

1995: 288). These conditions reflect the contribution of individual rights to the stability and value of the state system, as well as the value of community to the constitution of individuality. In Walzer's view:

> It makes moral sense to let membership be determined by the communities that actually exist and that are capable of regulating the life of their members. There are two provisos: that everyone be a member somewhere and that membership be a genuine good (autonomy must be real and extensive). (Ibid. p. 288)

Together, these provisos show Walzer's acknowledgement of the fact and value of membership in today's world. As we know, and as Walzer assumes, most people today are members somewhere. Chapter 5 demonstrates that the right of the individual to reside in, and return to, his or her own country has become an inalienable aspect of international relations. A sizeable number of people are, however, excluded from the distributions of territory and membership. In making the distinction between 'being a member somewhere' and membership being a genuine good, Walzer further acknowledges that 'mere' access to territory is not equivalent to membership in its fullest sense. Chapter 1 dealt with the often hollow nature of purely formal membership – Walzer's distinction is thus an important one. In making it, he acknowledges that there can be two levels of denial of membership. On the one hand, there is the kind of total denial, in which a person cannot be said to be a member anywhere; on the other hand, there is the kind of denial following which a person is excluded from the extensive autonomy membership has developed to protect and facilitate. I will deal with the first kind of denial first.

The aim of Walzer's first proviso is a world of practices and relationships from which 'no sizeable group of people is excluded' (Walzer 1986: 231). This requirement, as statelessness demonstrates, has proved particularly difficult to enforce. How should we understand Walzer's stipulation that we ought to be concerned when the walls which separate communities result in total exclusions? According to the premises of his theory, any attempt to protect or facilitate the right to be a member somewhere must be consistent with existing institutions and their social meanings. As we have seen, Walzer suggests that part of the existing value of the state system is the availability of alternatives and the possibility of refuge. He also argues that a basic principle of reciprocity can (and does) facilitate the acknowledgement by one group of another group's fundamental claim to be included in the basic protections of membership. He therefore elaborates a requirement that the borders of inclusion should match those of the state (Walzer 1995: 288); a principle which excludes the possibility of permanent alienage (Walzer 1982: 61). The importance of an appropriate 'fit' (Ibid. p. 49) between membership and residence is supported by the mutual value to individuals and groups of acknowledging each other's claims.

Walzer also provides an interpretation of mutual aid, which explains how, when and why states might be required to offer protected living space to persons 'who have no other place to go' (Ibid. p. 45). As we know, he maintains that 'the distribution of membership [. . .] in any ongoing society, is a matter of political decision' (Ibid. p. 40). In general, there are important factors weighing against the possibility of allowing the 'individual version of the right to a place in the world to override the collective version' (Ibid. p. 47). While in many cases, the collective right to a place in the world will necessarily override the individual version, Walzer acknowledges that there are crisis situations in which we may need to revisit the scope of the collective right. By reflecting on the reiterative universalism which might allow us to think constructively about situations where individual rights are severely threatened, Walzer suggests that we might be able to find ways to accommodate at-risk individuals and groups and, especially, refugees.

While Walzer uses the term 'refugees', it seems plausible that he would include stateless persons who have been forced to flee in this category. As refugees present themselves to us as individuals whose life and liberty are at risk, he argues that refugee claims can only be met 'by taking people in' (Ibid. p. 48); there is not time to ask them to wait for a territorial settlement. When other state communities decide to extend the distribution of membership to the inclusion of refugees, they are – Walzer suggests – applying a thin principle of mutual aid, derived from their acknowledgement of the basic rights of others to life and liberty. Even so, Walzer clearly sets out the limits of mutual aid as a distributive principle. While its basic form derives from the reiterated universality which grounds thin, emergency decisions, it still requires some content, in order to be made meaningful to the community implementing the principle. Walzer suggests that when deciding whether to extend membership to refugees, communities rightly look for some connection. Walzer gives the example of the US decision to extend membership to refugees fleeing Vietnam (Ibid. p. 49). We might equally think of the UK decision to extend membership to refugees fleeing Uganda, a former colony. Walzer argues in support of the principle of mutual aid, suggesting that the character of the state makes it easier for state communities than, say, families or clubs to admit new members (Ibid. p. 45). However, this fact does not make admission morally imperative (Ibid. p. 45). As Walzer has it, the right to protected living space 'cannot be enforced against particular host states' (Ibid. p. 50). When there are large numbers of refugees, in particular, 'we will look, rightfully, for some more direct connection with our own way of life' (Ibid. p. 49).

This possibility is constrained not only by the collective right of admission and refusal, but also by Walzer's additional acknowledgements that 'ideological affinity is a matter of mutual recognition' (Ibid. p. 50) and that there is a necessary connection between security and welfare (Ibid. pp. 64–7). The right of asylum seekers to 'a place in the world', therefore, very clearly depends on the existence of a connection, of some existing social meaning. The inherent 'vagueness' of mutual aid as a principle, as well as the fact that it might sometimes come up 'against the internal force of social meanings' (Ibid. pp. 33–4), means that the world today cannot offer any guarantees of membership, in spite of the constructive force of Walzer's reiterative universality. In the end, the 'presumptive legitimacy' (Walzer 1980: 214) of sovereign states restricts the scope of universal rights.

Walzer's second condition on the general right of communities to define membership required membership to be a genuine good. His account of membership is an interpretation of a world in which the general right (and, sometimes, requirement) to stay somewhere or other underlies a range of more specific rights and relationships. In practice, then, being a member somewhere has long been the prerequisite of a range of political and social relationships of inclusion and distribution. And yet, the relationship between being a member somewhere and full inclusion is a complex one, as we have seen. Central to his analysis is the claim that the separations which support local struggles for inclusion are part of what make membership a genuine good (Walzer 1980: 228).

States' membership rights are, therefore, limited by the requirement for membership to be a genuine good. Thus, for Walzer, it is illegitimate for states to have second-class citizens (Walzer 1982: 61). This prohibition is justified explicitly in terms of the limits to self-determination in the sphere of membership. These limits mean that immigration decisions are partially constrained, whereas naturalisation 'is entirely constrained: every new immigrant, every refugee taken in, every resi- dent and worker must be offered the opportunities of citizenship' (Ibid. p. 62). The limits to self-determination highlight the moral importance of having an individual stake in the production of social meanings. And yet, Walzer is nevertheless very clear that while this is a desirable end of community, it is not a requirement that can be enforced from without. Walzer explains, at great lengths, the requirement for any change to political orders to come from within (for example, Walzer 1980: 228). While there are a few crisis cases where this requirement (and, hence, the duty of non-intervention) can be overridden, these are very much the exception (Ibid. pp. 217–18). Of course, this means that many people will have to live in situations of exclusion and alienation; situations of *de facto* statelessness show only too clearly the hollowness of strictly formal membership.

Walzer has another suggestion which is helpful for thinking about the extreme lack of 'fit' between state and people in some parts of the world. In some cases, the members of the alienated group have not yet been compelled to flee and therefore still have some place to be, however unsatisfactory. Where such people remain excluded from the distribution of important goods, and where there is little prospect of improvement, Walzer suggests the possibility of secession. He suggests that secession might even improve the overall situation, replacing one ill-fitting state with dangerous entanglements (Walzer 1994: 66) with two secure and 'fitting' states. Here we are looking not at the redistri- bution of membership, but at the – perhaps, simpler – redistribution of territory. While states could not be expected to cede vital resources, Walzer acknowledges that many states control superfluous, or even unused, land. Perhaps surprisingly, Walzer's account suggests, if only speculatively, that secession (that is, the redistribution of territory) might be more straightforward than the redistribution of member- ship. As a way of ensuring that secession does not lead to worse states, Walzer suggests that there may be a case for the international protection of minorities:

> The nationality treaties of the interwar period were notable fail-
> ures, but some measure of success in protecting minorities ought

to be possible now that nation-states are more entangled with and dependent on one another. Suppose that the leaders of the European Community or the World Bank or even the United Nations were to say to every nation seeking statehood: we will recognize your independence, trade with you and provide economic assistance – but only if you find some way to accommodate the national minorities that fear your sovereign power. The price of recognition and aid is accommodation. (Ibid. p. 80)

There is much to be said for such a practice. Walzer believes that the opportunities for state building (Walzer 2004: xiii) are better today than in the past. If such a model were to be put into practice, it would help prevent a situation of infinite regression (Orend 2000: 169) in which states were prone to break down, rarely possessing the stability necessary for the provision of social goods to their members. At the same time, it would enable people to create their own mechanisms for enforcement of their individual and communal rights. To avoid digression, I am going to leave consideration of the obstacles to secession to one side.

Notwithstanding the potential problems, there is, therefore, something promising in Walzer's commitment to recognising statelessness and to his consideration of alternatives. Nonetheless, there is something quite limited in his recognition of statelessness as a real condition. In his rush to ensure the very basics of membership (that is, access to territory), he tends to underestimate the continued likelihood of restricted membership. As I hope to show in the last section of the chapter, he also underestimates some of the major obstacles to genuine membership and, especially, their international dimensions. He assumes too much, therefore, of the coincidence between members and states and, hence, between access to territory and real and extensive autonomy.

This section has sketched out the contours of Walzer's understanding of the practical and moral relationships between members and non-members. While a cursory reading suggests that these relationships are rather limited, I hope to have shown that Walzer elaborates on these relationships in some interesting ways. On the one hand, he claims that the thick moralities associated with membership are open to the construction of qualified, thin principles, which might ground the extension of membership to at least some refugees and stateless persons. Once membership has been extended, these new arrivals will be members, included in the thickly connected relationships of membership. On the other hand, Walzer suggests that there are also (inevitably, weaker) grounds for international action, on the basis of the prohibition found in our reiterative universality. International cooperation might be able to support the development of new states where territory has been redistributed to a newly sovereign nation.

This section has also tried to show that Walzer's theory is helpful for understanding the practical tension in which denials of membership can be both valid and unlawful. Walzer's interpretation of the world shows that denials of membership can often raise considerations of mutual aid in other communities. Denials of membership are also shown to be highly prejudicial for the individual affected. We might, then, want to say that such denials are unlawful. Indeed, Walzer suggests that importance of being a member implies that there can be universal agreement on the claim that residents have a rightful claim to 'live a reasonably secure life' in the state of residence (Walzer 1977: 54). However, the vital point that membership should be a genuine good suggests that there may be good reasons to allow individuals and groups to consider the denial valid and seek alternatives, either by recourse to political refuge or by recourse to the collective right of secession. What we find, therefore, in Walzer's theory, is a productive interpretation of this tension, which extends its basis in the individual rights abstracted to his thin, reiterative universality. His attempt to dig out values intrinsic to the practice and to find ways that these are, or might be, enforced or extended is also very constructive. The last section of the chapter attempts to further assess the constructive potential of Walzer's theory for thinking about membership in world politics.

III THE MEANING OF MEMBERSHIP

The first part of the chapter was intended to explore how Walzer envisages his own political theory. In distinguishing it from cosmopolitan theory, Walzer endeavoured to show that our claims about how the world should be organised must be based on empirical facts about the world as it is, rather than on external principles. For his theory to hold, then, it will be necessary for him to keep to these strictures. However, there has been some valid criticism of Walzer, in this respect. For one thing, Cochran has argued that Walzer goes beyond the bounds of his avowed interpretivism, constructing an ontological foundation in community which constitutes an inevitably constrained theory. This part of the chapter aims to see whether Walzer's theory is as coherent as he needs it to be, addressing the specific question of whether his ontological assumptions do, in fact, overstep the bounds of his avowed interpretivism. My assessment of Walzer's coherence will have important implications for his account of territorial separation and of the scope and limits of autonomy and self-determination – that is, of the universal implications of his particularist starting points.

It is probably not surprising that Walzer's critics disagree over the coherence of this theory. Orend questions whether the distinction Walzer wants to uphold between discovery, invention and interpretation is tenable. He suggests that Walzer might 'protest too much' (Orend 2000: 27) and suggests that there is good reason to see his theory as substantively inventive. Abandoning the search for 'a correct moral theory' in favour of theory which will make moral discourse 'the most fully understood' (Ibid. p. 29) is, in Orend's view, still a constructive endeavour. He therefore asks whether it might not be true that 'the best interpretation is a kind of invention?' (Ibid. p. 28) Cochran's criticism differs from Orend's, in that she suspects Walzer of the construction or invention of foundations, which, in fact, close off possibilities for interpretation. As this would be an important criticism of Walzer, I will address it in some depth in what follows.

Cochran makes several specific criticisms about the lack of fit between Walzer's ontological assumptions and avowed interpretivism, which I will address in turn. Recall, from Chapter 1, that in Frost's case, she found that 'pre-agreed institutional frameworks' over-determine his 'social critique and resulting ethics' (Cochran 1999: 106). In Walzer's case, she argues similarly that his conceptions of the self, community and social understandings unnecessarily circumscribe his ethical claims, closing off alternative avenues for exploration (Ibid. pp. 52–77). Pin-Fat offers a very interesting related reading of Walzer's 'binary universalism' and his inability to avoid making the moves of one 'metaphysically seduced' (Pin-Fat 2009: 85–6).

Cochran argues that Walzer's project relies on the concept of 'a person who is historically and socially constituted', in spite of the fact that he is 'reluctant' to elaborate on the importance of this conception (Cochran 1999: 57). From this basic concept of the person, Cochran shows how Walzer endeavours to go on to develop a theory which focuses on the 'significant question of the self's connections' (Ibid. p. 59). However, his theory remains, at base, a theory premised on a communitarian conception of the self. Cochran therefore finds his 'universalist utterances' (Ibid. p. 55) to be determined by this underlying ontology, in which justice begins from the 'shared meanings of community' (Ibid. p. 56) which constitute the self.

For my part, I find this particular criticism of Walzer to be slightly overstated. He has taken significant pains to demonstrate the mode of interpretation, which allows us to construct abstract versions of maximal moralities, seizing 'upon a single aspect, relevant to our immediate (often polemical) purposes' (Walzer 1994: 18). I am more wary than Cochran of the claim that Walzer's moral minimum is, in the end, ethnocentric (Cochran 1999: 72). I do, however, agree with her that if you scratch the surface of Walzer's theory, moral parochialism is privileged over and above the universality of 'every human parish' (Walzer 1985: 22) in his assumptions that being 'at home' will tend to be the best route towards full inclusion. This is problematic, because, as we know, particular parochialisms often conflict with individual rights to life and liberty. Cochran convincingly shows that a problematic implication of Walzer's communitarian ontology is its commitment to the state. For her and Orend, Walzer's 'state-based communitarianism' (Cochran 1999: 66) leads to the strong claim that the state is 'the necessary condition for that provision of shared, socially recognized needs that Walzer views as both the hallmark and the pinnacle of a just political existence' (Orend 2000: 59). He is far less attentive to the adequacy (or otherwise) of the state as a condition of justice. In assuming a general coincidence between states and members and between admission and autonomy, Walzer has too little to say in acknowledgement or mitigation of the frequent inadequacy of the state, in this regard.

An important consequence of Walzer's (implicit) conception of the self as socially-constituted is its implications for his ontology of community. In Cochran's view, his ontology assumes a certainty which he has explicitly rejected. In spite of his commitment to a narrow objectivity, she comments (rightly) that for Walzer, 'community is a permanent and essential feature of all human life' (Cochran 1999: 75). Thus, he simultaneously historicises the state and essentialises community in his claim that, while the state 'can always be replaced by some other structure', it is 'rightfully an instrument of the community' (Walzer 2004: 49). Cochran aims to show that the specifics of his conception of community form the basis of his 'eternal return to the state' (Cochran 1999: 74). This return sees him argue, for example, that any state is better than no state (Walzer 1980: 228). While the empirical realities of statelessness might appear at first glance to back this idea up, we know that according presumptive legitimacy to states in this way has often both sanctioned and obscured the gap between formal membership and genuine inclusion.

Cochran's final criticism of Walzer to be discussed here relates again to the way in which his conception of the self over-determines the foundations of his ethics. She challenges Walzer's assumption that we can meaningfully identify the shared understandings so vital to his theory (Cochran 1999: 71–2). Given that the right to self-determination which legitimises the state is based on an ostensibly 'empirical' (Walzer 1993: 176) foundation in social meanings, this is an important challenge. Cochran then suggests that Walzer's particularist foundations might have rather restrictive implications for individual rights. In the end, she argues that Walzer's position amounts to a decision to privilege the state over the individual as the proper subject of justice (Cochran 1999: xvi). It follows that his attempt to outline a more universalist scope for inclusion in the state and, hence, the state system is necessarily constrained by his particularist foundations.

Clearly, separation facilitates difference, supports communities and constitutes individuality. In this last part of the chapter, I suggest that it may be worthwhile to think more explicitly about the international institution of separation, rather than about the communities which it protects and facilitates. We have seen that for Walzer, one of the prime benefits of separation is that it allows for difference. However, it also plays a substantive role in constituting a realm of equivalence. While neorealist international relations (IR) theorists no doubt overstate the equivalence of states, recognised states all perform (to greater or lesser degree) some protective functions in relation to their territory. This gives membership a general meaning. Indeed, Walzer acknowledges the fundamental character of membership, in terms of the constitution of individuality. However, he remains committed to the idea that there is a best place for individuals to live, from which position they can work towards the kinds of mutual acknowledgement which sustain authentic autonomy. If membership does possess a much more general meaning, it is not clear why we should presume that individuals belong at 'home'. As Cochran suggests, Walzer's ontology leads him to overestimate the coincidence between given states and membership. It therefore also leads him to underestimate the international meanings and practices which constitute membership.

As we saw earlier, the goods of physical access to territory and of membership seem to be good candidates for universal values. In Walzer's view, membership is the 'primary good' that we distribute to one another (Walzer 1982: 31). It is a good which is both a source and consequence of plurality in today's world. However, there are distinctive features of the state system which are constitutive of the social goods of territory and membership. These arguably include substantive international social meanings, which attach to these goods. This relates to a dimension of empirical reality, to which Walzer pays little attention. Chapter 5 considers these international dimensions in detail. Here, I outline the parameters of the claim that distributions of membership and territory have clear supra-state dimensions. International theory can justifiably be concerned with distributions which are not 'authoritative', in the sense of being sovereign (Brown 2002: 6–7). Indeed, Walzer has already acknowledged the universal, international proviso that 'everyone be a member somewhere' (Walzer 1995: 288). In what follows, I will try to suggest that Walzer's interpretivism might, in fact, have greater scope than he imagines for understanding the connections between persons and for theorising inclusion. I will address the first part of this claim first, outlining the idea that meaningful criticism internal to the state system is now possible.

Of particular interest to the argument that I am trying to make here is Cochran's mention of the 'international forces of socialization', which might, in fact, complicate Walzer's ontology (Cochran 1999: 72). A key aspect of Walzer's theory is his claim that the world is not a political arena (Walzer 1980: 226). However, it might be possible to understand a politics beyond the state, without recourse to a foundational view of the individual or of some conception of politics prior to the polis (Frost 2002: 85). By depoliticising non-state arenas, Walzer goes further in essentialising the state. We can see this in the way that he describes the condition of statelessness as 'limbo-like' (Walzer 1970: 147). This kind of rhetoric has often been applied to statelessness[1] and, of course, there is something exceptional about their situation. However, as Chapter 1 began to suggest, it may be unwise – theoretically speaking – to dehistoricise and depoliticise the kinds of non-state arenas in which stateless persons are forced to act. I tend to agree with Walzer, that the experience of statelessness demonstrates the importance of 'even the most minimal kinds of social solidarity and legal definition' (Ibid. p. 147). I am less sure that these relationships should be left within the sovereign domain of states.

In places, Walzer seems to talk about the world as if it were akin to a state of nature. In a discussion of the situation of refugees, he suggests that they experience an 'unaccountable and peculiar freedom [. . .] without political obligations, at least without obligations to any state in the world of states, and their condition testifies to the wretchedness of such freedom' (Ibid. p. 147). For one thing, this explanation seems to be a flight of fancy. Empirically speaking, refugees have clear obligations to their states of residence and are often subjected to punishment for violation of the obligations of migration derived from international society. While Walzer claims that the 'limbo of statelessness' confers 'a freedom any of us would speedily exchange for membership and protection' (Ibid. p. 147), the idea of freedom seems overly-indebted to social contract theory in its failure to acknowledge the constraints posed by international society.

While I agree with Walzer, that political power within a particular community remains 'the critical factor in shaping the fate of the members' (Walzer 1980: 227), there are also vital international dynamics which constitute inclusion and exclusion. Walzer acknowledges the status of international society as a regime (albeit a weak one) which permits (and excludes) a range of practices (Walzer 1997: 19). Of course, as Walzer accepts, the international standing of governments is derived differently from their domestic standing. The mediated character of the relationship between foreigners and states means that the threshold for legitimacy is lower (Walzer 1980: 212). Nevertheless, international recognition has a vital role to play in the constitution of the moral standing of foreign states and foreign citizens. It is possible to understand international recognition's constitutive dimensions as generating connections between members and outsiders. In this case, the outsiders will remain outside of the community of members, but be included in a wider circle of recognition.

The circle of recognition of international society is already constitutive of a range of individual rights, and we can also say that there is a meaningful sense in which individual rights to life and liberty constitute the state and international society. While there may be no 'authoritative laws and commands' governing these connections (Walzer 1970: 147), Walzer's reiterative universality may allow us to go beyond the very narrow strictures of mutual aid. Perhaps, in the end, Walzer's thin morality is drawn too narrowly to apply to such relationships, which are not relationships premised on 'temporary alliances' (Walzer 2004: 88), but on institutionalised relationships of recognition. Walzer may, therefore, rather overstate things when he claims that outsiders are strangers, who we can only recognise as 'men and women' (Walzer 1982: 32). We surely know enough about the value of territory and membership to know at least something of 'who they are and what they think' (Ibid. p. 32). It may, therefore, be possible to articulate stronger rights, without moving beyond the bounds of constructivism and seeking to establish rights (Sutch 2006: 160). We may, rather, be able to find more solid ways to defend the rights Walzer already acknowledges as existing (and which may already have stronger grounds in international society), such as the right to membership. We may also be able to say more about the existing constraints on the immoralities of nationalism (Walzer 1989: 547), without recourse to the kind of settled norms Frost identifies (see Chapter 1).

Sutch agrees that there is 'a little more scope for the development of international politics' within the tradition of what he calls 'developmental communitarianism' than Walzer allows (Sutch 2006: 169). He makes the argument that this kind of approach might be suited to the elaboration of 'a more complete account of international relations' (Ibid. p. 169). I, too, am interested in how Walzer's interpretivism might provide for a more expansive background theory of membership, which might, in turn, help theorise greater opportunities for inclusion. Walzer argues that minimalism is both the product of international encounters, as well as a facilitator of such encounters, in turn (Walzer 1994: 18–19). While he provides a solid account of the first dynamic, he has relatively little to say about the latter. There is, therefore, something in O'Neill's charge that 'his particularism prevents him from accounting for the real connectedness of agents in world politics' (Sutch 2006: 148). Walzer's theory is helpful in outlining the particularist implications of cosmopolitan principles (Sutch 2006: 154), for example, the need for alternatives and space for political refuge. It is, however, less good when it comes to outlining the fullest interpretation of the universal implications (or, at least, implications for universalism) of his particularist values. Whereas Chapter 1 found Frost to say too much about the possibilities for reconciling universalism and particularism, this chapter has found that Walzer is insufficiently constructive in this regard.

IV SUMMARY

The chapter has set out two main claims. It has argued, first, that Walzer tends to overestimate the potential of thick moralities and arrangements to enforce rights and, second, that he therefore under-estimates the constructive potential of the existing links beyond and between states.

As we know, Walzer sets out a theory which begins with an empirical account of plurality and goes on – out of a concern with exclusion – to elaborate its universal implications. This is a task for which I have much sympathy. This book was also conceived as a way of identifying the ethical implications for individuals of the present organisation of the world. It also shares with Walzer the assumption that we have no way of discovering or inventing objective truths. However, it would appear that Walzer's underlying assumptions about the necessity of community to personhood underpin the strong claims he makes about the state and the weak claims he makes about individual rights. He therefore makes a range of ethical claims which are the clear result of his necessarily restricted ontology.

The middle section of this chapter showed that Walzer's ideas can help us understand what is at stake in being excluded from the values associated with moral and political particularism. The final section argued that we need to focus more on the relationship between the appeal and the limits of a particularist-inspired universalism. In the end, I briefly suggested that there may be scope in Walzer's work for the more constructive development of an appropriate background theory of membership in world politics. A theory of this kind would have to pay closer attention to the existing connections of international society and work from these towards the construction of some preliminary ethical claims about the possibility of greater inclusion.

Note

1 The stateless person has variously been called a monster (van Gunsteren 1988: 738), 'a god or a beast' (Bentwich 1962: 58), tragic and repulsive (Malkki 1996: 384) or, in Arendt's famous phrase, 'the scum of the earth' (Arendt 1973: 269).

Chapter 3

RICHARD RORTY ON THE KINDNESS
OF STRANGERS

In spite of the fact that 'Rorty is not generally regarded as an IR theorist' (Cochran 1999: 144), his work has often been discussed by international relations (IR) theorists. As Cochran says, his discussion of 'liberalism, antifoundationalism, the implications of liberalism and antifoundationalism for human rights, and the call to extend our "we" group' are significant for the way we understand world politics. This chapter explores the implications of his work for the question of 'where a liberal, yet antifoundationalist ethic might take normative IR theory' (Ibid. p. 144). It addresses this potential in three sections. The first part of the chapter assesses the extent to which Rorty, in fact, manages to articulate an antifoundationalist theory. The second part focuses, in particular, on his attempt to understand the experience of humiliation and its effects, in turn, on his understanding of the relationship between liberalism and humiliation. The final part of the chapter offers a critique of Rorty's failure to attend to the political implications of his theory of sentimentality, sympathy and solidarity, with its suggestion that the victims of cruelty must rely on the kindness of strangers.

I QUASI-FOUNDATIONALISM

In 'Human Rights, Rationality and Sentimentality' (Rorty 1998), Rorty argues that universalising discourses, like particularising discourses, rely, in the end, on contrasts between 'us' and 'them' (1998: 168–9). Drawing on examples from recent campaigns of ethnic cleansing, he demonstrates how claims to authentic humanity necessarily rest on suppositions as to inauthentic humanity or animality. Rorty is making two points here. First, that claims to universality cannot avoid the influence of particularism. Second, that there is something particularly risky in the dependence of claims to universality on an absolute 'us' versus 'them' distinction. These ideas are central features in Rorty's work and help explain his commitment to particularism, as well as his related caution about phrases like 'humanity'. He is similarly sceptical about claims to rationality, which have often implied either 'a distinction between adults and children' or between men and women (Ibid. p. 168). Such meta-distinctions have, in his view, been behind many shocking examples of brutality between human beings.

As well as being horrified by some of the excesses resulting from the division of 'featherless bipeds' (Ibid. p. 177) into humans and non-humans, Rorty is wary of philosophical endeavours to articulate objective criteria of humanity. He suggests that this kind of essentialism – the idea 'that human beings have a special added ingredient which puts them in a different ontological category than the brutes' (Ibid. p. 169) – has been shown by history to be a poor guide to our behaviour. Flexibility, rather than rationality or cruelty, seems a better way of understanding ourselves (Ibid. p. 170). This position has implications for the idea of the 'ontological trap' discussed in Chapter 1. Rorty encourages us to sidestep the impasse between authentic and inauthentic humanity, in the hope of avoiding the blind alleys down which it has led us. His attempt to show how we might approach this task centres on the idea of a human rights culture. In outlining the status of this culture, he refers to the idea of Eduardo Rabossi, that 'the human rights phenomenon renders human rights foundationalism outmoded and irrelevant' (Ibid. p. 170). The next section of this chapter will address the features of Rorty's liberal human rights culture.

Rorty argues that it is outmoded to continue to ask questions about whether human beings really have human rights (Ibid. p. 174). However, his wider argument suggests that they don't. His rejection of foundationalism is avowedly pragmatic (Rorty 1982), but does seem to reach towards anti-foundationalism, insofar as he argues that: 'All that separates us from other animals are 'historically contingent facts of the world, cultural facts' (Rorty 1998: 170). A common criticism of anti-foundationalism refers to its implications for ethical knowledge. Rorty faces head-on the criticism that letting go of the ontological foundations which anchor us leaves us adrift, unable to make any judgements at all. In simple terms, this criticism asks: how we can know anything if we let go of what we are certain we know? Rorty wants us to forget the idea that 'it is our ability to know that makes us human' (Ibid. p. 185).

He suggests that we 'brush aside' questions like 'How do you know that freedom is the chief goal of social organization?' (Rorty 1989: 54). His position is that there is no reason to believe that the senses that we hold and the judgements that we make must be rooted in anything transcultural. In his view, our claims to knowledge probably have no justification outside of cultural facts and the individuals that sense them.

As well as urging us to avoid the search for a foundational ontology, Rorty urges us to avoid the seduction of independent frameworks by which we might correct our moral intuitions (Rorty 1998: 172). In the absence of any certain framework for determining the community to which we have to be responsible (Rorty 1983: 583), we must work from the communities with which we, as individual persons, 'presently identify' (Ibid. p. 588). Chapter 1 disputed Frost's assumption that a satisfactory background theory might lead us towards correct decisions on what to do in 'hard cases'. Rorty's scepticism about the availability of this kind of knowledge and, hence, about epistemology more broadly, is therefore very helpful for thinking about what tasks, if any, a background theory might perform.

Rorty's pragmatism disputes the use of philosophical attempts to achieve such knowledge. Since – in his view – such endeavours have served no practical use, he concludes that the attempt is irrelevant to our moral choices (Ibid. p. 172). Rorty argues that, in practice today, many of us no longer seek to found culture on nature or on 'knowledge of transcultural universals' (Ibid. p. 174). He further claims that it is the 'extraordinary increase in wealth, literacy, and leisure' (Ibid. p. 175), which, instead, gives us contingent knowledge 'that we live in an age in which human beings can make things much better for ourselves' (Ibid. p. 175). We increasingly look, he suggests, to historical narratives, rather than philosophical metanarratives (Rorty 1983: 587). This is a positive move – the assumption that knowledge is contingent and the decision to give up the search for 'theoretically informed critical practices' (McCarthy 1990: 367) facilitates a more flexible approach to ethics. The liberating effect of this move is the removal of unnecessary structural constraints 'either of the mind or of the world – on the historical progression between worldviews' (Calder 2007: 66). Without 'stable criteria for determining the desirability of change' (Rorty 1983: 175), we are forced into contingency and experimentation.

Flexibility, or malleability, is vital to Rorty's understanding of the situation of privileged liberals today. The kind of ethics such people can grasp aims, as we shall see, at the possibility of extending our ethical horizons in a manner which acknowledges the inevitability of ethnocentrism. Given his 'legitimate concern [. . .] about totalizing narratives: the risk of suppressing difference and otherness with an imperialistic "we"' (Cochran 1999: 206), it is an ethics which must also be committed to the contingency of all judgements. Rorty therefore blends (limited) flexibility with fallibilism (Ibid. p. 206), in order to outline space for an experimental ethics (Rorty 1998: 228). In Cochran's view, fallibilism 'represents an interesting way of offering universals and the weak foundations on which they are based without the under-current of absolutes or fixity that is associated with a traditional philosophical understanding of a universal' (Cochran 1999: 206). While it might be depressing to accept that there is no standard for measuring the correctness of our intuitions, Rorty therefore enjoins us to be pragmatic, to 'downscale our goals and aspirations to a measure commensurable with the limited resources at our disposal' (Conway 2001: 75). He therefore carves out a niche for creative thinking, for 'unjustifiable hope' (Smith 2005: 76).

Rorty's writings on human rights represent his interest in avoiding the impasse between community and individuality. Like all similarly interested theorists, he shares the cosmopolitan concern for human dignity. However, in the end, his concern with totalizing narratives, outlined above, leads him to ally himself with the Hegelians (Cochran 1999: 154). I noted above that Rorty reaches for an anti-foundationalist position. Cochran agrees that he 'clearly prefers a narrative of one's relation to a community, not to humanity, as the way in which we describe ourselves and make sense of our lives' (Ibid. p. 154). However, as we saw in her critique of Walzer, positioning oneself in 'the shifting sand of the contingencies of history and social circumstances' (Ibid. p. 75) is still an act of positioning, which can, if we are not careful, seduce us into acting as if 'we can always rely' on these grounds 'for ethical critique and judgement' (Ibid. p. 75). In Cochran's view, Rorty does a better job than Walzer of avoiding that seduction. She argues that his pragmatism allows him to more successfully eschew communitarianism, which raises the exciting possibility that we can think beyond the impasse in theorising 'the ethical possibilities of forms of community between the state and humanity' (Ibid. p. 156). In spite of some reservations, which I will come to in due course, Cochran finds that Rorty's approach 'suggests another way of liberating normative

IR theory from the stranglehold of foundationalism and its search for universal, ahistorical, transcultural validity' (Ibid. p. 159).

Before coming to her reservations and their implications for how we should understand Rorty's implications for IR theory and for thinking about human rights, I will briefly outline Cochran's description of Rorty's work as 'quasi-foundationalist' (Ibid. p. 170). Key to her claim here is the idea that Rorty resorts, in various places, to a picture of the self. Therefore, in spite of his arguments that 'no idea of the self can serve as a foundation for liberalism' (Ibid. p. 152), she indicates that talk of the self makes 'numerous appearances in his work, and not simply in reference to its obsolescence' (Ibid. p. 152).

Cochran argues that in spite of Rorty's very valuable insights into the paucity of epistemologically-centred philosophy, he leaves 'in the shadows' the ontology at work in his own methodological assumptions (Ibid. p. 167). It seems that the move away from epistemology constitutes a return to ontology, with the consequence that an 'unacknowledged foundationalism remains' (Ibid. p. 167). This is not a damning criticism; for Cochran, Rorty's pragmatism remains an important innovation. In terms of theory, it suggests that the impossibility of anti-foundationalism does not preclude substantive moves within the 'contingent end of the spectrum of ways of defending ethical claims' (Ibid. p. 168). In simple terms, Cochran sees in Rorty the potential of a least-problematic approach to forwarding ethical claims, in light of the fact that we seemingly cannot avoid 'being weak foundationalists of one sort or another' (Ibid. p. 168). We can, however, avoid engaging in deep modes of justification and making claims as to the 'correctness' of our judgements about what to do in hard cases. These insights will be carried forward into the background theory under development in this book.

II SYMPATHY, SOLIDARITY AND HUMAN RIGHTS

This part of the chapter looks in more depth at Rorty's contribution to thinking about human rights. Rorty's discussion of the liberal human rights culture is useful for thinking in an experimental way about the relationship between individuality and states' rights and, therefore, about the practical relationships between exclusion and inclusion. His account of the 'moral progress' of human rights (Rorty 1983: 182) shows how it has become increasingly difficult for liberals to justify the marginalisation of others. In this approach to human rights, Rorty relies on specific understandings of the (liberal) agent of justice and of the under-privileged victim. As we have seen, Cochran finds this reliance on ontology to be largely unavoidable and, in any case, an improvement on attempts at deep justification. This is not to say that we should be uncritical of the methods Rorty uses.

In various places, Rorty discusses the experiences of humiliation, cruelty and vulnerability, in general (for example, see Rorty 1998; Rorty 1989; Rorty 1983). For obvious reasons (outlined above), this is as far down the path of generalisation as Rorty is inclined to go. Nonetheless, his commitments to fallibility and flexibility suggest to him that the progress of the world 'will not be determined by any large necessary truths' (Rorty 1989: 188). Our present-day liberal commitment to the idea of individual respect is therefore acknowledged to be 'fragile and perishable' (Ibid. p. viii). It is not a commitment which can rest on claims to truth or to empowerment (Ibid. pp. 90–1); Rorty therefore accepts that it is not a commitment which has at its disposal the necessary tools to speak truth to power. To read, in his commitment to the avoidance of cruelty, a foundational commitment to some independent human trait is, therefore, misguided. Rorty argues that his accounts of cruelty, liberalism and human rights are not dependent on the concept of 'something within human beings which deserves respect and protection quite independently' (Ibid. p. 88).

Instead, generalising about cruelty is an ethnocentric response to our sense of its existence. From this pragmatic starting point, Rorty makes several contingent claims about suffering, all of which hinge on a particular understanding of language. In *Contingency, Irony, and Solidarity* (CIS), he surmises that 'the best way to cause people long-lasting pain is to humiliate them by making the things that seemed most important to them look futile, obsolete, and powerless' (Ibid. p. 89). This claim relates clearly to Rorty's mistrust of totalizing narratives and to his attempt to find a way to 'redescribe' (Rorty 1983: 584; 1989: 53) the situation of others in ways that can make us think, without causing them humiliation.

Nevertheless, Rorty does work from some (contingent) generalisations. For example, he upholds the question 'what humiliates?' as vital to liberal purposes (Rorty 1989: 91). This question is connected to the goal of expanding 'our chances of being kind, of avoiding the humiliation of others' (Ibid. p. 91). It follows that 'the morally relevant definition of a person, a moral subject [. . . is] "something that can be humiliated"' (Ibid. p. 91). It is a sense 'of human solidarity [. . .] based on a sense of a common danger, not a common possession or a shared power' (Ibid. p. 91). I will turn later in this section to consideration of the 'liberal ironism' (Ibid. p. xv) which Rorty sees as a good way of expanding our chances of being kind and avoiding humiliation. For now, I want to remain focused on how, from his pragmatic standpoint, he understands the experiences of cruelty and humiliation.

In CIS, Rorty sets out a general claim to the effect that 'pain is non-linguistic' (Ibid. p. 94). Pain is 'what we human beings share that ties us to the nonlanguage-using beasts' (Ibid. p. 94). He offers up an analysis of George Orwell's *1984*, which suggests that, perhaps, its key lesson is that human beings do:

> share a capacity which other animals lack. They can all be given a special kind of pain: They can all be humiliated by the forcible tearing down of the particular structures of language and belief in which they were socialized (or which they pride themselves on having formed for themselves). (Ibid. p. 177)

On this account, the liberal concern with 'victims of cruelty, people who are suffering' is a concern with people who 'do not have much in the way of a language' (Rorty 1989: 94). That is why there is no such thing as the 'voice of the oppressed' or the 'language of the victims' (Ibid. p. 94). This is a very interesting characterisation. While Rorty has rejected the idea that there is some independent trait 'within human beings which deserves respect and protection' (Ibid. p. 88), he clearly depicts the experience of suffering as one which is outside of the scope of existing languages. When, for example, a relatively inclusive multi-ethnic society breaks down, the language of inclusivity has demonstrably broken. History has shown that an ethnic group whose members are now the victims of cruelty cannot use their existing cultural identity and language to somehow 'persuade' their oppressors that they are worthy of respect and protection, for it is that very identity and language which is often the cause of their dehumanisation and oppression (Rorty 1998: 167). In such cases, Rorty argues that:

> the language the victims once used is not working anymore, and they are suffering too much to put new words together. So the job

of putting their situation into language is going to have to be done for them by somebody else. (Rorty 1989: 94)

Two questions should be posed to Rorty at this juncture. First, is this foundation in cruelty problematic? That is, does it contradict his avowed commitment to a view of the self as historically constituted? Second, are the claims he derives from this (admittedly weak) ontology held contingently?

On the first question, there has been significant disagreement. Brown has suggested that one strength of Rorty's approach is that 'he is genuinely able to claim not to be privileging any particular voice in the dialogues' (Brown 2002: 207). However, he finds it to be a weakness that Rorty substitutes the notion of 'suffering' for other liberal ontologies. For the very 'problem with universal values in the first place' means that 'it is by no means clear that it is possible to establish' what constitutes unnecessary suffering (Ibid. p. 207). However, Rorty is not claiming that it is possible to establish what constitutes unnecessary suffering. This criticism misunderstands his intentions. I am therefore rather convinced by Cochran's argument that it may be impossible to avoid recourse to foundations and her suggestion that we aim for the contingent end of the spectrum in response (Cochran 1999: 168).

The second question requires more consideration at this point. Rorty is claiming two things: first, that a language can be broken and require rebuilding; and, second, that this can require outside assistance. To better understand Rorty's claim that languages can become useless, we need to explore the relationship he conceives between language and politics. He draws quite a sharp distinction between the conditions of parochialism and the conditions of liberalism, arguing in 'Human Rights, Rationality, and Sentimentality' that there is a direct connection between security and the extent to which a culture rests on a sense of what its members are not (Rorty 1998: 178). To define a culture in opposition to some other trait is not, Rorty tells us, the result of prejudice or irrationality. Instead, he urges us to think of it as a quite normal reaction to insecurity:

The tougher things are, the more you have to be afraid of, the more dangerous your situation, the less you can afford the time or effort to think about what things might be like for people with whom you do not immediately identify. (Ibid. p. 180)

Those most prone to parochialism typically 'live in a world in which it would be just too risky – indeed, would often be insanely dangerous – to let one's sense of moral community stretch beyond one's family, clan, or tribe' (Ibid. p. 178). Frustratingly, Rorty has little more to say about the experience of danger and insecurity. It is, therefore, necessary to try to reconstruct his idea as sympathetically as possible. The idea clearly rests on the common-sense observation that some degree of protection and stability are vital to peaceful relations between groups. Living with fear, unpredictability and want have tended to be sources of conflict. However, Rorty wants to claim that there comes a point at which the suffering of an individual or group renders their parochial culture and language unworkable. It is as if the differences on which these and their local rivals are based become unsustainable in their connection to, what 'we liberals' call, dignity.

What Rorty is telling us is that insecurity has often been a condition of parochialism. Implied in his account is the related idea that parochialism has often been a condition of insecurity. This vicious circle can easily be applied to situations of protracted conflict the world over. For Rorty, there is no easy way to avoid such seemingly deep-rooted clashes. What the liberal can try to do is pick up the pieces when a group's sense of itself, like that of the Bosnian Muslims during the Serbian onslaught (Ibid. p. 167), is fatally threatened by the cruelty of strangers. Rorty draws on the work of Judith Shklar and Ellen Scarry to demonstrate the connection between cultural humiliation and individual degradation (Rorty 1989: 89). He thereby shows how – at the individual level – it is possible to force someone into acceptance or embodiment of some 'fact' which contradicts their fundamental view of self.

In an earlier work, 'Postmodern Bourgeois Liberalism', Rorty makes use of a similar idea. Here, he sets out his view of dignity as contingent on social relations, accepting the criticism of strong foundationalists that this implies, strictly speaking, that 'a child found wandering in the woods, the remnant of a slaughtered nation whose temples have been razed and whose books have been burned, has no share in human dignity' (Rorty 1983: 588). The language he chooses to use here is instructive. We can probably ignore the possible charge that his use of the word 'child' is dehumanising or humiliating (cf. Rorty 1998: 168), as it is likely that Rorty refined his own vocabulary for thinking about suffering over time. More troubling, however, is the assumption that suffering, like torture, tends to obliterate language and culture. This is not an entirely novel idea. Douzinas – writing on human rights – similarly describes fear, pain and death as 'radically singular; they resist and at the limit destroy language and its ability to construct shared worlds' (cited by Chimni 2004: 62). In Rorty's case, however, the echoes of *tabula rasa* seem particularly ill-fitting with his substantive views of language and socialisation, in which the only necessary picture of the self is the 'centreless web' (Rorty 1990: 291). It seems that he may, in this instance, be slipping towards the non-contingent end of the foundational spectrum. While this idea of a human 'blank slate' who can be 'taken in' and 're-clothed with dignity' (Rorty 1983: 588) avoids 'portraying the individual as someone who exists prior to any community' (Burrows 1990: 326), it runs the very real risk of reverting back to the ontological trap in which being stripped of dignity equates to 'unqualified, mere existence' (Arendt 1973: 301).

This stark depiction – which might, as we will see, serve a useful rhetorical purpose – seems to lapse into a foundational opposition between being a moral subject and being a mere object of sympathy. As I noted in Chapter 2 in relation to Walzer, there is something unrealistic today about imagining the refugee or stateless person as a creature in a state of nature. The constraints of the state system (to be explored in more depth in Chapter 5) give the lie to this image. Pragmatically speaking, it is probably also easier to find examples of deeply-rooted and long-lasting enmity, than permanently razed temples and burned books. Here I want to suggest, preliminarily, that Rorty's understanding of victimhood might be problematic. In order to substantiate this idea, I will need to look at the way he understands the relationship between the victim and the secure, sympathetic 'liberal ironist'. In order to think critically about Rorty's view of suffering, it is necessary to assess the plausibility and constructive potential of liberalism for rebuilding broken languages without humiliating: a key objective of Rorty's approach. If it can set out a plausible account of reintegration into a moral community, it might make the culture-less child a less problematic foundation.

Flexibility, as we have seen, is a key aspect and merit of Rorty's approach. The extensive use he makes of the concept of flexibility refers to the potential malleability of humans, but also of liberal culture and liberal institutions. The basic idea is that the security and stability of liberal culture and institutions renders discussions about their foundations irrelevant. Because the idea of individual rights and the institutions which protect them are now stable, they are – if we move on from discussions about their 'essential' value – amenable to incremental change. With a view to the history, rather than narrative of individual rights, Rorty suggests that the emergence of 'the human rights culture seems to owe nothing to increased moral knowledge, and everything to hearing sad and sentimental stories' (Rorty 1998: 172). By offering up a summary of liberal culture which emphasises the value of individual rights, we are able to provide a contingent justification of its value, even though this is necessarily expressed in a non-neutral language. Rorty hopes that his flexible re-description of the human rights culture will help us find some answers, phrased in our existing vocabularies, to questions like: 'Why should I care about a stranger, a person who is no kin to me, a person whose habits I find disgusting?' (Ibid. p. 185). In the absence of grounds for obligation, we might still, therefore, be able to find reasons which are convincing to us.

Rorty's approach to human rights works from the idea that human rights are cultural. They are part of one historically situated, particular, moral vocabulary, which is shared by members 'of a community, speakers of a common language' (Rorty 1989: 59). Human rights are also, therefore, implicitly relational – created and sustained by feelings of 'love, friendship, trust, or social solidarity' (Rorty 1998: 176). Rorty sees the best potential for the expansion of the human rights culture to rest, therefore, in the possibility of facilitating interaction, in getting 'people of different kinds sufficiently well-acquainted with one another so that they are less tempted to think of those different from themselves as only quasi-human' (Ibid. p. 172). Language is the tool which we commonly use to explain and understand our relationships to others. By refining and improving upon the vocabularies we already use, Rorty claims that we can 'increase the predictability, and thus the power and efficiency, of our institutions' (Ibid. p. 171) and heighten 'the sense of shared moral identity which brings us together in a moral community' (Ibid. p. 180). The aim is not, therefore, to transcend 'the particular little things that divide us', but to compare them 'with other little things' (Rorty 1999: 86). By re-describing the suffering of others using sad and sentimental stories, we might create the kind of solidarity which makes marginalisation difficult to justify (Rorty 1989: xvi).

As noted so far, Rorty does not accept that pluralism, and, hence, particularism, are obstacles to the expansion of kindness. The fact that people use different vocabularies in order to make sense of their own lives and societies does not, in his view, necessarily preclude understanding of 'the actual and possible humiliation of the people who use these alternative vocabularies' (Ibid. p. 92). This point does not presuppose any geographical limits to the possibility of understanding. Indeed, education and civilisation are both factors in the expansion of understanding (Rorty 1983: 587). What we already know about the link between insecurity and parochialism does, however, suggest that this understanding might be one-way when it comes to those 'deprived' of security and sympathy, who are likely (on Rorty's account) to find it difficult to answer the question of why they should care about a person whose (liberal) habits they may find disgusting. Two-way understanding is likely to be dependent on mutual security. Rorty acknowledges that there might be a power imbalance in our attempts to address suffering. The onus for expansion is very much on the secure, sympathetic liberal, who benefits from the necessary conditions for increasing his, or her, identifications with others.

Sympathy is necessarily the privilege and possibility of the secure liberal, given that there is, for Rorty, no way for the oppressed person – caught up in tribal rivalries or in possession of a powerless language – to speak truth to power. What are the implications of one-way understanding? Well, firstly, it may be difficult to describe such sympathy as communication. Indeed, sympathy is depicted as a substantially private disposition, cultivated by poetry, literature and the like (Rorty 1989). An important part of Rorty's philosophy is its attempt not to reconcile, but to find some compromise between the strand of philosophy concerned with the flourishing of the self and the strand concerned with solidarity and the avoidance of cruelty (Rorty 1998: xv). In CIS, the compromise requires the 'liberal ironist' to privatise irony or the 'attempt at authenticity and purity, in order to prevent yourself from slipping into a political attitude which will lead you to think that there is some social goal more important than [the liberal goal of] avoiding cruelty' (Ibid. p. 65). Rorty therefore outlines a methodological (Cochran 1999: 151) public/private split, which allows a realm of self-creation in which individuals may pursue aesthetic ends, 'so long as they do it on their own time – causing no harm to others and using no resources needed by those less advantaged' (Rorty 1989: xiv). There are also psychological factors which limit the scope of private ironism. While Rorty sometimes depicts the self as a 'centreless web'

(Rorty 1990: 291), he does seem – as we have seen – to rely on some understanding of the web's centre.

Until now, I have suggested that Rorty's recourse to a conception of the individual's centre only becomes a problem when he veers into the theoretical territory which naturalises community and dehumanises those stripped of community. When discussing the scope for ironic re-description, Rorty argues that the individual centre demands coherence (Rorty 1998: 171; Rorty 1999: 37; Rorty 2000: 15). This demand is neither intrinsically transgressive, nor intrinsically conservative. Of course, Rorty hopes that it will tend towards the expansion of our ethical horizons. However, in the following discussion, I demonstrate that his understanding of the centre might operate in a more constrained manner than is (contingently) necessary.

The more clearly social or liberal effects of ironism arise when Rorty's imaginative liberal communicates her sympathy for the suffering to her fellow liberals, encouraging them to extend their own commitments to human rights. It follows from his quasi-foundationalism that giving up 'truth' would have a democratising effect on communication (Rorty 2002: 149), leading to more and more instances where the strong are induced to turn 'their piggy little eyes to the suffering of the weak' (Rorty 1998: 182). I share the sentiment that it seems problematic if the potential for change really rests on the inclinations of the powerful to gradually stop accepting 'the oppression of others' (Ibid. p. 181). As Rorty sees it, however, there is probably no other way. Even this hope is contingent; the progress of the human rights culture might just as easily be reversed (Ibid. p. 185). Nonetheless, there is at least some evidence that sentimental stories have, in fact, 'induced us, the rich, safe, powerful people to tolerate, and even to cherish, powerless people' (Ibid. p. 184). For Rorty, the contemporary power of the human rights culture is evidence of this social fact.

As the liberal broadens 'the size of the audience' she takes to be competent, she increases 'the size of the relevant community of justification' (Rorty 2000: 9). Extrapolating the political implications of this position suggests that liberals could come to feel it necessary to justify the effects of their policies to all relevant parties which are assumed to be competent. We can therefore see how a particularist morality can go beyond its existing community of justification. Rorty's lack of explicit attention to the state and state system make it difficult to infer much more about his view of the political implications of his hopes for solidarity. However, as the final part of the chapter argues, we can reasonably conclude, from his commitment to liberal democratic institutions, that Rorty implicitly accepts the state (Cochran 1999: 155). While he is very clearly open to the idea (within necessary limits) of moral community beyond the state, there is a lack of explicit interest in 'the institutional form which that scope takes' (Ibid. p. 155). It may be that this lack of concern constrains the potential of his work for understanding the international politics of states and of human rights.

The public/private split represents Rorty's desire to privatise Nietzschean selfishness and avoid conservatism, carving out a distinctive public sphere in which we can appeal against 'societal norms and conventions' (Ibid. p. 190). However, for Rorty, of course, there is no necessary tension between aestheticism and solidarity – he therefore imagines that the ironist pursuits of some liberals will be the source of solidarity, once communicated to their fellow liberals. That kind of communication will remind the community of 'the failure of our institutions and practices to live up to the convictions to which we are already committed by the public, shared vocabulary we use in daily life' (Rorty 1989: xiv). Throughout this book, I have been arguing that this gap between promise and reality might be a fruitful way of exploring ethics. As Rorty sees it, the gap cannot ground obligations. It might, however, serve as the catalyst for us to reshape and improve our existing institutions.

When communicating his or her utopian identifications, the liberal ironist will, of course, be bound by the (admittedly flexible) vocabulary he or she shares with their community. It has been suggested by some critics that Rorty may be unreasonably optimistic about the expansive potential of communal vocabularies. Calder, for example, suggests that Rorty's prohibition on humiliation and the resulting limitations on re-description are likely to support superficiality, if not conservatism (Calder 2007: 12). While Rorty makes much of the idea that existing languages can be improved through moments of rupture and discontinuity (Ibid. p. 65), the requirement for justification depends on existing forms of cognition (Ibid. p. 65). Put another way, the need to be communicable within a presumptively limited community of justification will tend to limit this transgressive potential. Indeed, the potential for conservatism is very clear in Rorty's account of liberal democracy, which makes it clear that liberals (ironists or otherwise) will have to 'abandon or modify opinions on matters of ultimate importance, the opinions that may hitherto have given sense and point to their lives, if these opinions entail public actions that cannot be justified to most of their fellow citizens' (Rorty 1987: 257). It seems that Rorty's emphasis on the transformative potential of liberal irony underestimates the potentially constraining effects of community. On this interpretation, Rorty's desire to anticipate communitarian criticisms of the potential amorality of the private sphere might have caused him to misjudge the communitarian constraints on romanticism. That is to say that by privatising irony, Rorty privatises sympathy. Without much greater attention to the public sphere, Rorty sets out a version of individual rationality (Rorty 1998: 177) which is never put to the test of communicability.

It is also at least possible that security, the embrace of contingency and Rorty's public/private split would create such distance between liberal members that their shared language would become hollowed out. It is at least arguable that discourse in liberal societies today has been reduced to empty slogans, divested of substantive agreement. Interestingly, these two rather brief objections to Rorty's ethics demonstrate the distance he has come in side-stepping the communitarian-cosmopolitan impasse. His ethic – both 'oriented to community' and with a 'will to universalization' (Cochran 1999: 194) – can be charged with being too committed to the community in its requirement for individuals to abandon unjustifiable convictions, even when these convictions are utopian. It can similarly be charged with being too committed to liberal separation, insofar as the consequence of privatising sympathy might be the hollowing out of shared languages. For all its quasi-foundational benefits, however, we are left with an ethics which outlines rather limited potential for cultural refinement. In the remainder of the chapter, I point to two more ways in which this potential is limited.

III THE POLITICS OF KINDNESS

It has been quite a common criticism of Rorty that he holds a 'light regard for the political' (Cochran 1999: 166). There has also been some quite significant criticism of his conclusion that the powerful must speak for the oppressed. Honi Fern Haber, for example, draws our attention to the way that our depictions of strangers have 'often served to reinforce that kind of seeing which strengthens the ideological grip of the status quo' (Fern Haber 1994: 55). These two major areas of criticism have only been explored in brief so far. Both are vital to this book's consideration of what Rorty's ethics might offer in the way of strengthening our understanding of membership and of the relationship between inclusion and exclusion in world politics. This last part of the chapter deals, first, with the unexplored political in Rorty, before moving onto consider the potential for his ethics to depoliticise the situation of victimhood. This task is undertaken in a spirit Rorty would probably welcome; namely, in the attempt to write a book which might 'help us see the effects of social practices and institutions on others' (Rorty 1989: 141), where 'others' is a category which is left presumptively open.

What, then, of Rorty's supposed light regard for the political? Certainly, his accounts of the liberal ironist and of the liberal human rights culture seem to rest on a range of unspecified political assumptions. To the extent that this limits the inclusivity of the human rights culture, the lack of attention might be of ethical concern. As we know (from Rorty and from experience), liberal institutions today are relatively authoritative. Rorty also tells us that they are inextricably related to liberal culture as it is, as well as to the public/private split, which he sees as central to imaginative identifications with needy victims. Liberal institutions are thus vital to Rorty's unjustifiable hope. Community is both a product and condition of language and, hence, of morality, and pluralistic communities are both a product and condition of liberal vocabulary and morality. Lurking in the background of the pluralistic liberal community with its authoritative institutions is a state system premised in part on the state right to exclude. Acknowledgement of this background condition of separation does crop up in a few places in Rorty's work – for example, in his claim that 'each community should so far as possible be protected from harm caused by other communities, and in particular from deprivation of the resources necessary to its members' (Ibid. p. xiv). Given that necessity is socially determined, we might say that liberal communities – in fact, and in Rorty – are particularly resource-hungry. Without closer attention to the social and political contexts and implications of those needs, Rorty's justification of liberal morality and the public/private distinction on which it rests is necessarily more arbitrary than he concedes. Habermas has made this point in a particularly convincing way. He argues that:

> With the orientation towards 'more and more', 'larger and larger', and 'increasingly diverse' audiences, Rorty brings a weak ideali-

zation into play that, on his premise, is far from self-evident. As soon as the concept of truth is eliminated in favor of a context-dependent epistemic validity-for-us, the normative reference point necessary to explain why a proponent should endeavour to seek agreement for '*p*' *beyond the boundaries of her own group* is missing [. . .] If something is 'true' if and only if it is recognized as justified 'by us' because it is good 'for us,' there is no rational motive for expanding the circle of members. (Habermas 2000: 51)

The big question that I have identified is whether there is a vocabulary for discussion of these needs (and their implications) which might be more persuasive than that attributed to Rorty's liberal ironist.

Rorty's acknowledgement of the connection between plurality and individuality is fairly minimal. He has almost nothing of substance to say about the constitutive relationship between individuality, solidarity and the plurality of the state system. This could seem an unreasonable criticism; every ethics has its limits. Nevertheless, I want to suggest that in excluding such considerations, Rorty underestimates the means available for outlining the effects of institutions on others. Our appeals against 'societal norms and conventions' (Cochran 1999: 190) needn't stop at the boundaries of the state, as Rorty implies. As I argued above, working within these constraints leads Rorty to overestimate the possibilities of extending the liberal community of justification. However, it may be that extending his theory to include consideration of the constitutive effects of the state system can provide for stronger interjections against the exclusive effects of the state system from which 'we liberals' derive such benefits.

There is one final question to be addressed in this chapter. This relates to the question of whether the constraints I have just outlined do unnecessary harm to the prospects for Rorty's utopia. In order to answer this point, we need to reconsider the potential relationship between Rorty's liberal ironist and culture and the insecure victim. This relationship is already one-directional on Rorty's account. Recall that neither the tribally defined person at risk, nor the 'child found wandering' are able to speak to the secure liberal (or any other stranger). It is therefore vital for the privileged liberal to have some reasonably effective chance of understanding the suffering of these strangers. Rorty is committed – more than to anything else – to the avoidance of humiliation. In the case of the child found wandering, he is able to achieve this, insofar as our attempts to 're-clothe' him or her with dignity (Rorty 1983: 588) begin with a blank slate, given that it is 'the tools of language [. . .] which enable us to impose ourselves on the world' (Calder 2007: 100). This is problematic for reasons I have already outlined. Briefly, it relies on a kind of foundational dualism which Rorty would be best to avoid, as well as depoliticising the, in fact, highly political experience of extreme marginalisation. The case of the tribally defined stranger raises other issues. Here, we can imagine the situation of a *de facto* stateless person, who retains the very basic security which sustains language, but whose existence lacks the predictability necessary to the kind of self-authorship (see Rorty 1998: 77) which represents the fullest form of autonomy. How could Rorty's liberal understand her predicament without paying critical attention to the world beyond the liberal state? I have tried to argue that she couldn't and that it is therefore necessary to incorporate the wider political implications of the human rights culture much more fully into discussions of its future.

IV SUMMARY

This chapter has assessed the potential of Rorty's 'quasi-foundationalism' (Cochran 1999: 170) for thinking about the relationship between exclusion and inclusion in world politics and, in particular, its instantiation in the relationship between individuality and the state. In doing so, it has identified some potential benefits which derive from Rorty's approach, as well as some things to be avoided. I will conclude by briefly making some recommendations on the constructive potential of his overall theory.

A clear advantage of contingent theorising is the caution it urges. Thinking contingently leads us away from the temptation to posit 'correct' theories, allowing for a more flexible approach to ethics. In terms of the specific task at hand, it suggests that there are good reasons to avoid talking about the 'settled norms' (Frost 1996: 9) of international relations. If we apply the guidance of quasi-foundationalism to the discussion of the ethics of denationalisation, we are shown that there may be no way out of the tension between its validity (justified in terms of the state right to exclude) and its unlawfulness (justified in terms of the individual right to inclusion). By rejecting both types of argument, we might be set free to think more critically about the international politics of exclusion.

On that basis, Rorty's own lapses into non-contingent theorising are rather regrettable. Particularly when thinking about victimhood, there seem to be good reasons to resist the urge to depoliticise the experience of humiliation. Rorty's attempt to articulate humiliation leads him to make the claim that there are cases in which no further humiliation is possible. This kind of claim has parallels with Walzer's claim that any state is better than no state (Walzer 1980: 228) in its recourse to a non-contingent claim about abjection. Of course, it differs in that Rorty avoids spelling out the political implications of his accounts of humiliation and sympathy. It is never clear what the practical response to humiliation should be. Indeed, in spite of its anti-foundationalism, Rorty's theory wants for a more rigorous engagement with pluralism. As it is, he does not succeed in removing the structural constraints on ethical knowledge (Calder 2007: 66), but, rather, obscures them, to the extent that the state system still informs the character of his own claims. As such, the vaunted malleability of the liberal ironist and liberal human rights culture are, in fact, rather limited.

Specifically, I have argued that Rorty tends to underestimate the ways in which liberals can, and do still, justify the effective marginalisation of others by reference to their liberal 'needs'. Even so, it may be that we already have recourse to a more transgressive vocabulary than Rorty imagines. I want to suggest that first shining a light on the political implications of our existing languages of justification might lead to a more critical, more contingent ethics. While there can be no way of knowing whether future vocabularies will induce us to extend the scope of our justifications in dialogue with strangers, the increasing rejection of internal justifications might be a good step in this direction. Cochran has argued that a Rortian-inspired approach might entail 'better capacity to theorize the attachment persons have to the practices shared within communities' (Cochran 1999: 170). If the goal is to better theorise the attachment persons have to the practices shared within and between communities, we will be required to pay closer attention than Rorty does to the realm outside of the liberal state. If we want to avoid an ethics in which the humiliated must rely on the kindness of strangers, we may have to better understand how our privilege relies on their exclusion.

Chapter 4

ONORA O'NEILL: FIXING THE SCOPE
OF ETHICS?

At first glance, Onora O'Neill may appear an odd choice for inclusion in this book. Back in Chapter 1, I set out a broad framework, which, it was said, would orient my attempt to construct some kind of background theory suitable for helping us understand the relationship between inclusion and exclusion in world politics. In that chapter, I stated my commitment to weak foundations, and in Chapter 3, I wrote positively about 'quasi-foundationalism' (Cochran 1999: 170). In the preceding chapters, I have argued consistently in favour of theory which explicitly acknowledges the contingency of its judgements. And yet, O'Neill is most well-known for her Kantianism and for her attempt to outline a strain of practical reason which might be capable of formulating universal judgements. There are, however, very good reasons for her inclusion in this book. While O'Neill is both a Kantian (and, hence, universalist) and a cosmopolitan, her work is rigorous in its constructivism. Her philosophical approach means that she has lots of interest to say about the way in which 'pre-agreed institutional frameworks' over-determine much writing in ethics (see Cochran 1999: 107). She is therefore very open-minded about the possible value of alternative social arrangements and has engaged scrupulously with the weaknesses, exclusions and inequalities of our present institutions.

This chapter is arranged in the following way. The first section offers a discussion of O'Neill's constructivism and Kantianism, with a focus on the importance of determining the relevant scope of actions and institutions. It addresses O'Neill's use of the concepts of plurality, connection, finitude and vulnerability, in relation to scope. The second section explores the cosmopolitan claims she herself puts forward, before offering my own views on the potential of O'Neill's work for helping us understand the connection between inclusion and exclusion in world politics.

I CONNECTIONS, CAPABILITIES AND ETHICAL SCOPE

The two previous chapters have outlined some of the problems associated with allowing pre-determined institutions to exercise undue influence on our attempts to think critically about the world. O'Neill's response to the limits of communitarian theorising has two key elements, which I will discuss in turn here. First, she uses Kant's conception of autonomy to criticise theories which begin from arbitrary, 'hence unreasoned', moves (O'Neill 2003: 9). Second, she develops a conception of practical reason, which, she claims, has universal relevance. At first, O'Neill's commitment to the abstract principle of followability might seem jarring in the context of this book's commitment to the avoidance of unjustifiable, non-contingent claims. However, Chapters 2 and 3 related the limited implications for inclusion of theory starting from what O'Neill calls internalised commitments (O'Neill 2000: 23). Her position is therefore worthy of detailed attention.

O'Neill uses Kant to defend the possibility of autonomous justification, arguing that there is a distinction between autonomous and heteronomous justification. The heteronomous chooser 'makes some arbitrary, hence unreasoned, move', which seeks to justify a principle 'by imputing authority to something or other, for whose standing or authority either no reasons, or (at most) incomplete reasons, are given' (O'Neill 2003: 9–10). In general, particularist appeals seek this kind of conditional justification – limited, in terms of comprehensibility. O'Neill argues that appeals:

> to the actual norms of a society or tradition, or to the actual sensibilities, attachments and commitments of individuals will seem at worst incomprehensible to those who do not grasp those norms and commitments and at best merely conditionally reasoned to those who grasp them but do not share them; in either case they will seem arbitrary. (O'Neill 1996: 51)

The conditionality of such justifications is a limiting factor. An obvious objection, which we have already discussed, would be to respond that surely all justifications derive from somewhere (O'Neill 2003:

9). O'Neill anticipates the objection: 'surely justifications must begin somewhere else' (Ibid. p. 9). In other words, perhaps 'all reasons for action are ultimately conditional' (Ibid. p. 10). This is the line of argument which has been developed so far in this book. The use of Kant's heteronomy/autonomy distinction offers a particularly interesting response to pluralism. While she acknowledges the empirical motivation of internalised commitments, she argues that 'it does not follow that it is rational to live lives that express whatever commitments happen to have been internalized' and asks whether it is not 'intrinsically arbitrary to view existing commitments, and their internal revisions, as intrinsically justifying?' (O'Neill 2000: 23).

O'Neill's response to the idea that all justifications begin somewhere else sees her differentiate between idealisation, which assumes transcendent vindication, and abstraction. In her view (and again, following Kant), abstraction serves as a justifiable ethical response to pluralism. The fact of ethical pluralism requires the liberal to be tolerant. However, contrary to other theories, toleration here is not derived from 'a strong form of individualism' or from a distinction between self-regarding and other-regarding acts (O'Neill 1989: 28). The ability for an actor to abstract from the particularities of his or her own thick morality makes for a constructive, practical version of reason. Reason, on this account, is neither transcendental, nor groundless (Ibid. p. 28), but rooted in practice. It is, nevertheless, constructive, insofar as it makes increases in the scope of justification possible (O'Neill 1988: 711). O'Neill therefore argues that it is 'indispensable to all communication that succeeds in the face of disagreement' (Ibid. p. 711).

As discussed in the preceding chapters, neither Walzer, nor Rorty have much time for abstraction. For both, the pursuit of justice beyond state borders is inescapably parochial (though this connection is more implicit in Rorty's work). Given the criticisms that have been raised against both, in particular, in respect of their failure to appreciate the existing connectedness of different agents in world politics, it is worth considering whether abstraction might be compatible with a quasi-foundationalist approach to theory. The chapter as a whole sets out to assess whether there is substance to the claims that O'Neill's theory ends up in the kind of relentlessly uniform prescription and ethical insensitivity which her account of abstraction seeks to avoid (O'Neill 2001a: 16). For, if so, we might conclude that she drags us back into the realm of foundationalism 'proper', with its associated risks of oppression. I will, then, suggest that, in any case, we might be able to dispense with any non-contingent aspects of her theory. I will argue that this move has two advantages. First, it undermines the charge that her theory is insensitive to ethical plurality. Second, it allows for much greater engagement with 'strangers'.

As I have suggested, O'Neill values abstraction (which is connected to justifiability) over idealisation (which implies arbitrariness) (O'Neill 1988: 714). While the former is potentially expansive in scope, the latter leads back to arbitrary judgements, which 'disable' us from reaching other audiences (Ibid. p. 714). By contrast, abstraction can help in the formulation of accessible arguments. Accessibility is a possible outcome of practical judgements. Practical reason requires us to strive for accessibility. In seeking to act ethically, in this sense, actors are required to engage in a two-step process. For a given act, they are required first to identify the relevant scope – that is, to identify the other actors who will be affected. They are then required to choose actions based on 'followable' principles. Together, these provisos form a kind of guideline for ethical action. As a Kantian constructivist, O'Neill accords 'a justificatory role to the issue of scope' (Besch 2009: 1). Acts and decisions therefore 'depend for their authority on being suitably acceptable within the right scope' (Ibid. p. 1).

How are actors to determine the scope of a particular action? O'Neill makes the empirical claim that actors must make some assumptions about relevant others when they act 'for the solid reason that inaccurate assumptions [. . .] may lead to failure, to retaliation or to other harm or injury' (O'Neill 1996: 106). Of course, in many cases, we won't know much about the individual attributes of those others. When I choose to buy a fair-trade brand of coffee, for example, I know little, if anything, about the people who might benefit. Nevertheless, I can make reasonable assumptions that there are specific agents who benefit from being treated more fairly than they would by alternative arrangements. Whereas Rorty and Walzer make assumptions about the difficulties of circumventing strangeness, O'Neill observes that a degree of strangeness does not preclude actors from making 'adequately accurate assumptions about others who can be specified', if not fully individuated (Ibid. p. 115). Her account rests on an abstract account of ordinary capabilities and vulnerabilities 'that can be taken for granted in all others for whom the reasoning is to count' (Ibid. p. 56). She is therefore more optimistic than either Walzer or Rorty about the intelligibility of descriptions and principles, seeing the kind of 'thickness' that Walzer advocates as limited in its arbitrariness (Ibid. p. 68). All rational actions, she assumes, rely on some assumptions about those that will be affected, our connection to them and their capabilities (Ibid. p. 100).

On the basis of this arguably empirical assumption, O'Neill makes the normative claim that our understandings of a given situation 'cannot be assumed for action or in taking up attitudes or in supporting policies and relying on practices, but then denied when ethical questions arise' (Ibid. p. 100):

> In particular when agents commit themselves to the assumption that there are certain others, who are agents or subjects with these or those capacities, capabilities and vulnerabilities, they cannot coherently deny these assumptions in working out the scope of ethical consideration to which they are committed. Commitments to others' ethical standing are taken on as soon as activity is planned or begun: what is needed is a procedure for working out what these commitments are in a given context. (Ibid. p. 100)

It is worth taking a moment to consider exactly what is being argued here and to consider the extent to which this foundation can, in fact, be justified. O'Neill appears to be relying on the concept of coherence in a dual sense. On the one hand, she is making the empirical claim that rational actors operate on assumptions which are largely, or as far as possible, accurate. On the other hand, she is making the normative claim that ethical coherence requires us to openly acknowledge those assumptions as constituting the proper scope of ethical consideration. Denying the practical assumptions on which we act is claimed to be 'ethically disreputable', manipulative and prone to distortion (Ibid. p. 107). If, by contrast, we are to act reputably, we will be required, first, to acknowledge this scope and, second, to strive for universality in determining the relevant ethical considerations to which we are therefore committed.

Of course, one of the main objections to principle-based accounts of ethics is that they are overly prescriptive. O'Neill has dealt with this objection in various places. She takes the view that principles do not entail actions; they 'do not give us algorithms for living. They identify broad requirements that we must live up to, but they do not actually tell us what to do' (O'Neill 2001a: 15). She would also defend her account of the assumptions on which actions rest. For her theory to make sense, she must hold that this depiction of agency is 'banal' and undemanding (Sutch 2006: 168); her theory cannot be consistent with an idealised foundation. I will come back, later in this chapter, to the question of whether she, in fact, avoids perfectionism.

A second long-standing line of criticism argues the opposite – that is, that formal, abstract principles of this sort are, in fact, too indeterminate (O'Neill 2001a: 16). In responding to this objection, O'Neill stresses the importance of judgement. Of course, principles must always be applied to particular groups of people and to particular actions and, hence, used as the basis for more specific judgements (Ibid. p. 16). She argues that actions and institutions entail assumptions about other 'agents or subjects with these or those capacities, capabilities and vulnerabilities' (O'Neill 1996: 100). On that basis, the need for reasoning to be accessible requires actors to 'find ways of deliberating that connect these abstract principles of justice to the more specific and accessible categories of discourse of particular communities' (O'Neill 1988: 718). This process is exactly the reverse of Walzer's thin morality discussed in Chapter 2. There are, however, clear parallels here with the Kantian constructivism of Ronald Dworkin taken up and developed by Mervyn Frost (see Chapter 1). The major difference between Frost and O'Neill is that O'Neill is explicitly committed to followability as an external principle. It is her belief that by striving for the kinds of autonomous judgements Kant outlines, we might be able to reconcile the commitment to 'starting points which are available and reasons which are convincing' (O'Neill 1996: 8) with a more radical cosmopolitan agenda of institution-building, unconstrained by the internalised logic of the state system. The next section comes to her cosmopolitanism.

As we have seen, O'Neill is committed to the idea that practical ethics 'depend for their authority on being suitably acceptable within the right scope' (Besch 2009: 1). This scope is not pre-determined, but is, rather, determined by an actor's appreciation of the context of a specific action or institution. The implications for international justice are that it 'makes more sense to start with functional rather than territorial divisions of the tasks of government' (O'Neill 1994: 72; O'Neill 2000: 172):

> A better set of just institutions might be one that is constructed in the light of considering carefully to whom and to what (to

movements of persons, of goods, of information, of money) any
given boundary should be porous. (O'Neill 2000: 200)

As she notes, principles of justice 'have different implications in differing situations; [. . .] institutions and practices that are just and feasible
under one set of conditions may be neither in another' (O'Neill 1993:
118). In her discussion of scope, O'Neill says much that is relevant
to the idea of interconnectedness, which is central to this book. We
have seen, so far, that practical reason, rather than a thick account of
individuality, provides the foundation of O'Neill's theory. While she
avoids giving a full account of personhood or of the state, she does
make some observations about the interconnections between agents,
which are a feature of acts, decisions and institutions. On this basis, she
makes some assumptions about the role of these interconnections in
determining the ethical scope of these acts, decisions and institutions.
Specifically, she uses the concepts of plurality, connection and finitude
to address the interconnections which characterise action, making
the observation that 'connected lives become selectively, variably and
sometimes acutely vulnerable lives' (O'Neill 1996: 192). In her discussion of interconnection, we get something much closer to what I have
argued is missing in Walzer and Rorty. Neither of these two theorists
has much (indeed, enough, in my view) to say about the ways in which
the arrangements of plurality can 'disable agency' by restricting independence and through the demands of interdependence (O'Neill 2000:
163). O'Neill's attention to the capability and vulnerability sustained by
practical interconnectedness is, thus, extremely valuable.

Having determined the relevant others to be included in the scope
of our ethical considerations, we are required to identify action-guiding
principles which could be followable by those others. Of course, any
principles relying on arbitrary authorities will be out of bounds. We
are, therefore, required to seek out autonomous principles which
could be acceptable to all relevant actors – that is to say, principles
which could hold universally in the given domain. In O'Neill's hands,
practical reason becomes a pathway to the construction of widely
(indeed, universally) accessible claims (O'Neill 1988: 714). It is sharply
distinguished, in her account, from 'private reason', which relies on
arbitrary premises and leads to relativistic conclusions (O'Neill 2000a:
54). Practical public reason is grounded in the importance of communicability and the claim that 'communication has [. . .] to meet sufficient

standards of rationality to be interpretable to audiences who share no other, rationally ungrounded authorities' (O'Neill 1989: 35).

The Kantian idea of practical reason is constitutive of a first-order prohibition, which requires actors to reject the institutionalisation of unfollowable second-order principles. O'Neill cites deception as an example of an unfollowable second-order principle: nobody, she argues, 'can coherently view deception [. . .] as an inclusive principle that could be available for all' (O'Neill 1996: 174). If all were to engage in deceit, the very basis of trust and, hence, of on-going interaction, would be undermined. It would therefore be unreasonable for a government or other actor to choose a path requiring the institutionalisation of deception. The overall goal of O'Neill's first-order principle of followability is the ability to assess our existing institutions, in terms of the extent to which 'they implement or obstruct the rejection of injury' (Ibid. pp. 209–10). Followability is also a principle which should prevent actors from choosing actions based on insincere reasoning about the existence and capabilities of relevant others. It will prohibit actions which 'take advantage of the very limitations they deny' (Ibid. p. 110).

When actions are based on principles which are not followable, they will tend to substitute distorted accounts for the actors' practical understandings about the existence and capacities of relevant others (Ibid. p. 107). Nevertheless, followability is not a perfect action-guiding principle. O'Neill acknowledges that it is probably not possible 'to establish that all activity of a type that cannot be done universally is wrong' (O'Neill 2003: 231). In an imperfect world, it may not be possible to dispense wholly with 'coercion, with deception or with certain other types of activity that create victims' (Ibid. p. 231). Our concern when building new institutions should therefore be the rejection of avoidable injury (O'Neill 1996: 173). Given the practical difficulties of doing so in an imperfect world, any improved institutions will be required to 'compensate for any systematic or gratuitous injuries' (Ibid. p. 173). While it may not always be possible to fully reject injury, it should be possible to avoid 'making a principle of injury fundamental to lives, institutions or practices' (Ibid. p. 166). 'Systematic' is used here to refer to the kinds of 'species' injury which result from our shared vulnerabilities to hunger, pain and so on (Ibid. p. 173). Systematic injury often affects groups on the basis of these persistent vulnerabilities. These are distinguished from the more 'variable and selective' vulnerabilities, which are the result of specific relationships (O'Neill 1996: 192). 'Systematic' injury can be applied, in particular, to the kinds of injury likely to affect others about whom we may know relatively little. It rests on only 'a rather abstract account of the ordinary capacities and capabilities and the routine forms of vulnerability that can be taken for granted' (Ibid. p. 56). She is concerned with both direct and indirect injury (Ibid. pp. 167–9) and with active injury, as well as the injurious effects of 'indifference or neglect' (Ibid. p. 204).

O'Neill's theory both strives for universality and rests on assumptions about the nature of the link between interconnections and action and, hence, between interconnections, cognition and wider intelligibility. I will come, later in this chapter, to a more critical assessment of the role and function of these assumptions in her work. For now, it is of particular interest to consider the way in which O'Neill's philosophical arguments about scope can be applied to world politics.

Chapter 5 of the book looks at the extent to which membership practice is institutionalised and hence open to criticism, in terms of its coherence and its relationship to avoidable injury. At this stage, however, it may be useful to try to apply O'Neill's method to the 'system of states' more broadly (Ibid. p. 172). Statelessness seems to be evidence of a persistent, species-wide vulnerability to injury. Part of my argument in this book as a whole is that there are good reasons to think about the practice of membership as relying on international networks of meaning. When states develop membership policies (conceived broadly as including citizenship policies, immigration policies and so on), they generally do so on the basis of some assumptions about their connection to other states with varying capacities. States often, for example, close their borders to asylum seekers fleeing weak states. One way of trying to press governments to act more inclusively would be to argue that their acknowledgement of these interconnections commits them to ethical consideration of those affected by these same relationships. According to O'Neill's theory, the way in which the state system limits 'access to the means of life' (Ibid. p. 172) clearly suggests that questions of membership entail a cosmopolitan view of ethical standing. Taking this view into account, it will be extremely difficult to justify institutions which leave some vulnerable to the serious injuries associated with statelessness. In practice, as Chapter 1 noted, denationalisation remains both 'valid' and 'unlawful' (Weis 1979: 242) within the present institutions which frame membership practice. To the extent that it remains valid for states to exclude those without any alternative source of protection, O'Neill would surely conclude that such exclusion is unjustifiable. While there is no *a priori* way of knowing whether statelessness is avoidable, it is presuppositions about the value of state borders which make it seem unavoidable and make denationalisation seem valid. The following section addresses O'Neill's rejection of presuppositions about state borders, assessing her political cosmopolitanism.

II ON COSMOPOLITAN SCOPE

O'Neill's incredibly interesting critique of the Universal Declaration of Human Rights (O'Neill 2001) illustrates in more detail her views on the justifiability (or otherwise) of the state system. In this article, she explores the way in which the declaration expressly fixes the scope of rights to the anti-cosmopolitan state system (Ibid. p. 185). She shows how presuppositions about the validity of the bounded state system inevitably restrict the ostensible cosmopolitanism found elsewhere in the declaration. The importance the declaration places on the right to a nationality (Article 15) clearly demonstrates its basis in what is, for O'Neill, an arbitrary political arrangement. The tension between this arrangement and the delivery of universal rights (O'Neill 2001: 185) becomes manifest in several places in the declaration. She points, in particular, to the distinction between the right to asylum (Article 14) and the right to freedom of movement (Article 13). In separating out these two rights, the declaration makes explicit the fundamental difference between the rights of members and of non-members. As she says:

> In a world without bounded states, these distinctions would make no sense. Here it becomes quite explicit that the Declaration views states as the primary agents of justice: a cosmopolitan view of rights is to be spliced with a statist view of obligations. (O'Neill 2001: 185)

The attempt at 'splicing' anti-cosmopolitan assumptions with a cosmopolitan view of moral standing fails. It fails, inasmuch as it is incoherent. In O'Neill's view, it would be much more appropriate to strip out the implicit presumptions about states in favour of a more complete understanding of the relevant actors. It might, then, be possible to think more constructively about the relationship between connected and mutually vulnerable agents and the possible institutionalisation of justice.

Instead, by presuming that any rights will be 'assigned primarily to states' (Ibid. p. 186), the declaration:

> takes too limited a view of the implications of connection and finitude, and is hence likely to say far too little about inclusive requirements for those who are mutually vulnerable and connected in specific and variable ways that not merely mitigate but restructure, alter and heighten vulnerability. (O'Neill 1996: 193)

The implied reliance on states has the effect of obscuring many of their limits as agents of cosmopolitan justice. A more rigorous foundation in connection and finitude would, in fact, have highlighted some of the problems associated with reliance on the state; it would, in particular, 'have exposed the problems created by rogue states and weak states, and the predicaments created for other agents and agencies when states fail to support justice' (O'Neill 2001: 186). The declaration therefore remains wedded to an incomplete view of the state, which is contradicted by more critical understandings. As O'Neill notes:

> Often when we speak of [. . .] 'states,' the term is used in a merely formal sense, as a largely honorific appellation, and it is widely acknowledged that they lack capabilities that would be indispensable in any primary agent of justice. (Ibid. p. 190)

Insofar as the Universal Declaration 'masks' what other activity readily acknowledges, it can be seen as based on 'a distorted account' of activity's presuppositions (O'Neill 1996: 107).

O'Neill contends that many theorists (and, in particular, communitarians) merely acknowledge plurality by identifying other relevant agents (O'Neill 1996: 193). Her argument is that by adding connection and finitude into the equation, we can achieve fuller ethical coherence with the actual assumptions actors make about those others in their routine actions. The idea is that by better understanding the specific capabilities and vulnerabilities of those connected to us, we might be able to say far more 'about inclusive requirements for those who are mutually vulnerable and connected in specific and variable ways' (Ibid. p. 193). With this more solid understanding in mind, we will be better able to construct new institutions which 'aim to avert and mitigate many of the injuries to which characteristic and persistent vulnerabilities lay people open' (Ibid. p. 192). Plurality, connection and finitude are held to apply to all spheres of action, including the state system. While different acts and decisions in the state system will entail different scopes, O'Neill is sceptical of the claim that connections are concentrated within state borders. Empirically speaking, there is clearly a wide range of activity in which connections between individuals and groups transcend state borders, in addition to the wide range of interstate activities with which all IR theorists are familiar. By applying the notion of followability to this broadly conceived domain, O'Neill argues that we should, as far as possible, seek to build institutions which avoid systematic or gratuitous injury and compensate any exclusion, which is their result (Ibid. p. 173). Only in this way will the requirement for the ethical scope of actions to cohere with their practical scope be satisfied.

O'Neill's cosmopolitanism is closely connected to her universalism. The kind of autonomous judgement for which she strives is shown to be incompatible with any theory which presupposes territorial boundaries (O'Neill 2000: 178). Given her claim that actors and actions determine scope, it cannot be justified for a theory to rest on 'definitional strategies' which undercut the more important goal of 'vindicating' specific arrangements (Ibid. p. 178). In this sense, O'Neill's theory clearly overlaps with Cochran's criticisms of Frost and Walzer (discussed in Chapters 1 and 2, respectively). O'Neill makes an important point about the way in which arbitrary foundations inevitably and unnecessarily restrict the scope of ethical claims. By presupposing the shape of boundaries, communitarian reasoning overlooks the practical and ethical malleability of existing boundaries (O'Neill 2001a: 48), as well as many of the harms which these boundaries cause. Therefore, far from being sensitive to pluralism, she makes the claim that 'particularists are largely blind to it, since they see ethical life as encapsulated in distinct domains by rigid grids of categories and sensibilities' (O'Neill 1996: 20). When it comes to more radical particularists (such as Rorty) who 'ground ethics on individual sensibility or perception', she argues that they still 'have little of use to say about interaction with those whose sensibility differs' (Ibid. p. 20). This criticism underpins her cosmopolitanism:

> It seems to me that [. . .] an adequate account of justice has to take seriously the often harsh realities of exclusion, whether from citizenship of all states or from citizenship in the more powerful and more prosperous states. Why should the boundaries of states be viewed as presuppositions of justice rather than as institutions whose justice is to be assessed? (O'Neill 2000: 4)

While Walzer settles on the claim that any state is better than no state (Walzer 1980: 228), O'Neill argues that 'tyranny can be worse than insecurity' (O'Neill 2001a: 58). Her position offers a more flexible understanding of the vulnerabilities which the state and state system help sustain. O'Neill has much to say about these vulnerabilities and about the injuries which are often the result. Her points raise important questions for the way we think about the 'fit' between peoples and states by highlighting the harm caused by any, and all, proposed alignments 'of identity to territory', be they through demands for assimilation, departure or – at the extreme – extermination (O'Neill 2000: 178). By separating out existing borders and the demands of personhood, her theory allows us to grasp the common-sense point that 'if identities matter, minority identities matter' (Ibid. p. 173). O'Neill thus has rather solid philosophical and normative reasons for suggesting that we 'keep the legal and political notions of state and citizenship and the social and cultural categories of community, nationality and identity quite separate' (Ibid. p. 175).

The two previous chapters found that the tendency to assume rigidity is rather widespread in political theory. Those chapters also pointed to some of the undesirable implications of this kind of inflexibility. I charged both Walzer and Rorty with underestimating the existence and potential of meaningful interconnectedness across state borders. While I am not fully convinced by O'Neill's arguments about deriving authority from our 'undeniable' practical connections to others, it does seem undeniable that we can (and do) communicate 'if not perfectly, still a great deal' (O'Neill 2000a: 48) with 'outsiders'. By contrast:

> Where some actual boundary is taken to be the horizon of thought, what lies beyond that pale must be either incomprehensible to insiders, or no concern of theirs. In this case the legitimacy not merely of boundaries but of certain actual boundaries has been built into the very account of political discourse – or even of all

discourse [. . .] any attempt to vindicate boundaries from 'within' cannot take seriously – indeed may not be able to acknowledge either the predicaments of those who are excluded, or the alternatives for those who have been included. (O'Neill 1994: 66)

Presuppositions which rest on assumptions about incomprehensibility have been shown to lead to inflexible ethical claims which tend to exclude a range of important actors and processes from consideration. O'Neill has been a key voice in the move to include what she calls 'networking institutions' in political theory (O'Neill 2000: 182). Many of these institutions 'exercise substantial power' which 'is not confined within any bounded territory' (Ibid. p. 182).

O'Neill's theory is therefore very constructive in its rejection of the inequalities of the state system and in its criticism of the way so many theories, in turn, rest on these inequalities. However, given the framework of this book, there remain questions to be asked about the premises on which her theory rests. While I argue that it is important to avoid assumptions about strangeness which restrict the scope of ethical justification, it will be important also to acknowledge the limits to the relationship between empirical interconnections, cognition and intelligibility. These limits might have their own implications for the scope of practical ethical justification. In thinking about the assumptions of O'Neill's theory, I intend to keep in mind Cochran's claim that it is probably impossible to strive for anti-foundationalist ethics (Cochran 1999: 168).

As we saw in the first section of this chapter, O'Neill outlines an account of ethical universalism which is said to be 'neither self-evident nor given' (O'Neill 1989: 36). The authority of practical reason does not derive, in her view, from arbitrary premises. It is, however, a fully universal account of reason. She argues, following Kant, that practical reason is neither 'merely pragmatically necessary', nor a conventionally established assumption (Ibid. p. 36). Of course, this is a foundational claim, though one which O'Neill believes can be given autonomous justification. An often-raised objection to Kantian thinking of this kind claims that it seeks, in the end, to vindicate unjustifiable claims. While O'Neill acknowledges the inherent risks in appeals to autonomous judgement and, especially, the risks of the power/knowledge nexus (O'Neill 2000a: 54), she is nevertheless optimistic about the possibility of structuring thought and speech 'in ways that others can follow'

(Ibid. p. 54). At a very practical level, the attempt at 'followability' can dislodge the assumption that:

> Only arguments conducted in bureaucratic terms can reach bureaucracies; only arguments using standard capitalist economic categories can reach transnational corporations and their executives; only arguments in terms of national interest and standard political categories can reach governments and government agencies. (O'Neill 1979: 39)

She argues that followability is 'a principle capable of guiding the interactions [. . .] of beings whose coordination is not naturally guaranteed' (O'Neill 1989: 44). It emerges, therefore, as a principle appropriate to the international domain and to the search for arguments which convince across functional and territorial boundaries. The 'warrant that we have for following and trusting' procedures based on practical reason 'is that they are always subject to self-scrutiny and correction' (Ibid. p. 36). She therefore rejects the idea that it reintroduces contentious premises to ethical reasoning, offering up a qualified defence of fallibilism, which assumes the possibility of progress or a gradual process of Enlightenment (Ibid. p. 37). Any progress in communicability will 'have to develop and be instituted in the course of human communication' however (Ibid. p. 43), for there 'is neither a natural nor a pre-established harmony in the conversation of mankind' (Ibid. p. 43).

On the one hand, right action is clearly shown to be conditional on actors identifying the appropriate scope and on their choice of followable (or authoritative or universal) principles within that scope. On this account, right action is quite clearly contingent, to the extent that it is conditional on fallible cognitive processes. Indeed, O'Neill explicitly rejects the argument that practical reason relies on (or could have) some transcendent vindication (Ibid. p. 28). In her view, one of the idea's key strengths is that it is not derived 'from any source that transcends human life' (Ibid. p. 43). Instead, the potential achievement of consistency is 'an unending and exacting task, whose limits remain unclear to us' (Ibid. p. 47). Our assumptions are necessarily 'corrigible' (O'Neill 1996: 121), 'may or may not be present to agents' consciousness and may be ignored, disputed or repressed' (Ibid. p. 121). As Thomas M. Besch points out, 'activity can presuppose assumptions that are false or misguided, or that are made blindly or without due care'

(Besch 2009: 9). O'Neill seems, however, to accept that there can be no guarantee that any actor will determine the right course of action. Nevertheless, more effective recognition of the existence and implications of interconnections may still be possible (O'Neill 1996: 101) in the absence of any transcendental commitment. The practical character of her ethics means that the question of rightness tends to arise only 'when agents commit themselves' to assumptions about plurality, connection and finitude (Ibid. p. 100).

There may, however, remain something problematic in O'Neill's recourse to non-contingent theorising, in spite of her criticisms of other theories, in which 'remnants of undefended perfectionism are often evident in the background' (Ibid. p. 94). For her to meet her own high standards of autonomy, she will have to rely on the distinction between abstraction and idealism, outlined earlier. In trying to assess whether she meets this challenge, I intend to focus on the assumptions she herself makes about agents' cognitive abilities. Besch argues that even accepting the existence of 'adequately accurate' assumptions (O'Neill 1996: 115), there is a problem in O'Neill's move to the claim that we must 'by pain of incoherence or unreasonableness, include them in the scope of practical reasoning' (Besch 2009: 10).

How do the vices of incoherence or unreasonableness commit actors to followability and, hence, to right action? Some external account of coherence or reasonableness is clearly vital to O'Neill's theory. Indeed, as we have seen, she strives for an autonomous theory that goes beyond convention and pragmatism (O'Neill 1989: 36). Her account is therefore based on what she claims are abstract and uncontroversial assumptions about actions and agents. However, when it comes down to it, on the constitutive dimension of O'Neill's theory, it is the case that our assumptions, even where they are misguided, are the only available sources for constituting ethical consideration. This contingency makes the concept of coherence hard to square with a more abstract or universal conception. By equating practical assumptions with ethical guidelines (Besch 2009: 9), she makes ethical action contingent on the uncertainty of agents' actual assumptions. It follows that a more plausible (contingent) theory of coherence would need to let go of the claim to universality and acknowledge the contingency of fixing a coherent ethical scope on empirical judgements and on the agent's motivation to act coherently in the prescribed manner. As Besch has it, it remains unclear 'why it should be incoherent, or unreasonable, not to endorse such a view of ethical standing in the first place' (Ibid. p. 10). His preferred solution is very different to mine, and I leave the detail of the former aside for now. We both agree, at least, that there is an incomplete assumption of harmony implied in O'Neill's aspiration to universality, in spite of her acknowledgements of fallibilism.

We have seen, on the one hand, that O'Neill acknowledges that 'achieving consistency is an unending and exacting task, whose limits remain unclear to us' (O'Neill 1989: 47). She accepts that actors 'may be stupid or thoughtless or calculate poorly' (Ibid. p. 92). On the other hand, she sticks to the claim that it is generally possible (and desirable, given the fact that we are not self-sufficient beings) to calculate intelligibly on the 'normal and foreseeable results' (Ibid. p. 93) of our chosen actions. She therefore clearly rejects perfectionism. And yet, it is not clear that all that remain are uncontentious and abstract assumptions about agents' abilities to reason. I agree with her that there need be nothing transcendent in the claim that reason can provide 'a way of discovering whether we are choosing to act in ways (however culturally specific) that we do not in principle preclude for others' (Ibid. p. 104).

While the specific judgements of practical reason will always be contingent on a range of assumptions, they are grounded in the relatively uncontentious basis of human activity in interconnectedness and non-self-sufficiency. Nevertheless, there is something problematic in her claims that this basis can provide a universal warrant for the theory of practical reason. She may well be seeking to bolster what are, in fact, weak foundations with an unavailable supporting structure. I would suggest that it may not be feasible to determine either the conditions of right action or the rightness of a given action. It may, nevertheless, be possible for us to make constructive use of interconnections and of O'Neill's ideas about scope by viewing them as constitutive, in the sense that they can criticise and re-imagine existing institutions in an open way.

A more contingent view of coherence retains various practical applications. It remains suited, for example, to the kinds of criticism O'Neill wants to make of agents who make clashing promises and commitments (O'Neill 1996: 118). While these outline modifications would significantly constrain the likely scope of ethical coherence as a concept, they would potentially make more constructive use of O'Neill's ideas about vulnerability and inclusion. I will argue later in this book that this modified position provides a more constructive grounding for appreciation of the injuries of statelessness than either Walzer's state-based account of the denial of membership or Rorty's disconnected view of victimhood. Taken alongside her detailed attention to vulnerability, a major benefit of this kind of approach might be its suitability for thinking about the persistent, avoidable injury of the state system.

In the two previous chapters, I found that Walzer and Rorty were unnecessarily restrictive in their appreciations of international meanings. Following Cochran, I found that the ethical claims of these two thinkers were, in the end, too conditioned by their respective commitments to deeply held particularist starting points. O'Neill seeks to improve on this situation by identifying a mode of practical reason which is capable of producing autonomous judgements. However, my concern with the scope and limits of justification has, as its starting point, the idea that there is no ethical knowledge that is necessarily or universally true, whether discoverable or the subject of invention. Nevertheless, there are attributes of O'Neill's theory which might prove very helpful for thinking constructively about inclusion and exclusion in world politics. I want to suggest that it might even be possible to conceive of a more contingent approach to understanding connection and vulnerability in the state system.

In the last chapter, I discussed Cochran's conception of fallibilism (Cochran 1999: 206) in some depth. Fallibilism not only helps temper ethnocentrism (through the acknowledgement that our internalised commitments could be otherwise), it also requires us to accept that there may be no grounds for ethical judgements 'on which we can always rely' (Cochran 1999: 75). And yet, it doesn't require us to give up theorising. Rather, Cochran suggests that quasi-foundationalism allows for moves within the 'contingent end of the spectrum of ways of defending ethical claims' (Ibid. p. 168). At first sight, O'Neill's Kantianism positions her at the non-contingent end of the foundationalist spectrum. However, her constructivism makes it more difficult than it first appears to position her adequately on this spectrum. As we have seen, the abstraction/idealism distinction which she sets out and her conception of autonomous judgement preclude the straightforward claim that she is a moral perfectionist (see O'Neill 1996: 93–4). Indeed, it is precisely her sensitivity to ethical plurality which causes her to reject claims based on arbitrary starting points and to seek autonomous and accessible principles and justifications.

And yet, the present work starts from a position which is sceptical about the possibility of strongly autonomous judgements. In it, I have, so far, demonstrated a commitment to the view that there are probably no principles and, hence, no judgements, which are fully accessible in the strong sense. Theorists who start from this assumption tend to be wary of assuming too much about accessibility, especially in contexts characterised by significant inequalities of power. I therefore want to argue that O'Neill cannot avoid – any more than any of us can – recourse to somewhat contentious claims and that it is (pragmatically speaking) a mistake to assume otherwise. However, I also want to argue that it is extremely valuable to aim, as far as possible, for accessible reasoning, even if this 'accessibility' will always be contingent. This suggests an addition to Cochran's arguments about the merits of quasi-foundationalism. Perhaps, in the light of O'Neill's theory, our assumptions, however unavoidably, should strive for as much intelligibility as possible. I want to suggest that we focus less on O'Neill's proposed abstraction and more on her account of existing understandings and interconnections. There may be potential here to argue for the limit of 'unanswerable exercises of power and the more damaging sorts of vulnerability' (Ibid. p. 171) and the aversion of groundless exclusion (O'Neill 2000a: 46). To the extent that all foundations are arbitrary and hence contingent, Cochran is right about the need to acknowledge their contingency in the theoretical use we make of them. We can, all the same, strive for more accessible judgements and conclusions in specific contexts. Some conception of accessibility or intelligibility might, indeed – as she suggests – provide a critical counter to this tendency and its risks of arbitrariness. Accessible debates may, in some cases, benefit from existing networks of shared meaning and will, in other cases, require supporting meanings to be constructed (O'Neill 1996: 185).

III SUMMARY

O'Neill deals extensively with the risks of grounding ethical claims on arbitrary foundations. And yet, in the end, she is unable to avoid the same trap. I want to argue that this is not a damning criticism of her work. As Cochran suggests (Cochran 1999: 170), it may be impossible to avoid fallibility, even for those who are desperate to avoid the seduction of arbitrariness. If this is true, we should be more relaxed in our acknowledgements of the contingency of our starting points and, hence, of our ethical claims. Therefore, while O'Neill's constitutive account of coherence reveals that her political programme, too, is 'open to question' (O'Neill 2000: 178), this is not a fatal flaw. It might, nonetheless, require us to make some modifications to her theory. O'Neill claims that:

> If today we are committed by some of our routine activities to a more or less cosmopolitan view of moral standing, then whatever our account of justice, we shall need to work towards an implementation of its requirements that takes account of that scope. (Ibid. p. 200)

A more modest rendering of this claim might say that when the scope we attribute to our routine activities fits a more or less cosmopolitan view of moral standing, we will be able to work towards an implementation of some relations that take account of that scope. I am not sure that this reimagining would please O'Neill, although there are places in her own work where this less stringent image of cosmopolitanism emerges. In *Bounds of Justice*, for example, she depicts cosmopolitanism as 'a background picture which frames and sets standards for attempts to work towards an appropriate degree of institutional cosmopolitanism – that is towards institutions which take seriously the obligations that approximate moral cosmopolitans have reason to acknowledge' (Ibid. p. 201). In any case, it offers a more contingent basis for cosmopolitan theorising.

Each of the chosen theorists (Walzer, Rorty and O'Neill) agrees that it is vital to start with us as the relevant ethical actors. In different ways, each demonstrates a substantive concern with the avoidance of contested foundations and, yet, each – as we have seen – grounds their own theory in some unprovable foundation. Each therefore highlights the importance of taking a constructive, flexible approach to ethics, which acknowledges our fallibility and the limits of ethical reasoning. O'Neill's constructivism retains the concern with intelligibility found in Rorty and Walzer. However, I have argued that her approach is more useful than either alternative, insofar as it avoids assumptions about strangeness. It may, indeed, be possible to understand our connections to others without recourse to a foundational view of personhood. Even if our knowledge about others will always be conditional and limited, awareness of these limits can also help us avoid imposing arbitrary claims on those others. The ability to work towards some concrete understanding of our connections to others within the state system is central to O'Neill's arguments that we might be able to identify 'claimants' (O'Neill 1996: 135). While she accepts that it is not possible to construct an accessible picture of these 'claimants', she argues that it will often be possible to know something about the vulnerability of strangers to which our actions connect us. These vulnerable persons may, by contrast, 'grasp the air' (Ibid. p. 135). It will be the job of those making decisions to work towards policies which do not grasp the air, but rather, grasp the connections and vulnerabilities which are always already at stake. I have suggested that it is neither possible, nor desirable to finally 'fix' the scope of ethics. I have, nevertheless, found O'Neill's commitment to intelligibility instructive and constructive. By letting go of the claim to universality, it is possible to reorient her approach in a more rigorously contingent manner.

Chapter 5

TOWARDS A BACKGROUND THEORY
OF MEMBERSHIP

This chapter is somewhat different to the preceding chapters. The last part of this chapter attempts to piece together the various insights of Chapters 1 to 4, to the end of producing an outline background theory of membership in world politics. However, I leave this task to one side for now, in order to focus more explicitly on the practice of membership, which has, until now, remained in the background. Though the bulk of the chapter offers an account of this practice, I will try to avoid making any ethical claims about it in the first instance. I will, however, attempt to sketch the parameters of inclusion and exclusion, exploring the relationship between membership and individuality. These focuses relate to my interest, outlined in Chapter 1, in the way that political and social practices constitute and constrain individuality. Towards the end of the chapter, I discuss the way in which concepts outlined in Chapters 1 to 4 (such as flexibility, fallibility and communicability) might help shape an ethical response to (or 'background theory' of) membership in world politics. As Chapters 2 to 4 have shown, different political theories rest on (differing) assumptions about the connection between individual persons and the present reality of a plurality of states. For now, I leave aside the task of theorising, in order to try to locate the empirical grounds of membership. For reasons that might already be clear, I try to offer a relatively uncontroversial analysis of the practice of membership as it currently operates in the world.

I MUTUAL RECOGNITION IN THE STATE SYSTEM

This book is partly inspired by the Hegelian turn in international theory and, in particular, by its interest in the 'concrete practical' expressions of the 'system of mutual recognition within which individuality comes to be of value' (Frost 1996: 141). This chapter offers, first, an analysis, then an ethical response to the ways in which individuality has come to be of value within the state system. In doing so, it focuses on the inclusionary and exclusionary dynamics of membership. First, then, a reconsideration of the fundamental parameters of membership, as it is organised today, is in order. It will become apparent that for the individual, membership or 'personality' is constituted by widespread practices of identification, based on reciprocity or mutual recognition of interests. That is not to assume that these interests are prior to the practice, but rather, to emphasise the mutually constitutive relationship between fact and value in world politics.

Any analysis of the state system will tend to make some reference to plurality. At the very least, plurality signifies that the domain is one in which agreement is not guaranteed and in which there is some degree of interdependence. Accounts of plurality generally focus, to some extent, on two related conditions: cooperation and separation. Explanatory IR theory, for example, is a field in which there is sub-stantive disagreement about the scope of cooperation and the scope of separation. Nevertheless, it is a field in which there is underly-ing agreement that states sometimes act separately and sometimes act co-operatively. Constructivist IR theory has encouraged greater analysis of the relationship between norms and interests and of the implications of this relationship for our explanations of the scope of separation and cooperation in the state system. Without engaging any further in theoretical debates here, it is worth saying something about the basic approach, which structures the analysis to come. Throughout this chapter, it will be assumed that it is difficult to sepa-rate out what happens and why it happens. This difficulty requires the analyst to consider the outcomes of political and other regulative proc-esses alongside the meanings which are commonly used to explain or legitimise the practice or process. To be clear, this approach does not imply that those meanings or norms are justified or authoritative in any sense at all; it merely seeks to explore the practice as a whole in a fairly uncontroversial and unstructured way.

There is much that can be said about the constitution and regulation of membership in the system of states. Without offering a genealogi-cal account of membership practice, it is nevertheless possible to make some basic observations. There is, for example, almost unlimited evi-dence of a widespread state interest in exclusion.[1] An early UN study on statelessness testified, therefore, to states' shared 'desire to guarantee order and security' through mechanisms of expulsion and repatriation (United Nations 1949: 16). One only needs to look to recent developments in state security policy and immigration and asylum policy to see this interest manifested. One way in which this interest is institutionalised is in the regulation of inter-state movement of persons. There is now almost universal acknowledgement of states' responsibilities, in respect of their citizens. Whether or not we can identify any *a priori* interest in the citizen-state relationship, it is demonstrably a relationship with important implications. Attention to statelessness and, hence, to the limits of this relationship can help us make sense of the present day importance of states' commitments to their citizens.

One key feature of the state's institutionalised responsibility to its citizens is the international legal requirement for states to take ultimate responsibility for the permanent residence of their own citizens. Even in a world which is – arguably – highly globalised, inter-state travel is premised on a formalised commitment to this effect. Taking an international approach to the analysis of membership helps illustrate the relationships of recognition which constitute and limit the relationships between states and individuals. For most people, individuality today entails some (greater or lesser) possibility of leaving their own state. States have forged a degree of cooperation, making it possible for them to accommodate visiting non-citizens, who are, in the end, the ultimate responsibility of their own government. In the famous words of Arendt, states have come to recognise a shared interest in deportability (Arendt 1973: 283).

To elaborate, we might say that states' recognition of shared but differentiated commitments enables them to confer certain privileges on identifiable persons. This explanation makes no judgement on the legitimacy or moral worth of those privileges; it only points to a contingent part of the existing meaning of the practice as a whole. While Frost discusses these 'settled' norms in a way that suggests their authority (see Chapter 1), I am, for now, steadfastly trying to avoid imputing any authority to the norms or effects of membership as a set of processes and practices. Nevertheless, I want to point to two existing norms which now play a part in governing inter-state travel and citizen-state relations. The first institutionalised norm holds, as already suggested, that it is a good that states recognise certain basic commitments to their citizens. The second holds that it is a good, in certain conditions, that individual persons are permitted to travel between states and is encoded in the International Covenant on Civil and Political Rights (ICCPR), under which a person has the freedom 'to leave any country, including his own', (United Nations 1966: Article 12.2). Of course, it is a norm that runs into potential conflict with other ostensibly settled norms, and there may (contra Frost) be no clear way to reconcile these contradictions.

Nevertheless, attention to the general legal permission, in respect of inter-state travel, demonstrates some of the more-or-less universal implications of the existing arrangements of plurality in the system of states. It also demonstrates the extra-territorial effects of membership in a recognised sovereign state. Membership itself has become a status with significant, because limited, extra-territorial effect. Substantial cooperation on the regulation of inter-state travel has emerged alongside plurality as a way of balancing the practical tension between the demands of inclusion and the demands of exclusion. As we will see in due course, this tension has not been resolved; indeed, final resolution may not be possible. For now, however, I want to remain focused on the extra-territorial effects of the citizen-state relationship. As I will show, this dimension has become strengthened in various ways. On the other hand, it will be clear, also, that there is a limit to this status, which may prove problematic when it comes to attempting to offer a critical reading of membership in world politics.

In contemporary world politics, nationality (or membership) denotes a distinct relationship, implying not only 'the right of sojourn and return' and, hence, the possibility of exit, but also 'the enjoyment of diplomatic protection abroad' (Weis 1944: 4). Arendt also points us to the way that the modern state has 'tended to protect its citizens beyond its own borders and to make sure, by means of reciprocal treaties, that they remained subject to the laws of their country' (Arendt 1973: 280). In a domain where dominance is not possible (that is, there are no enforceable, or even agreed, universal laws), reciprocity has often been the guiding principle. Recognition in the system of sovereign states is not guaranteed, but is sustained by its conformity with common interests and, as this chapter will show, by the effect of its constitutive achievements in the field of nationality.

Complex relationships of recognition presently exist and these confer contingent (and uneven) benefits on states and individuals. Common reciprocal practices that reward behaviour consistent with these norms have also developed. In its bilateral form, reciprocity has allowed states to grant additional privileges to each other's nationals and to restrict privileges in retaliation of the same. Reciprocity can be seen, therefore, as a response to states' awareness of the challenges imposed by their mutual dependence. At the highly symbolic level, states grant diplomatic privileges and immunities to each other's senior functionaries, exempting them from domestic jurisdiction. Even so, these privileges can be withdrawn, highlighting not only states' mutual dependence, but also their rights over non-national residents. States retain the liberty to rescind their recognition of overseas diplomats, declaring them *persona non grata* (Higgins 1985: 649), as in 2010, when the United Kingdom expelled an Israeli diplomat, not on account of his own behaviour, but on account of his government's complicity in interfering with the status of UK nationals resident in Israel (see Borger 2010). States also generally recognise each other's competence to protect their members overseas, but reserve the right to intervene on behalf of their own, in case of unjustifiable harm. If, as a British national, I am subjected to arbitrary detention overseas, that government (and I) can reasonably expect my government to intervene on my behalf. There are also specific tasks which are, in general (I will consider the major exceptions in due course), within the remit of one's 'own' state, for example, the provision of passports for international travel. Again, these practices can be understood as related to a plural context in which neither cooperation, nor agreement are guaranteed and in which the units are substantially interdependent.

Everyday reciprocity in recognition of states' mutual dependence can also be read as 'fundamentally a threat of retaliation' (Rubinstein 1936: 726). In a very simple example, the United States 'retaliates' when a foreign government imposes visa fees on its citizens. At this point, a 'reciprocal' fee is imposed on nationals of that country (US Department of State 2011). This retaliatory dimension notwithstanding, it remains clear that reciprocal recognition is constitutive of individual and collective value. The threat of retaliation has also been mitigated by the institutionalisation of bilateral and multilateral agreements. The demands that states ordinarily make on each other rarely cause each other, or the wider practice, serious harm. As retaliations go, neither 'ordinary' expulsions, nor the imposition of reciprocal fees impose particularly high costs on states or on the wider value of mutual recognition. Isolated incidents apart, it is clear that recognition of states' interdependence has routinely made sustained cooperation possible, with positive effects for states and individual travellers. The advance of cooperation can be seen in the development of quite strong bilateral ties, which often encourage 'good' behaviour. While the majority of states tended historically to provide only basic (if any) unilateral assistance to foreigners (Hathaway 2005: 203), reciprocal bilateralism has encouraged agreement on better standards of treatment.

Reciprocity, especially in the tit-for-tat sense, is not the only concept that helps explain state practice in relation to membership. While states have reason to fear defections from the commitment, in principle, to the permanent residence of citizens, the shared value of adherence has underpinned substantive cooperation. In many places, an alertness to the constitutive role of identity has developed alongside further cooperation over the conditions and status of visiting and resident foreigners and, hence, in relation to the status of membership. Practices incorporating aspects of regional identity (for example, European Union citizenship) not only sustain diffuse reciprocal adherence to valued norms, but also strengthen the individual status of membership. By codifying the contingency and equivalence often said to be a vital aspect of reciprocal arrangements (Keohane 1986: 4), regional solutions building on a sense of common identity can help to achieve and sustain multilateral practices of recognition. That is, they support the sort of regional membership practice in which states 'behave well towards others, not because of ensuing rewards from specific actors, but in the interests of continuing satisfactory results for the group of which one is a part, as a whole' (Ibid. p. 20). In clarifying together the extra-territorial effects of European citizenship, for example, states have not, in fact, loosened their commitments to each other in respect of their own citizens, but rather, achieved the still greater regularisation of sojourning non-citizens' status and, hence, strengthened norm-governed behaviour, as well as the extra-territorial status of citizen-members.

Recognition – as a reciprocal arrangement – coincides, in general, with state interests, as well as providing international status to the individual. Explicit (diplomatic or contractual) agreements in respect of non-nationals tend to build on the minimal standard of general treatment accorded to aliens. The very structure of reciprocal recognition in the system of sovereign states is such that it doesn't work 'from an underlying presumption that aliens should receive full rights' (Hathaway 2005: 195). Of course, stateless persons, in addition to being undeportable, lack a government willing and able to advocate on their behalf. Stateless persons tend, therefore, to be at the mercy of state authorities, which, in some states, only afford a minimal standard of treatment to aliens generally. The limits of reciprocity seem clear enough. Even so, states present at the drafting of the 1954 Convention Relating to the Status of Stateless Persons sought to institutionalise these limits even more solidly. Delegates at the Convention insisted that any treaty be developed in strict conformity with existing practice. The majority of state delegates, therefore, insisted that no exemption from diplomatic reciprocity was even implied in the wording of the Convention (Robinson 1955: 20). In the case of states which ordinarily presumed to treat outsiders as if they were members, it is also made clear in Article 7 that this is not to be expected prior to a period of three years lawful residence (Hathaway 2005: 195). The explicit limits to the individual benefits associated with alienage are shown very clearly here.

We might even want to say that the wide institutionalisation of guaranteed temporary status for foreigners has represented deterioration in status at the limits. This backs up Arendt's claim that 'only with a completely organized humanity could the loss of home and political status become identical with expulsion from humanity altogether' (Arendt 1973: 297). So far, I have outlined the inter-state context of recognition, in which norms associated with individual personality, inter-state travel and citizen-state relations have developed, with a focus on the standards of treatment of aliens. I now turn to look in more detail at the individual effects of the relationship between recognition in the system of sovereign states and individual personality. Doing so will again help explore the constitution and limits of individual personality.

Given that reciprocity requires certainty about the proper source of responsibility for an individual, the assumption remains that 'every individual [. . . can be] recognized as having a legal personality' (United Nations 1949: 11):

> When one considers the occasions for invoking the relationship– emigration and immigration; travel; treason; exercise of political rights and functions; military service and the like – it becomes evident that certainty is essential [. . . and that there] must be objective tests, readily established, for the existence and recognition of the status. (International Court of Justice 1955)

The distinction between members and foreigners (and, hence, between those with legal personality and those without) has, indeed, tended to rest on objective criteria, which are formally institutionalised in identity and travel documents. States' acknowledgement of their ultimate responsibility for their own nationals requires persons to have a verifiable identity, such as that found in the passport, which serves to identify 'each individual traveller', as well as his point of origin and 'the State to which he can be deported' (Salter 2004: 72). The passport can be seen as a formal representation of an individual's verifiable identity, which enables states 'to allow the bearer to pass freely without let or hindrance, and to afford the bearer such assistance and protection as may be necessary' (UK passport). Allied to this identity, there are a range of additional claims 'that a person can legitimately expect to have socially met because he or she participates, with equal rights, in the institutional order as a full-fledged member of a community' (Honneth 1996: 133). If we take the institutional order to be international in scope, it becomes clear that individual recognition is constituted in an important way by the less than fully-fledged, but inescapably important, membership equivalent to nationality status – that is, legal personality (United Nations 1949: 11). The claim to recognition under consideration is the claim to recognition while away from home, at the very least, of one's claim to safe conduct. Membership can be seen, therefore, as embodying a claim by the state for recognition of the person and property of its nationals. Generally speaking, states recognise such claims (even where, for example, visas or passport stamps impose some control over the sojourn of the bearer). Reciprocity therefore serves, in practice, to mitigate the problems of plurality, as regards membership.

What, then, can be said with confidence about the relationship between individual 'personality', or membership, and the state-based relationships of recognition that help constitute it? It is clear that states recognise each other and recognise, in turn, bilateral and multilateral commitments to each other. It is also clear that these commitments require certainty about the connection between states and citizens. The confirmation of an individual's identity proceeds, therefore, by confirmation of their nationality or legal personality. Personality, as it is presently constituted, requires that states can recognise the connection of individual persons to given states, which requires, in turn, that states make these connections clear and at least minimally effective. States act as more-or-less equivalent parties to a range of reciprocally-based practices of identification, and it remains clear that, in general, it is 'the sovereign right and responsibility of each State to determine, through the operation of national law, who are its citizens' (UNHCR 2004: 124). States, then, are the ones who do the recognising, in acknowledgement of the links between states and persons (Batchelor 1998: 174). This recognition is facilitated by identification documents and practices and generally confers upon individuals the right (even the duty) to return to their 'own' country. For the individual person, these practices have tended to facilitate commitments to the protection of non-citizens and, hence, enhanced the protective scope of state-membership.

As Frost makes clear:

> As this practice is presently organized, we who are citizens of sovereign states know that it is always appropriate to ask for the identity of the state within which a person claims citizenship rights for him or herself. It may sometimes happen that a person turns out to be a citizen of more than one state. But citizenship always implies membership of some or other state or states. (Frost 2006: 8)

The reason that it is 'always appropriate' to seek verification of membership relates to the character of international recognition already discussed. The implication for the individual is that not only citizenship, but also diplomatic protection and recognition by other states, always imply 'membership of some or other state or states'. Thus, we see that the value of the general permission to travel between states is dependent on the individual's embodiment of the certain commitment to him, or her, of some or other state. It appears also that part of what is valuable today about belonging to some or other state is precisely its extra-territorial purchase, which is to say that the value of being a member cannot now convincingly be isolated from the value of states' mutual recognition. I am suggesting here that the value of membership in world politics rests, in part, on the fundamentally individual potential for identification (and, hence, recognition) around the world. This positive point comes with a caveat which a satisfactory background theory must take into account: the very international practices which are constitutive of these valued and valuable norms aggravate the impact of being denied a proper place in the state.

That I might (should I need or want to) leave my own state and travel to other countries in the world in an attempt to better flourish as an individual, seems to support the constitutive claim that each level of the world's institutional hierarchy 'creates a moral standing which remedies some of the deficiencies experienced at the lower level' (Frost 1996: 158). However, states' mutual recognition of each other and the concrete embodiments of recognition in reciprocal practices have also created a minority standing, which exacerbates some of the deficiencies experienced at the lower levels. The practices which offer value to many, or even most, persons not only exclude, but actually worsen the situation of stateless persons. From an ethical point of view, the limits of recognition will require attention to the possibility of extending international recognition, in order to avoid the conclusion that exclusion from the state is necessarily 'identical to expulsion from humanity altogether' (Arendt 1973: 297). As things stand, membership practice entails two contradictory points. It has tended – on the one hand – to facilitate certain commitments to the protection of non-citizens and, hence, enhanced the protective scope of state-membership. And yet, it has also served to endanger life at the limits.

II THE LIMITS OF PERSONALITY: REFUGEES

The focus of this chapter, so far, has been on the normal practices in which states participate that allow them to exclude non-citizens and which also constitute a domain of extra-territoriality, in which states and individuals are subject to recognition. In the normal course of events, adherence is supported by bilateral and multilateral reciprocal arrangements, as well as by commitments to regional identities. There is a harder case that poses distinct challenges in respect of the permanency of residence for citizens and has, hence, required distinctive practices for balancing the reality of inter-state movement with states' interests in exclusion. Again, understanding of this 'problem' requires attention to the plurality of the state system, as well as the role of norms and individual identity. The first section of this chapter considered the possibility, retained by states, to make a claim against another in respect of the duty of readmission and mentioned the recent case of the Israeli diplomat. Indeed:

> Under international law, every state is, in principle, competent to expel at any moment any alien who has been admitted into its ter-

ritory. It does not matter whether the alien is there on a temporary basis or has settled down for professional or business purposes. (Robinson 1955: 60)

However, in day-to-day practice, acts including the issue of removal orders and deportations are used only rarely and are consistent, even then, with a widely valued norm. If the worst states can do to each other is invoke the commitment to the residence of members, the reciprocal value of the practice holds pretty firm. However, there is a further 'harm' states can do to one another. States that persecute their own citizens will often impel those members not only to exercise the possibility of exit, but also to disrupt the host state's ordinary recourse to their possible return. The reader will perhaps be familiar with the practices which together make up the regime for refugee protection. However, the approach taken here should highlight certain key features of international practice in relation to membership.

The particular challenges associated with individuals and groups unwilling to be repatriated in fulfilment of the state commitment to re-admit its nationals relate, in part, to states' mutual interest in this norm. The same basic interests, norms and institutions underlie practice on refugees. There are implications here for the extra-territoriality of protection, which is shown to be contingent not only on the connection to one's 'own' state, but also on assumptions about the durability of this connection. In conformity with the norms and practices already considered, determinations of refugee status converge both on explicitly agreed criteria, but also on the less explicit shared interest in exclusion. Goodwin-Gill's fascinating piece on the politics of refugee protection gives a clear historical insight into states' reluctance to 'upset' countries of origin (Goodwin-Gill 2008: 21), as in the case of Algeria, where it is suggested that client governments 'did not want France accused of persecution' (Ibid. p. 20). The present framework for refugees, thus, to some extent, goes beyond the constraining effects of reciprocity, situating decisions with the office of the United Nations High Commissioner for Refugees (UNHCR) as an international agency. In this way, states are relieved of the demand to make judgements on each other, with the effect that exceptions to the general permanence of the connection between citizen and state are dealt with in a manner that treats them clearly as exceptional.

Commitment to the norm has also, at various times, been mitigated by ideological factors, as well as humanitarian concerns, although it is clear that 'self-interest [. . .] cannot be ignored or washed out of the picture' (Ibid. p. 21). However, given the Cold War political and ideological posturing in which states vindicated claims of persecution and criticised other states, the growing reluctance to make 'contentious judgements' (Ibid. p. 18) suggests a progressive hardening of states' shared interest in exclusion and, hence, in the tie between individuals and a given state. There has, correspondingly, been a clear shift away from the durable solution of resettlement:

> The recent years have witnessed a far lower level of resettlement arrivals as compared to the late 1980s or 1990s. In particular following the events of 11 September 2001, the number of refugees accepted by countries decreased significantly due to specific screening procedures put in place by some countries [. . .] Whereas resettlement levels increased again during 2004 [. . .] this appears to have corrected the effects of 2001 and put the level back to its pre 2001 levels showing a pattern of steady decline since numbers have gone down again in 2005 [. . .] and 2006. (UNHCR 2007: 40)

A good part of the value of current practice rests, in an obvious sense, on the (actually immensely varied) goods that states afford their members. Yet, in the case of rejected and returned refugees, much of this individual content is stripped. The possibility of exit is also undermined in these cases; cases where its promise as a norm (conferring the possibility of sanctuary) is, arguably, most valuable. What this suggests for 'understanding of the link between free individuality and the system of sovereign states' (Frost 1996: 151) is that the individual value of states' mutual recognition is subordinate or subsidiary to the value which accrues to states. It also suggests the possibility that the individual value is contingent on a normal, healthy relationship between the individual and a given state, which is to say that the possibility of leaving one's own state is contingent not only on its temporariness, but also on an already existing 'coincidence between what the state requires of them and what they require in order to be free' (Ibid. p. 150). It is becoming clear that 'the link between free individuality and the system of sovereign states' is limited by the very nature of the practices which sustain it (Frost 1996: 151).

The practices which distinguish members/foreigners from stateless persons effectively exacerbate the pluralism of the state system at its limits. This exclusionary limit is demonstrated by the stark contrast between the situation of the citizen of a 'good' state, generally able to travel between countries, and the persecuted member of a 'bad' state, often forced to remain there. An interesting aside is that in many parts of the world, foreigners are, by virtue of the diplomatic protection of their own state, better off than members. At its best, then, the system of sovereign states extends the benefits of state membership, consolidating the state's commitments to members and allowing for the possibility of exit. At its worst, it aggravates the experience of the individual whose relationship with his, or her, state does not function as it should.

III THE LIMITS OF PERSONALITY: STATELESS PERSONS

Stateless persons, too, pose 'problems' so far inconsistent with agreed norms and resistant to reciprocal recognition practices. The 'valid' but 'unlawful' character of denials of membership has already been mentioned as demonstrating the tensions associated with the breakdown of the citizen-state link. In Chapter 1, I referred to various attempts to institutionalise the unlawfulness of denationalisation. The interest in its validity remains vital, however. There is some debate today about the extent to which states retain 'almost unfettered discretionary power', in respect of the right to confer nationality (International Court of Justice 1955). However, as recently as 2009, lawyers accepted that 'international law still does not, with few and vague exceptions, seek to regulate the sovereign competence of states to designate national or juridical persons as their nationals' (Sloane 2009: 7). As one commentator on Africa has noted, in the current situation:

> States can no longer legally deprive citizens of rights, but they can shortcut their obligations by limiting the very existence of citizens. Because international norms on the granting and deprivation of citizenship and those defining the rights of noncitizens are weak or non-existent, states can legally limit the number of individuals to whom they guarantee key rights. Remarkably, state actions to lift or limit citizenship are not prohibited by human rights law, despite their decisive impact on individual human rights. (Harrington 2005: 25)

Therefore, while the ostensibly basic tension between individual rights and sovereignty rights may not be as fundamental as has sometimes been imagined, there remain difficulties in reconciling these two types of norm. The remaining challenges represent the important role states still play in mediating individuality.

When a government denationalises, removes or 'deports' one or more of its own citizens and refuses to take him or her back, a host of problems arise. A state that forces one or more of its members out violates the general pact among states to take ultimate responsibility for the residence of their citizens. Such breaches of comity generally serve some domestic political end of perceived importance. States that withhold nationality from persons with a good claim to it (such as birth, descent or residence) and/or subsequently deprive such persons of it, therefore diverge from the general practices associated with membership in international politics. In principle, all states have a secondary self-interest in the possibility of excluding even their own members.[2] In fact, the value accorded by states to the right to determine the parameters of membership means that, still today, there is no clear and unambiguous agreement on a proposal that 'stateless persons should be admitted to the territory of the State to which they formerly belonged on request of the State of residence' (Kuhn 1936: 496).

While this permission is circumscribed for states that are party to the 1961 Convention on the Reduction of Statelessness (for example, Articles 5 and 6), it can help account, in part, for the limited number of states parties (thirty-eight as of June 2011). Given that the recognition of competency is a necessary precondition if governments are to engage in reciprocal practices, states in crisis will sometimes inevitably have a strong self-interest in consolidating power by excluding a minority or dissident group. And even well-intentioned governments can fail to uphold their municipal and international commitments to those with a proper claim to membership, especially during or after periods of conflict, given that:

Documentary requirements may compound these problems. Wars, other conflicts, and administrative mistakes often create insuperable obstacles to documenting birth, marriage, parentage, or residence. Children born in a refugee area outside of their parents' state of citizenship during an armed conflict may later find it difficult or impossible to document their parentage or date and place of birth. (Weissbrodt and Collins 2006: 258)

However, as we have seen, the value of the general norm has made acceptance of the right to residence and return widespread, with state-lessness remaining a minority problem, albeit one that can help clarify what is at stake in membership and in its limits.

The existence of stateless persons undermines the basis of states' shared commitment to the residence and return of members and poses a challenge in respect of the continued ordinary possibility for individuals of moving between states. Stateless persons are not deportable – a long-recognised complicating factor (see Arendt 1973: 283) which fatally undercuts the general freedom to leave one's country, a right which is not – in principle – 'restricted to persons lawfully within the territory of a State' (United Nations 1999: paragraph 8). In most cases, this right does not cause problems. However, states are often wary of the presence of persons who can be neither deported, nor expelled. In an attempt to contain the 'spreading lawlessness' (Arendt 1973: 447) of statelessness, it has been affirmed (in conformity with the practices of recognition discussed early in this chapter) that no country is legally 'bound to receive a stateless person in respect of whom an expulsion order has been issued' (United Nations 1949: 16). Robinson outlines the related norm that 'once a stateless person has been admitted or legalized, he is entitled to stay in the country indefinitely and can forfeit this right only by becoming a national security risk or by disturbing public order' (Robinson 1955: 61). Thus, while in theory, according to the ICCPR, the stateless individual may leave the state of residence, the reluctance of other states to receive him or her means, in practice, that stateless persons are often either quietly pushed out or else remain 'stuck' where they are. In the end, the vast majority either remains stuck in situ or caught in the push-pull of states equally unhappy with their presence. This renders the stateless person an inevitable outlaw (United Nations 1949: 16); 'confronted by two sovereign wills, that of the State that says "go" and that of the State that says "stay out"' (Rubinstein 1936: 852–3). In neither situation can the stateless person realistically be said to enjoy the individual attributes of membership at stake in the norm which facilitates inter-state travel. In fact, his fate is often, in the end, to be stuck 'in the country of his "unlawful" stay [. . .which] may apply to him such restrictions as are necessary in his case to safeguard the interests of the state' (Robinson 1955: 63). Even the Human Rights Committee, which monitors compliance with the ICCPR, affirms that domestic law 'may subject the entry of an alien' to restrictions compliant with the state's international obligations (United Nations 1999: paragraph 4). The stateless person, by contrast to the refugee, enjoys no legal exemption from penalties for unlawful entry.

The 1954 Convention Relating to the Status of Stateless Persons represented a major attempt to clarify the burdens of statelessness. As of June 2011, there are sixty-six states who are parties to the Convention, seventy-eight fewer than to the 1951 Convention on the Status of Refugees. The drafters of the 1954 Convention faced significant difficulties in minimising and distributing the perceived burdens arising out of the entry of stateless persons. The Convention attempted to open up the possibility of international recognition in a manner which would also provide individual value, allowing stateless persons to exit and enter countries more easily. Article 28 requires contracting states to provide travel documents for travel outside of its territory to lawful stateless residents and, hence, requires other contracting states to recognise such documents 'if they are prepared to admit him' (United Nations 1954: paragraph 8, schedule to Article 28). This requirement follows from the 'general rule of international courtesy that acts of one government are given credence else where [sic] except when there are valid reasons to assume an error or abuse' (Robinson 1955: 11). It cannot, of course, require the same of non-contracting states, and, hence, the status implied in the travel documents is acknowledged by a much more limited reciprocity than that governing 'normal' inter-state travel. The presumption for such travel documents is that they entitle the bearer to re-enter the territory of the issuing state during the period of validity, which must not be less than three months (unless the destination state waives this entitlement, which might seem unlikely, given the value of the norm which proscribes expulsion) (United Nations 1954: paragraph 12, schedule to Article 28). The assurance of the right of re-entry requires acknowledgement, on the part of the state of residence, of a semi-permanent connection to the (probably unwanted) stateless resident. There are, however, ways around this, given that the Convention imagines that travel documents may contain 'a statement to the contrary' and that the Article is open to reservations.

While the provision received considerable opposition at the time, the British representative pushed the point that it was 'one of the most important in the whole Convention and that its elimination would be highly undesirable' (Robinson 1955: 51; see also, Weis 1961: 263). It does, therefore, provide clear benefits to the individual, even while it in no way entitles 'the holder to the diplomatic protection of the diplomatic or consular authorities of the country of issue, and does not ipso facto confer on these authorities a right of protection' (United Nations 1954: paragraph 12, schedule to Article 28). In spite of the extra-territorial effect of the limited right to travel and of the subsequent provisions for legal assistance outside of the country of habitual residence, the legal framework under the Convention in no way satisfies the right set out in the Universal Declaration of Human Rights to 'recognition everywhere as a person before the law' (United Nations 1948: Article 6).

The general international approach to statelessness reaffirms not only the right of the state to determine who are (and are not) its members (insofar as there are limited sanctions applicable to states who rid themselves of members), but also the common value of exclusion, insofar as states are prohibited from expulsion of stateless residents. In any case, the inference has been that the state of residence subsidises these wider interests, to the extent that it is expected to waive its self-interest and 'put up' with its stateless residents. The only way in which the state could normalise this relationship would be for it to nationalise its stateless residents, who would then benefit from recourse to the right of exit. Even so, to recognise statelessness in this manner would be unequal from the point of view of the system of sovereign states, given that it would be an effective challenge to the agreed upon norm that it is for each and every state to determine who gets to be a member.

Early on, the International Law Commission proposed a solution that would be practically equivalent to naturalisation, for while it could have allowed states to continue to exclude stateless persons from the aggregative benefits of citizenship, it would have gone far beyond treatment of non-nationals and provided for much of what is at stake in membership. The Commission suggested that states of residence might consider granting the status of 'protected person' to anyone stateless. This status would include the core entitlement to diplomatic protection (Weis, 1961: 257). The Conference of Plenipotentiaries, tasked in 1954 with drafting an agreement on the status of stateless persons, did not devote much attention to this suggestion. The reasons are unclear from contemporary reports (Ibid. p. 257), although there are two clear possible constraints. On the one hand, the diffuse reciprocity which sustains states' recognition of each other's members requires the widespread and on-going commitment of states to existing, rather than new, connections between individuals and a given state. On the other hand, the depth of this connection means that a commitment to naturalisation would impose significant burdens on the naturalising state. It has, indeed, been noted that at the time of drafting, states were reluctant to constitute provisions which might be 'the impetus for persons to attempt to secure a second nationality' (Weissbrodt and Collins 2006: 253). Consequently, the requirements for naturalisation are weak in the resulting Convention Relating to the Status of Stateless Persons, which holds under Article 32 that: 'Contracting States shall as far as possible facilitate the assimilation and naturalization of stateless persons'. The clear ambiguity of the phrase 'as far as possible' is reflected in the fact that the Article did not provoke disagreement in the Conference of Plenipotentiaries which drafted the Convention (Robinson 1955: 64).

IV THE LIMITS OF RECOGNITION

When one looks at the state system, it seems to be clear that the very 'system of mutual recognition within which individuality comes to be of value' (Frost 1996: 141) itself circumscribes not only the right of residence, but also the possibility of diplomatic protection in cases of statelessness. More can be said about these limits, and the chapter turns now to consideration of the ways that mutual recognition in the state system further complicates recognition of statelessness. There are good reasons that it has often been known as 'rightlessness'. Agreement on the domestic status of stateless residents has been another difficult thing to achieve. It is generally assumed that 'the basic human rights of stateless persons are, in principle, to be respected in the country of habitual residence' (UNHCR 1995: paragraph 19). It follows that such persons 'are not, therefore, assumed to be in acute need of international protection' (Ibid. paragraph 19). This assumption is institutionalised in the ICCPR, which commits states to certain standards of treatment for 'all individuals within its territory and subject to its jurisdiction' (United Nations 1966: Article 2). Likewise, the development of international human rights, according to which, governments 'have the primary responsibility for implementing [. . .] human rights in their own countries' (Donnelly 2003: 160), is now generally accepted as entailing duties to persons 'whether they are citizens or not' (Ibid. p. 159). This development in international relations has almost certainly brought benefits to individuals. I want to suggest, however, that it is a development which fails to resolve the continuing tension between statelessness and individual personality. Diplomatic reciprocity can be seen as having been substantially replaced by international guarantees of human rights. And yet, there remain limits to the promise of these ostensibly universal human rights. A close reading of the ICCPR, for example, shows that in places it is dependent on presumptions about personality. It reaffirms the ordinary liberty of states to restrict political rights to citizens, with the result that stateless persons lack all political rights. The preamble also assumes that the individual has an effective relationship with 'the community to which he belongs', while Article 12 restricts liberty of movement within a territory to the condition of lawful entrance. While the covenant also cites the claim that all 'persons are equal before the law' (Article 26), this seems to apply to persons in the strict legal sense, rather than to any more fundamental conception of personhood.

Thus, while the assumption that 'the basic human rights of stateless persons are, in principle, to be respected in the country of habitual residence' (UNHCR 1995: paragraph 19) makes sense when seen from within a foundational theory of individuality, a constitutive theory would emphasise the special vulnerability of stateless persons to state interests. Constitutive theory's emphasis on the situation of individuality within an institutional whole constituted by recognition (Frost 1996: 142) helps show that there is no basic respect in the country of residence and that this lack of respect is intimately connected to the ways in which we constitute one another as holders of the rights stressed here. In terms of the concrete practical expressions of recognition in the system of states, it is more accurate to say (elaborating on Donnelly 2003: 159–60) that, as it stands, governments' responsibility for implementing human rights entails duties to persons, whether they are citizens of that state or some other state. It remains important that they can be identified as a member of some state. International human rights, though undoubtedly valuable, are not equivalent to the general guarantees enjoyed by members, which, though imperfect, offer particular protections from injury. It is not clear, for example, that the Human Rights Committee can act as a substitute for the diplomatic interventions of one's own government. This power to intervene – which is more a possibility or threat than perfect individual remedy – is vital to understanding membership practice in the contemporary world. Tacit acknowledgement of the fact that there is presently no respect for the human rights of stateless persons can be interpreted in UNHCR's continued attempts to encourage states to accede to the 1954 Convention (UNHCR 2010a), with its specialist and specified standards of treatment.

So far, this chapter has intended to demonstrate the extent to which states' mutual recognition constitutes and constrains individuality. It has done so by considering general practice and the challenges posed by refugees and stateless persons. Given the institutionalised importance of inter-state travel and the extent to which stateless persons are excluded from it, some have been tempted to say that state recognition of individuals serves as 'the basis of human subjectivity itself' (Heter 2006: 24). In any case, it is obvious that we are constituted today as persons through international processes of reciprocal recognition. From the perspective of international politics, these reciprocal processes can be seen to operate often at a distance from us, within the institution of the system of states. And yet, this distance does not minimise the impact of the practices upon us as individuals. In fact, inter-state reciprocity – which, in general, follows the norm that it is a good that states recognise each other's members – is central to the constitution of personality. Its present limits are, therefore, of real ethical concern.

It is often imagined that the society of states is an improvement on the plurality of the state system, extending universal rights. And yet, in a very real way, societal constraints on state sovereignty can be seen to constrain individuality, insofar as they represent a refusal to recognise statelessness. We can't escape the interests of the state parties to international society. Status in the constitutive sense of a 'state of being recognised' within specific institutional practices (Ikäheimo and Laitinen 2007: 50) cannot easily be substituted by unilateral guarantees of status 'independent both of official grantings and of attitudes of recognition' (Ibid. p. 50). Membership, then, in the final analysis, entails the possibility of permanent residence in a given state, as well as the possibility of temporary residence in other states throughout the world. In a meaningful sense, membership emerges as an exercise concept, in the sense that it requires actual recognition. Membership provides, then, for diplomatic protection by a given state and the option (if not necessarily the ability) of refusing that protection and leaving the place of permanent residence in the case of persecution. I have also suggested in this chapter that the international practices of recognition which make this possible, at the same time aggravate the deficiencies of the state, in particular, its necessary exclusion. The resulting inequality is ethically troubling, showing that those without an advocate party to the reciprocity, which sustains recognition in international politics, are excluded from the individual value of membership. And yet, building on the theoretical assessments set out in the first part of this book, I want to suggest that there may be scope within our existing practices of recognition for greater inclusion. The last part of this chapter explores this potential.

V A BACKGROUND THEORY OF MEMBERSHIP IN WORLD POLITICS

The ostensible tension between universal and particular, embodied in a practical tension between individuality and sovereignty, was the starting point of this book. As the first chapter showed, statelessness has long been seen as a practical demonstration of this tension. The book has, however, taken a different approach to the association between individuals and states and the relationship between inclusion and exclusion. Beginning with a constitutive approach, it set out to examine the close links between human rights and sovereignty. This chapter has explored the way in which the state system constitutes and limits personality. By focusing on practices in this way, I have made myself reliant on empirical foundations. A corollary of the constitutive approach is that these practices are not external to our understanding of them. As such, much as I have strived to avoid wildly controversial claims, my starting points are unavoidably contentious. There is, I have argued, no way to provide an objective account of the world or of any of the practices which we shape and which shape us.

Following Cochran's arguments about foundationalism, we might say that my account rests on weak foundations. Mindful of her criticisms of Frost and Walzer, I have sought to ensure that any claims made about the ethics of membership are made conditionally. I have therefore rejected the terminology of 'settled norms' (Frost 1996: 9) to describe the ways in which individuality is constituted within the state system. This kind of conditionality makes it easier for us to be sensitive to the exclusions and inequalities of the practices we want to better understand. A further implication of this approach is that it will not be possible to reconcile or synthesise dignity and sovereignty in the manner that many other theorists suggest. This does not necessarily lead us back to the conclusion that there is an inescapable tension between the two kinds of norm. By rejecting foundational thinking, we might – I have suggested – be able to avoid imprisoning ourselves within such ontological traps. In this way, we will avoid reaching the conclusion Walzer does, that 'any state is better than no state' (Walzer 1980: 228). Chapters 2 to 4 set out in detail the potential contributions for understanding membership of Michael Walzer, Richard Rorty and Onora O'Neill. It remains for me to draw these insights together into a patchwork background theory. I will first recap the general points made, before shaping these into a background theory.

In Chapter 2, I showed that Walzer tends to overestimate the potential of thick moralities and arrangements to enforce rights by assuming too much about the foundational value of community. He therefore says too much in justification of the current arrangements of plurality. As a result, he underplays the practical tension between individuality and the state system. As such, he pays insufficient attention to, and, hence, arguably underestimates the constructive potential of, the relationships and networks of meaning which go beyond and between states. On the basis of this assessment of Walzer, I argued that we should focus more on the relationship between the appeal and limits of his particularist-inspired universalism. Put another way, we should look to understand the ways in which particularism is formed by, and informs, exclusion. We are most likely to be able to say something meaningful about this connection if we pay explicit attention to the existing connections of international society and, in particular, to the international institution of separation and what Cochran calls the 'international forces of socialization' (Cochran 1999: 72). Doing so might lead to a richer account of 'reiterative universality' (Walzer 1989: 514), which can say more about the types of encounter that minimalism might facilitate.

Chapter 3 explored Cochran's account of Rorty's 'quasi-foundationalism' (Cochran 1999: 170) in some depth. The benefits of this approach were said here to include caution, flexibility and the ability to better avoid the seductions of 'correct' theory. A Rorty-inspired 'quasi-foundationalism' might therefore provide us with an additional means of side-stepping the definitional tension between sovereignty and individuality. Applied to the impasse in which state-lessness is held to be both valid and unlawful (Weis 1979: 242), it can free us to think more critically about the international politics of exclusion. While Rorty himself was said to yield to the temptation to make foundational claims about exclusion from humanity, I argued that it might be possible to learn from this mistake and to ensure a more rigorous engagement with the actual relationships which sustain and limit personhood. Doing so would also make us more able to look critically at our existing, internal languages of justification.

This theme was developed in Chapter 4, which explored O'Neill's suggestions for rejecting arbitrariness in our ethical claims. O'Neill offers better awareness of the real seduction of arbitrary foundations than either Walzer or Rorty. And yet, in the end, she is unable to attain the kind of autonomy she wishes, in respect of the ethical claims she makes. In light of the constitutive framework set out in Chapter 1, it will be difficult to vindicate the distinctions she makes between autonomy and arbitrariness and between abstraction and perfectionism. If, however, we can let go of the aspiration to universality, we might be able to strive for enhanced accessibility on the basis of the international connections which O'Neill says so much about. Her account had the best potential for avoiding assumptions about ostensibly *strange* others. I argued that it might, therefore, be possible to understand our connections to others, without recourse to a foundational view of personhood. Even if our knowledge of others will always and inevitably be limited, it is self-reflexive awareness of these limits which is vital.

What, then, are the weak foundations on which the background theory of membership offered here rests? This chapter has set out a range of points, which I will recap here. It should be said that these are selected features of international relations, which I have chosen to emphasise on the basis that they tell us something interesting about the practice of membership and are relatively uncontroversial. First, I chose to emphasise the state interest in exclusion and in regulation of the inter-state movement of persons. The chapter then considered related developments in the citizen-state relationship. A permanent population is central to the constitution of the modern state (International Conference of American States 1933) and was historically manifested in concerns about emigration, taxation and loyalty, as well as concerns about national identity. Today, many argue that the postmodern state has an interest in the biopolitical management of its population (for

example, Foucault 2008). A more benign view might also emphasise the development of human rights, which has clearly shaped and
been shaped by the citizen-state relationship. A wide range of rights,
including the right to leave and re-enter one's own state, the right to
a nationality, the right to recognition everywhere as a person before
the law and the right of non-refoulement are all important dimensions
of membership practice today. In spite of the important differences
between states, there are common functions which they either perform
or are expected to perform. The practices of plurality therefore have
more-or-less universal implications. We are therefore able to speak
with some degree of meaning about the international dimensions of
membership, inclusion and exclusion. In terms of a background theory
of membership, it is therefore possible, by focusing on the universal
implications of plurality, to identify important international norms and
institutions.

The international institution of separation has been constitutive of a
range of important capabilities and capacities, as well as of some conditions of persistent vulnerability. Practices of separation and cooperation in the state system have developed alongside what Cochran calls
'international forces of socialization' (Cochran 1999: 72). Of course,
states retain substantial powers within these international frameworks.
A fundamental characteristic of international membership practice
remains the 'absence of general rules for the attribution of nationality and the discrepancies between the various national legislations'
(United Nations 1949: 4). We have, of course, witnessed the effect of
mutual recognition in establishing higher standards of treatment for
nationals and non-nationals. However, statelessness serves as evidence of the limits of international norms and institutions. It shows
that contrary to Frost's hope for a progressive resolution of the tensions
associated with sovereignty (Frost 1996: 158), international society has
– at the margins – exacerbated its worst excesses, including the possibility of exercising arbitrary and unlimited power over minority groups
and individuals. The exclusionary effects of progressive inclusion have
been studied in various fields. It is, for example, commonly argued that
there is a correlation between successful welfare provision and closed
societies and systems. At the very least, it seems possible to argue that
the costs of exclusion rise with the institutionalisation of inclusion.
While this might not vindicate Arendt's suspicion that statelessness is
equivalent to expulsion from humanity altogether (Arendt 1973: 297),

it certainly demonstrates the widespread regulation of individual recognition in today's world. All told, the continuing impasse in institutionalising for stateless persons the basic international rights associated with membership demonstrates an ethical problem when it comes to the international practice of membership.

This patchwork assembly of observations about the organisation of membership in international relations might not seem like much of a background theory. It certainly doesn't match the claims made by some theorists. Frost, for example, claims that it is possible to work towards a 'satisfactory' background theory (Frost 1996: 112), which will provide 'proper' understanding of 'the link between free individuality and the system of sovereign states' (Ibid. p. 112). This book doesn't make this kind of promise. It doesn't offer to tell us anything certain about the concrete implications of 'being a rights holder of a certain sort' (Ibid. p. 140). As I have already said, it will be similarly unable to claim either that denial of membership is fundamentally valid or that it is essentially unlawful. But by stepping outside of this kind of oppositional thinking, it could help in putting forward some conditional suggestions about the kinds of encounter that our existing connections might facilitate and link these to the possibility of reducing the injury and vulnerability which presently characterise statelessness. Doing so won't allow us to finally reconcile the tensions of the state system. It won't enable us to demonstrate that existing practices can be justified in any strong sense or to argue that they lack all authority. Therefore, in the next chapter's case study discussion, no assumptions about the proper scope of inclusion will be made. We cannot 'fix' the scope of theorising as communitarian or cosmopolitan. Instead, I will try to carry forward my understanding of inclusion as constituted and limited by a range of recognition practices, some of which operate between states and some of which remain contained within states.

More specifically, I will endeavour, in the remaining chapters, to explore what is problematic in the assumptions on which existing practice operates. It is still a presumption of international law that 'every individual [. . . can be] recognized as having a legal personality' (United Nations 1949: 11). Other actors also presume 'that it is always appropriate to ask for the identity of the state within which a person claims citizenship rights for him or herself' (Frost 2006: 8). In spite of the now-improved international legal status of the individual, I have tried to demonstrate the extent to which it is still generally presumed that individuals are recognised 'by international law only in exceptional circumstances' (Brown 2002: 115). As Brown notes, this was historically bad for pirates and good for diplomats. It remains bad for stateless persons. While I argued in Chapter 4 that it is only possible for the quasi-foundationalist to make conditional claims about the unreasonableness of these presumptions, it is, though contingent, not controversial to say that there is something mistaken in the presumption of states 'that everyone has been assigned an advocate/protector' (Goodin 2008: 275). To the extent that this presumption is used to explain the state-citizen link, it is important (and possible) to shine a spotlight on the contours of recognition which would counter the present exclusions of statelessness.

It is my hope that at the end of this book I will have said something constructive and intelligible about the potential for greater inclusion. The inescapable fallibility of theorising does not preclude constructive ethics. Indeed, by focusing on the value and limits of existing practices, we may, as Frost says, be able to talk meaningfully about 'the moral dimension that is already implicit' in them (Frost 1996: 141). For as long as we accept the conditionality of these claims, this will be a helpful undertaking.

Note

1 There is no new evidence to dispute Weis's claim that while 'it would certainly be desirable to lay down the rule that no national can be deprived of his nationality against his own volition by a unilateral act of the State of which he is a national [. . .] it is doubtful whether the States will be willing to accept such a far-reaching rule in the near future' (Weis 1944: 23).

Chapter 6

CONTEMPORARY STATELESSNESS IN EASTERN DEMOCRATIC REPUBLIC OF CONGO

The framework background theory set out at the end of Chapter 5 is not the kind of theory compatible with providing a full and final assessment of the nationality laws, citizenship practices or institutional responses central to contemporary statelessness. It is, however, intended to be the kind of theory which can help us understand the impact of existing institutions of mutual recognition on individual lives and, hence, the implications of laws, practices and institutions. As such, this chapter and the next set out to explore the individual implications of relevant membership practices in two contexts today. This chapter looks at the dynamics of statelessness in Eastern Democratic Republic of Congo (henceforth DR Congo or Congo). The next looks at the statelessness of the Rohingya resident in Burma, Bangladesh, Malaysia and Thailand. In each case, the discussion of the dynamics of statelessness is intended to be as up to date as possible, given that my background theory is imaginative, rather than aimed at retrospective criticism or justification. Because they are demonstrably important, there will be a specific focus on the rights associated with international personality, outlined in Chapter 5. By the end of both chapters, I hope to have said something interesting about the scope and limits of existing frameworks of recognition for inclusion of those who are presently stateless.

In the case of Congo, the weakness of the central state apparatus cannot be neglected (International Refugee Rights Initiative 2010: 30). In the most recent Failed State Index, the country ranks fourth overall, fourth on the 'demographic pressures', 'refugees/IDPs' and 'security apparatus' indicators and first on uneven development (Foreign Policy 2011). The country ranks third in the Brookings Institute's 2008 Index of State Weakness in the Developing World, landing in the bottom quintile for all indicators and designated a failed state (Rice & Patrick

2008: 10). As we will see, the inability of the national government to exercise a monopoly in the use of force has proved a fertile ground for the establishment of armed sub-state groups. This chapter will focus, in particular, on the implications of state weakness, competition for economic and political resources and of embedded ethnic essentialism. It will also consider the relationship of these factors to the wider institutional demands for loyalty and certainty in citizen-state relations, outlined in Chapter 5.

I BELONGING AND EXCLUSION IN EASTERN DEMOCRATIC REPUBLIC OF CONGO

In spite of the scarce media attention to it, the 1998–2003 conflict in Eastern Congo 'has been the most deadly' since the Second World War (Jacquemot 2010: 6). 'Africa's Great War', as it is often described, followed the First Congo War, which erupted in 1996, and has been followed in turn by continuing conflict, including in North and South Kivu, in the east of the country, bordering Rwanda, Uganda and Burundi (McGreal 2008). A major catalyst in all of these conflicts was the Rwandan genocide of 1994, which led to heightened ethnic tensions among Congolese groups, between Congolese citizens and Rwandan refugees and between Hutus and Tutsis of Congolese and Rwandan origin. Continuing ethnic tensions are both the source and the continuing outcome of fighting. According to the International Crisis Group in 2010, 'repeated failures' to achieve peace are now 'increasing the risk of ethnic clashes and disintegration of the national army in the Kivus' (International Crisis Group 2010). As we will see, the weakness of Congo's centralised state institutions, and the related militia competition for control over land, are essential factors in understanding belonging and exclusion in the country.

Ethnic tensions in the region are so serious that, in 2008, the UN's Special Adviser on the Prevention of Genocide highlighted the situation, pointing to the risks of 'genocidal violence' (United States Department of State 2009). Whether or not genocide can be substantiated, it was also noted that even the rhetoric of genocide 'had drastically increased tensions between ethnic communities' (Ibid.). The UN Special Adviser concluded that the major underlying cause of conflict in the region was 'the risk of individuals being targeted because of their ethnicity' (Ibid.). Relationships between the various parties to the Kivu conflict have shifted over time. However, the historically pro-Tutsi CNDP (National Congress for the Defence of the People), the pro-Hutu FDLR (Democratic Forces for the Liberation of Rwanda) and the FARDC (Armed Forces of the Democratic Republic of Congo) are all constituted in part by an essentialist ethnic discourse, which is, in turn, perpetuated by the actions of each group and by the conflict more broadly.

An additional factor in the wider context of the Kivu conflict is the way in which citizenship has, in much of Africa, been 'manipulated and restricted to deny rights to those whom the state wishes to marginalize' (Harrington 2005: 23). The manipulation and restriction of citizenship has gone hand-in-hand with democratisation in Africa. Exclusionary conceptions of citizenship have been used by 'incumbents bent on prolonging their stay in power' (Nzongola-Ntalaja 2004: 403), both to bar rivals and to control the contours of the electorate. In the case of DR Congo, the crisis of citizenship has been driven by the Rwandan conflict and by democratisation and 'the intensification of plural electoral politics' (Open Society Justice Initiative 2007: 5; Mamdani 2002: 2). It is claimed that in Congo, 'reference to ethnic identities had become the guiding principle of politics' (Vlassenroot 2002: 505). Mobutu Sese Seko (President of the country between 1965 and 1997) has been accused, in particular, of 'on-again, off-again manipulations' of the national citizenship of peoples of Rwandan descent in preceding years (Geschiere and Jackson 2006: 3). These 'Rwandophones', Kinyarwanda speakers or 'Banyarwanda' (people from Rwanda) are the major focus of this chapter.

Throughout the 1980s and 1990s, 'Mobutu and his cronies [. . .] manipulated the anti-Rwandan feelings in Eastern Congo to inspire ethnic cleansing' (Nzongola-Ntalaja 2004: 405). The incumbent president Joseph Kabila's 'predilection for virulent anti-Rwandan rhetoric' (Jackson 2006: 105) can therefore be seen as part of an on-going politicisation of inclusion and exclusion, which has scarred the country now for decades. At the local level, too, 'strategies of divide and rule by unscrupulous' politicians (Jackson 2007: 487) impact on individual and group recognition. Presidential and parliamentary elections are scheduled for November 2011. It is feared that the elections 'will only make the situation more volatile' (International Crisis Group 2010). Democratisation in DR Congo and other parts of Africa has drawn on exclusive notions of identity which hark back to pre-Independence notions of belonging and alienage (Open Society Justice Initiative 2007: 7). There are, however, also more structural resonances. In one expert's view, the 'very democracy that tended to create a majority across ethnic lines, tended to pit a self-consciously "indigenous" and Congolese majority against what many increasingly came to think of as a "non-indigenous" minority' (Mamdani 1998: 8). Questions of land, timing and indigeneity are frequent attributes of state membership practices and are subject to political direction in all cases. In places with weak state institutions, their exploitation by political elites and other military forces can have particularly devastating consequences.

Disputes over citizenship in DR Congo are particularly fraught in North and South Kivu, where questions of legitimate membership revolve 'around ascertaining the date of arrival of various groups of Kinyarwanda-speaking peoples, a highly contentious process' (International Refugee Rights Initiative 2010: 13). In spite of fierce disputes about the heritage of the different groups of Kinyarwanda-speaking people, there is widespread agreement among scholars and NGOs that there have been Kinyarwanda speakers in Congo since at least the mid-nineteenth century, when migration was encouraged by the Belgian colonial rulers (Manby 2009: 8). A new wave arrived in the 1960s, fleeing Burundi and Rwanda as refugees (Ibid. pp. 8–9). In 1972, the Kinyarwanda people in Congo were granted citizenship. In 1981, this citizenship law was rescinded, leaving them stateless (Open Society Justice Initiative 2007: 9). Whatever the objective facts, then, it is the way that these are legitimated in legal and political mechanisms of acknowledgement and recognition that gives them meaning.

Tensions between other Congolese peoples and the Kinyarwanda speakers were exacerbated by the arrival of over two million refugees fleeing the Rwandan genocide in 1994 (Mamdani 1998: 14). In the wake of rapidly worsening conflict, there were concerted efforts on all sides to redefine ethnicity and claims to legitimate membership. Those Kinyarwanda speakers born in Congo – many of whose families had been in the country for generations – began to define themselves defensively, not by language, but by reference to territory (International Refugee Rights Initiative 2010: 29). The term Banyamulenge (people from the hills of Mulenge) was the chosen term for those 'seeking to redefine [. . .] ethnic allegiances in such a way as to make them accept-able to the Congolese national discourse on identities' (Ibid. p. 29).

As well as marking a differentiation from more recent arrivals, the term Banyamulenge also served to distinguish those of Tutsi origin from Congolese Hutus, in response to the deepening hostility between the two groups, which had spilt over from Rwanda with the arrival of refugees after 1994's genocide. Banyamulenge has been an incredibly contentious label; to some other indigenous Congolese groups, it is 'nothing but a transparent attempt at faking autochthony in order to stake a primordial claim to Congolese territory' (Jackson 2006: 109). Serious hostility towards the Banyamulenge and towards non-Congolese Tutsi migrants and refugees has been acknowledged by the refugee agencies of various countries. The United Kingdom Border Agency has reported some improvements since 2004, when the post-war Transition Government deployed around 5,000 troops to 'protect displaced Tutsis threatened by other ethnic groups in eastern DRC' (United Kingdom Border Agency 2008: 10). I will leave aside, for now, the Agency's problematic interpretation of events, which sees this as evidence of the government's capacity to protect Tutsis. It should, however, be noted that there is a significant protection gap in Eastern DR Congo, by comparison with the capital, Kinshasa, and surrounding areas (Minorities at Risk Project 2006).

The mixing of 'old' and 'new' inhabitants is construed as problematic within a wider institutional context, which demands certainty and loyalty, and a domestic context characterised by essentialist ethnic claims and conflicts between rebel groups claiming to represent these rival ethnicities. Rival interests in controlling the demographic make-up of the Kivus play out in a particularly deadly way. The parameters of the national discourse are, of course, conditional, rather than fixed. Continuing clashes over land and resources, entitlements and political power mean that the grounds of 'legitimate' membership are always shifting. Even so, claims based on date of arrival serve as conditional mechanisms for accessing power and protection. For those who do not meet the criteria, they serve as mechanisms of vulnerability and exclusion. At the point of contestation in DR Congo, 'vehement' protests and aspersions of doubt come from all sides (Jackson 2007: 484). The underlying frameworks, which demand certainty, make doubt and ambiguity powerful tools in conflict situations, in particular.

Perhaps inevitably, given the Tutsi genocide in Rwanda in 1994, many media reports and much popular bile 'has focused with particular intensity on the Tutsi population' (Jackson 2007: 482). However, as this chapter will show, some of the most significant exclusions target all Kinyarwanda speakers: 'Hutu and Tutsi alike' (Ibid. p. 482). For the Hutus, like the Tutsis, ethnic identity has come to transcend Congolese identity (International Refugee Rights Initiative 2010: 24). As we have seen, much is at stake in the possibility of establishing one's historical connection to Congolese territory. And yet, the entanglement of different groups and their relation to rival rebel forces have made such claims difficult: '[t]he label "Hutu" has become increasingly dangerous for many: the conflict has become one in which the category of "Hutu" supersedes Congolese identity, often defined simply by the fact that they speak a common language' (Ibid. p. 24). Nevertheless, in comparison with the generalised hostility towards the Banyamulenge – seen as a 'Trojan horse' for Rwandan claims to the Kivus – the position of Congolese Hutus 'has remained more ambiguous' (Jackson 2007: 488). However, for Hutus as much as Tutsis, subsequent waves of refugees have blurred 'the distinction between Congolese and Rwandan [. . .] drastically altering the ethnic calculus of regional politics' (Manby 2009: 38).

When it comes to those Hutus of Rwandan origin, there are, of course, also claims on the part of Rwanda that those responsible for the genocide should be returned to face justice. However, in practice, questions of justice and of protection have tended to be pushed aside by an international logic which demands verifiable territorial distributions of individuals. Even so, it remains incredibly difficult to find an acceptable answer to the question of where Hutu refugees from Rwanda (a group which is known to include genocidaires) and the rebel Hutu FDLR militia 'can legitimately belong' (International Refugee Rights Initiative 2010: 5). The risks of Hutu identity can be seen in the treatment of a group of FDLR insurgents repatriated to Rwanda in 2010. According to the International Crisis Group, the returnees' claim to Rwandan nationality was denied 'and since then they seem to have vanished' (International Crisis Group 2010). Hutus have faced decades of hostility in Rwanda, exacerbated, of course, by the actions of the genocidaires and their supporters. Without agreement between the governments of Rwanda and Congo, the likelihood of establishing meaningful status is severely limited. As we will see, there are also good reasons to be wary of the individual implications of political agreements about where the various groups of displaced persons in Rwanda and Eastern DR Congo, 'in fact', belong.

The international institutional context of displacement and refugees in the Great Lakes region is worth mentioning briefly here. In 1994, an estimated one million 'mainly Hutu' refugees crossed from Rwanda into DR Congo (Stevens 2006: 60). For various reasons too complex to address here, UNHCR – under the leadership of Sagado Ogata – took the decision to promote their return to Rwanda. Given that many were trying (without success) to escape Rwandan troops, this decision was widely criticised on humanitarian grounds (Forsythe 2001; Stevens 2006). The Rwandan leadership forcibly dispersed the refugee camps in DR Congo and negotiated the dissolution of camps in neighbouring Tanzania, 'leading to half a million refugees being forced to return' (Stevens 2006: 61). In Stevens' view, UNHCR was actively complicit in 'forcing refugees back into a volatile Rwanda' (Ibid. p. 62). Since then, Ogata has herself expressed regret about this policy (Morris 2007: 9). In the light of the practices outlined in Chapter 5, it becomes possible to interpret the tripartite agreement between the two governments and UNHCR as a predictable response to a framework of international relations which demands and facilitates a degree of exclusivity in states' relationships to their citizens. In this case, it could be argued that the returnees were not stateless; how could they be when Rwanda recognised them as citizens? However, much will rest on how we understand statelessness. Chapter 8 will return, in detail, to this question. For now, I want to suggest that it is a bad-faith recognition which facilitates arbitrary and discriminatory treatment and precludes the possibility of alternatives.

Many Rwandan refugees have been subject to extreme violence and degradations, most recently as a result of the rapprochement between the governments of Rwanda and DR Congo, which formed the basis of armed attacks on FDLR rebels and their supposed co-conspirators (Human Rights Watch 2009: 13–14). The question of protection of the Rwandan Hutu refugees especially has been neglected. This group, 'who have been isolated and preyed upon for years by all sides' (Human Rights Watch 2009: 17), seem to be unwanted on both sides, with the potential for their return to Rwanda blocked by the government in 2009 (Ibid. p. 22). In 2011, the Rwandan government was once again exerting pressure on its refugee-hosting neighbours to repatriate those remaining. UNHCR duly announced that 'a cessation clause for Rwandan refugees in the Great Lakes region could be invoked by the end of December 2011, meaning that they would lose their refugee status' (Amnesty International 2011: 276). While the agency has been clear that this would only happen 'if certain indicators of progress were attained' (Ibid. p. 276), there remains considerable concern in the scholarly and humanitarian communities about an institutional shift from a more protective paradigm of voluntary repatriation to one of safe return (see, for example, Aleinikoff 1992; Chimni 2004; Haddad 2003; Zetter 2007). Elsewhere in the Great Lakes region, there has again been serious criticism of the involuntary nature of repatriations, achieved under a 2007 tripartite agreement between Rwanda, Uganda and UNHCR (Hovil 2008: 17). However, in the case under consideration, UNHCR has outlined its commitment to 'the local integration of those refugees who opt to remain in the country' (UNHCR 2010b: 4). In the absence of any of the effective rights associated with individual personality, it may well be difficult to make sense of 'opting' to remain. Absent the possibility of making an individual choice to re-enter his or her country, it may not make sense to talk so confidently about individual agency.

The 'choice' to remain in Congo is also constrained by the continuing and widespread insecurity in the east of the country (International Refugee Rights Initiative 2011), as well as by the general weakness of the state. While UNHCR has recently stated its commitment to supporting the Congo government's 'efforts to find an alternative resident status for displaced Rwandans' (UNHCR 2010b: 4), it remains unclear what the content and results of any such efforts might be.

From a distance, there are worrying similarities between what happened in the 1990s and what may be happening again. At the very least, the potential for returnees to Rwanda to access the protections of citizenship is ambiguous:

> In an article published in October 2007, the Kigali Newspaper New Times declares that 'all members of the Rwandan Diaspora' were able to return to Rwanda after July 1994 and 'automatically and unconditionally' regain Rwandan nationality if they wanted to. However, a 2005 Open Society Justice Initiative (OSJI) document specifies that Banyamulenge people who have lived in the DRC for 'generations' can 'theoretically' obtain Rwandan nationality, whereas a subsequent British Broadcasting Corporation (BBC) report refers to an agreement reached between the DRC and Rwanda in November 2007 with a provision for the return of Hutus to Rwanda. (Immigration and Refugee Board of Canada 2008)

In any case, there is little sense in studying the law outside of the way it is implemented.

There have been similar difficulties for Congolese refugees stranded in Rwanda, many of whom are Banyamulenge who fled Congo or were pushed out with Rwandan Tutsi returnees. In February 2010, a tripartite agreement between UNHCR and the governments of Rwanda and DR Congo was signed. It was intended to provide for the official return from Rwanda to Congo of tens of thousands of Kinyarwanda-speaking Congolese refugees. Refugees International estimates that around 50,000 refugees were repatriated under the agreement (Refugees International 2010: 1–2), which applied only to refugees registered in Rwanda with UNHCR (Lange 2010: 48). Being a registered refugee is clearly constituted by the acknowledgement of UNHCR that a person has a well-founded fear of persecution, under the 1951 Convention meaning of persecution. It therefore confers a form of recognition-based status which can be meaningful to the individual. Nonetheless, it is a limited status compared to citizenship 'proper', given that it is not underpinned by the same internationally relevant norms. It is therefore especially prone to manipulation, to being doubted and discredited and to generating particularly vulnerable categories of cumulative exclusion.

The relative weakness of the status conferred by UNHCR's unilateral acknowledgement of an individual's justified claim to asylum is demonstrated when it comes up against alternative attempts at verifying individual status. The next chapter considers what happens when UNHCR is not recognised by relevant state actors. In Congo, the status of even UNHCR registered refugees is often doubted. 'Real' motives, including 'a Rwandan plot to take over land in North Kivu' (International Refugee Rights Initiative 2011: 25), are commonly ascribed to Rwandophone refugees. Returnees and IDPs are often pitted against each other in disputes over access to land, which are expressed in claims about the 'true' identity and loyalties of the returnees (Ibid. p. 25). Rival claims to control the process and content of inclusion also threaten to overrule the determinations of UNHCR. Refugees International has reported inconsistencies between UNHCR's lists of refugees and CNDP lists of returnees (Refugees International 2010: 3), fuelling speculation of manipulation. It is, indeed, likely that the CNDP is engaged in efforts 'to seize lands and shift the demographics' in favour of Kinyarwanda speakers, to thereby 'consolidate their political and economic control of the area' (Bafilemba 2010). The power of the CNDP, relative to the refugee agency, cannot be ignored here, and Refugees International has tried to challenge this arbitrary power, claiming that the only 'legitimate' returnees will be Congolese Tutsis (Refugees International 2010: 3). The question of certainty is, however, itself a very interesting one, which does not appear to have objective content beyond the recognition of claims by competing forces.

In the context of a weak state, loyalty takes on special importance as a way of securing access to up-for-grabs economic and political resources. There are further suspicions that the returns are being manipulated in such a way as to strengthen the position of the CNDP – since 2009, a legitimate political party – in the 2011 elections (Ibid. p. 3). There is also widespread unease among many non-Tutsi Congolese at the relationship between the Rwandan government and the CNDP. In fact, the relationship between the two has been through various incarnations. Until 2009, and in spite of denials by Rwanda, it was widely accepted that the government had considerable influence over the CNDP leadership (Amnesty International 2008). In a 2009 deal struck between the governments of Rwanda and DR Congo, it became clear that the Rwandan government saw the CNDP as a 'bargaining chip' which it could play. By sacrificing the leader – Laurent Nkunda – and paving the way for the incorporation of CNDP members into the FARDC, the government of Rwanda gained access to FDLR rebels in Eastern Congo (Bafilemba and Heaton 2010). Beneath the agreement of both governments to cooperate in trying to neutralise the rebel militias, there is a clear economic interest: control over the lucrative mineral deposits in the region. In spite of this accord, substantial sections of the CNDP remain outside of government control, testament, in particular, to the weakness of Congo's state institutions. The CNDP still enjoys significant power in North Kivu, in particular, where it is said to retain *de facto* control over much of the region (Hege 2010: 52; International Crisis Group 2010; Refugees International 2010: 3). The result in the area around Lake Kivu has been a further deterioration in inter-ethnic relations (Human Rights Watch 2010). Continuing CNDP influence is also a key factor in the widespread displacement occurring in the region since 2009. Refugees International estimates that around 600,000 people have been displaced (Refugees International 2010: 1–2) in the last two years. While many have subsequently returned home, it is, as I have suggested, not sensible to construe this as evidence of an assertion of the right to return.

II MEMBERSHIP IN DR CONGO: BETWEEN TWO STOOLS?

The importance to states of being able to identify each other's nationals can be understood as connected to a recent institutional emphasis on the return and repatriation of refugees. Seen alongside this demand for certainty, democratisation in Africa can also be understood as part of a wider practice of consolidating statehood. The inevitable exclusionary effects of international membership norms are therefore often exacerbated by political elites' attempts to formalise the criteria for citizenship, which is to say that certainty can lead to zero-sum distributions of benefits and burdens. In the case of DR Congo, there are, however, additional layers of inclusion which operate at a remove from the formalities of legal personality. As we will see, these layers of protection and inclusion carry their own risks. However, they go some way to making the promise of belonging more meaningful for certain groups. In the end, though, they highlight, once more, the limitations of collective grounds for entitlement in providing for individuals.

According to one of the foremost scholars on citizenship in DR Congo, the unprotected fall 'between the two stools' of a divided membership practice (Mamdani 1998: 3). Mamdani pinpoints a distinction between 'civic space' and 'customary space' (Ibid. p. 3), while Jackson uses the terms 'ethnic' (or local) citizenship and 'empirical' (or lived) citizenship (Jackson 2007: 483) to help explain the situation in the country. People of Rwandan origin (however long they might have been in the country) are often excluded from national citizenship (or 'civic space') and customary local space. An important lesson is that 'the law is unlikely to succeed fully in eradicating the uncertainty around the legal status of Rwandophones as nationals' (Ibid. p. 482). The limits of law, in the case of the Congo, need to be understood, both in terms of the importance of local custom based on ethnicity and of the political dynamics which constitute and constrain 'existential security for the individual' (Ibid. p. 482). The critical idea of empirical or 'lived' citizenship offers a sharp contrast to the often-hollow promise of Congolese national citizenship. There is considerable evidence that although 'Congolese identity is a nice idea in theory [. . .] in practice it fails to deliver on many of the basic elements of effective citizenship' (International Refugee Rights Initiative 2010: 30).

The 1981 Nationality Law, rescinding the nationality of Congolese Kinyarwanda speakers, effectively denationalised an entire ethnic group, reversing the group provision of the 1972 amendment (Open Society Justice Initiative 2007: 9). In the years since 1981, as we have seen, the ability of Kinyarwanda speakers in Congo to make effective citizenship claims has been drastically circumscribed. Even though the legislation was not actively enforced by the central government (Immigration and Refugee Board of Canada 2008), due, in part, to the latter's weakness, Congolese Rwandophones have faced significant practical obstacles in a range of fields, including the registration of births. What this means, in practice, is that those who leave the Congo, voluntarily or otherwise, are often unable to return. While in exile, they are unable to call on the protection of their home state. They lack recognition before the law when it counts and are particularly vulnerable to involuntary returns.

In 2004, the Transition Government enacted a new nationality law. The new legislation has yet 'to bring any meaningful improvement to the situation for the Banyamulenge', even according to the conservative interpretation of the United Kingdom Border Agency (United Kingdom Border Agency 2008: 15). The 2004 law combines individual and group entitlements, though, as we will see, the latter are more fundamental. The revised constitution of DR Congo (effective since 2006) also specifies a set of individual rights 'located in the political and civil domain' (Mamdani 1998: 4). Nationality claims are to be considered, according to national law, on an individual, case-by-case basis (Jackson 2007: 490). However, the core criterion for inclusion remains collective, as the constitution 'still refers to ethnicity as the core expression of national identity' (International Refugee Rights Initiative 2010: 18) over and above 'birth, residence or other objective criteria' (Manby 2009: 9). There is, furthermore, a tendency to interpret the ethnic criterion in a singular, exclusionary sense. On the ground, understanding focuses on:

> a popular interpretation of the description of Congolese nationality as 'une et exclusive' [. . .] a description viewed as undermining the broader inclusionary threshold [. . .] The fact that this is the most popularly accessible element of the law is not surprising – it is a provision that has survived through multiple iterations of the national legislation. The more recent evolution of the law, which has added the word 'nationalities' to the definition of the group that, if present on the territory at independence, should be

considered to be members of the national community, has been less well absorbed. (International Refugee Rights Initiative 2010: 28–9)

The nationality law of DR Congo offers a striking example of the individual implications of arrangements of difference, especially where such arrangements are expressed in universalising language. In Congo, to be of Rwandan origin is to be fundamentally on the outside. And yet, it is not clear that the language of particularism by itself offers any solution to this kind of exclusion. As the very existence of statelessness shows, presumptions of collective entitlement tend to legitimise exclusion and neglect the practical importance of individual patterns of recognition. In the words of one NGO: 'protection based on ethnic allegiance alone is both transient and dangerous' (Ibid. p. 24).

In the end, the legal framework emphasises the mutually constitutive relationship between ethnic groups and the state to the detriment of the reciprocal relationship between the state and the individual. The law states explicitly that the constitutive source of the state is 'the ethnic groups and nationalities whose people and territory constituted that which became the Congo' (cited by Jackson 2007: 491).

As Jackson has noted, this clause permits rather exclusionary interpretations in practice. The law leaves a range of exclusionary arguments open, as he notes (Ibid. p. 491). It remains perfectly lawful to argue that the individual Kinyarwanda speakers present in the country in 1960, on account of their lack of national status, did not constitute DR Congo. It can equally be claimed that the Rwandophones' governance by other ethnic groups in 1960 precludes their consideration as a constituent people (Jackson 2007: 492). In any case, there is no unambiguous provision for the individual or collective recognition of the Congolese Kinyarwanda.

Operating below the level of national legislation is the 'customary space' (Mamdani 1998: 3) of 'ethnic' (or local) citizenship (Jackson 2007: 483). This level of recognition in Congo is intimately connected to the distribution of land. 'Indigenous' groups, acknowledged unambiguously as one of the country's constitutive peoples, are represented by Native Authorities. Since 1933, the Banyamulenge have been denied this level of autonomy, severely compromising their local political influence (Vlassenroot 2002: 503). These authorities hold customary access to land and are therefore the principal source of social and economic rights (Mamdani 1998: 4). In Kivu, the *Chefs de Groupement* – which head up the Native Authorities – 'have the power to confirm ethnic belonging and issue identity cards, oversee administration, allocate customary land for livelihood, hold tribunals through which customary justice is meted out, run local markets, and so on' (Ibid. p. 9). The ability of groups like the CNDP and FDLR to circumvent the state in their attempts to exert *de facto* administrative power becomes clearer in light of the importance of this customary space. In particular, the local source of power over land is vital to understanding membership in DR Congo.

The grave demographic pressures affecting the country are both the cause and the result of disputes over land. In the absence of access to land through the Native Authorities, many Banyamulenge and more recent Tutsi migrants have acquired land by purchasing it from local chiefs. There are, however, disadvantages to this approach. On the one hand, it is clear that 'land "ownership" has limited benefit if not accompanied by political rights or access to power to defend such rights' (International Refugee Rights Initiative 2010: 4). On the other hand, land purchases have fuelled grievances among other Congolese groups in Kivu. Purchases have once again led to charges against the Rwandophones of 'infiltrating' local power structures (Lange 2010: 48). And yet, purchasing is the only way for many to achieve any measure of material security. In such cases, 'existential security for the individual' (Jackson 2007: 482) is sought outside of both civic and ethnic practices of citizenship. The connection of the Rwandophone Tutsis to the CNDP can also be understood in this way. It is not necessarily to be understood as disloyalty to the Congolese state, but rather as evidence of people's practical acknowledgement of the importance of recognition, especially where more established forms of recognition are closed off. In many cases, Congolese Tutsi residents have multiple loyalties. Ironically, however, their 'transboundary loyalty' is both a source of (imagined) protection and a threat (International Refugee Rights Initiative 2011: 25). Many Congolese have suggested that 'Kinyarwanda speakers could only legitimately be recognised as Congolese if they renounce their ethnic ties' (International Refugee Rights Initiative 2010: 4). To do so, however, would not only mean renouncing the only protections they have, it would also be inconsistent with the essentially collective basis of Congolese citizenship.

A key theme in the literature on citizenship in DR Congo is the fact that:

> Nationality has not afforded people the protection that they believe to be their right. And it is this lack of protection that has forced people to create their own protection mechanisms along localised and ethnic lines. (Ibid. p. 30)

In Jackson's view, there are problems not only at the legal level, but also at the level of implementation (Jackson 2007: 481). This book has already discussed the problem of 'legal fiction' (Weis 1979: 241, see Chapter 1). Jackson also raises the important question of how far the relationship between the state and the individual really encompasses 'everything that it means to be a full "citizen"' (Jackson 2007: 481). In the context of DR Congo, there are particularly good reasons to doubt this.

For all of the reasons discussed in this chapter so far, Democratic Republic of Congo remains a state in which many people must currently live as stateless persons. Statelessness remains an issue, in spite of UNHCR's involvement in repatriations and in spite of a nationality law ostensibly designed to clarify entitlement to citizenship. Among the existing mechanisms for improvement of the situation of the stateless, perhaps the most interesting is the use of local pacification committees (LPCs) (Hege 2010). One of their primary challenges is 'determining the nationality and origin of [. . .] potential returnees' (Ibid. p. 52). Verification (International Crisis Group 2010a: 5; Refugees International 2010: 4) of refugees' nationality is also part of the UN's stabilisation regime, set up alongside the government of Congo's own plans for stabilising the east of the country, 'known as STAREC' (Refugees International 2010: 4). The assumption that the nationality and origin of these people can be determined seems premised on an underlying supposition that many (if not most) of them will indeed have a nationality, be it Congolese or Rwandan. However, as this chapter has shown, it is likely that many (if not most) do not. There is no guarantee that clarifying the legal grounds of entitlement will be an inclusive process. Although it does not sit well with foundational approaches to theory, it is difficult to avoid the conclusion that sometimes, people's status is just unclear.

At first sight, the language of 'determining' status implies a declaratory logic, following which our task is to establish – using objective criteria – whether one is or is not a national and assert this status. In fact, the approach taken by the LPCs is more sophisticated. These committees – established under a 2010 peace agreement – are 'composed of local authorities, customary chiefs and civil society actors, along with equal representatives of all ethnic groups present' in the relevant territory (Hege 2010: 51). By going beneath the state and engaging with the real structure of power, it seems that the committees are set up to acknowledge that in cases of statelessness, 'the most crucial question is one of protection' (Weis 1961, cited by Batchelor 1995: 252), rather than one of legal formality. Insofar as meaningful personality is today conditional on recognition by relevant others, it will be important to look at the existence and possibility of practical relationships of recognition.

Status, on this approach, is understood as conditional on recognition (Ikäheimo and Laitinen 2007: 50). It is an approach which can help highlight the limits of more obviously formal, documentary practices. The Data Centre for IDPs in North Kivu is engaged in some important work. Its aims include 'to undertake individual registration of camp-based IDPs, ensuring individual documentation, such as Voluntary Return Attestations, producing accurate beneficiary lists for assistance purposes and ensuring individual registration of returnees' (Church 2010: 36). However, recognition and local powers are vital. One NGO expresses this idea particularly well, in respect of Congolese refugees:

> Ultimately, if they are to be recognised as returning Congolese citizens (as opposed to Rwandan migrants) who are entitled to live in a specific area by others living in the communities to which they hope to return, the legitimacy of their return needs to be acknowledged by both the government and local community structures. Belonging at both of these levels is crucial to ensuring their access to both livelihoods and security [. . .] one without the other is simply inadequate and makes return and reintegration impossible. (International Refugee Rights Initiative 2011: 21)

As well as emphasising the need for government and local acknowledgement, the International Refugee Rights Initiative argues – following the views of the potential returnees – that any future return will have to be return 'as a group' (Ibid. p. 23). This position reflects the importance of combined group standing and the group nature of resource entitlement in the country. It also demonstrates people's understanding of the practical importance of having claims – for example, to access to land – recognised by others (Ibid. p. 23). The land question, so vital in the Congo context, is also being addressed jointly by UNHCR and UN-HABITAT, who have stated their commitment to a 'participative and community based' approach (Raymond 2010: 20).

Another important lesson of the Congo case, however, is the extent to which collective entitlement can be a double-edged sword, constitutive of threats, as well as protection. My background theory emphasises, in addition, the risks associated with granting too much authority to what are often arbitrary and exclusive powers and practices and the importance, therefore, of paying special attention to the likely individual implications of existing relationships. When we instead presume too much about the legitimacy of these powers, we can become blind to significant violence and exclusion, as the critics of UNHCR have pointed out. It is always, therefore, worthwhile expressing concerns about existing recognition powers. In Eastern DR Congo, Hege notes that there are perhaps valid doubts about the ability of the LPCs to act impartially, 'in view of the territorial expansion and dominance of the CNDP in return areas' (Hege 2010: 51). Of course, partiality is central to determinations of nationality, even if the implications for individuals are much more troubling in countries where a weak state combines with embedded ethnic tension and struggles over resources, including the fruits of monopoly state power.

The situation of stateless persons in Eastern DR Congo is shaped by a range of local social, political and economic factors. Here, I have focused on the ethnic dimensions of citizenship and statelessness and on the way in which the weak and decentralised nature of the state constitutes dynamics of inclusion and exclusion. What we see in the Congo case is that the state is not the only party to individual recognition. Its weakness both problematises civic and legal remedies and facilitates local practices of recognition and inclusion (and, hence, non-recognition and exclusion). Having traced the fiendish complexities of belonging in Eastern DR Congo, the chapter will now turn finally to consideration of the effects of these tensions on the membership rights discussed in Chapter 5. The rights emphasised there were the right to leave and re-enter one's own state, the right to a nationality, the right to recognition everywhere as a person before the law and the right of non-refoulement. It will become clear that these key attributes of international personality are denied to people in Eastern DR Congo, as a result of particular local dynamics.

The UDHR declares or asserts a very wide range of rights. I have chosen to focus on four of these. Article 13 affirms that everyone 'has the right to leave any country, including his own, and to return to his country'. When it comes to those deprived of nationality in Eastern DR Congo, it is clear that this right is inaccessible. For example, the attempt of Congolese refugees to exercise the right to re-enter their own country is currently threatened not only by insecurity and persecution in the country, but also by their deliberate exclusion from membership. Article 15 asserts that everyone 'has the right to a nationality'. Clearly, this right is circumscribed in Congo, where many people have limited prospects for obtaining a nationality. Article 6 declares that everyone 'has the right to recognition everywhere as a person before the law'. Stateless persons in Eastern Congo are not recognised at home as legal persons. Denied the 'means with which to prove their nationality' (Open Society Justice Initiative 2007: 7), they are therefore unable to enter into legal relationships of recognition in the countries, including Rwanda, in which they have settled. Customary international law upholds that states are customarily obliged not to forcibly return a person to a territory where he or she may be exposed to persecution (Duffy 2008: 373). This restriction is related to Article 14 of the UDHR, which holds that everyone 'has the right to seek and enjoy in other countries asylum from persecution'. In Eastern DR Congo, we see concern that individuals may be returned (to Congo and Rwanda) in the face of vulnerability, insecurity, discrimination and persecution (on Congolese refugees, see United Kingdom Border Agency 2008: 15).

Of course, the absence, in practice, of the means to claim these so-called rights does not necessarily undermine their meaning or scope. What the case of the Kinyarwanda speakers from, and in, Congo does show us is the importance of effective recognition to these rights and immunities. It also shows us that the state is not the only party relevant to mutual recognition when it comes to understanding the contemporary meaning of these attributes of international legal personality. It therefore highlights the importance of political understandings of rights regimes. Jackson's reference to Robert Cover's idea of 'nomos' is useful here in its claim that: 'No set of legal institutions or prescriptions exists apart from the narratives that locate it and give it meaning' (Cover 1983, cited by Jackson 2007: 495). In the Congo case, these narratives go above and below the state. The state, however, remains vitally important to proper understanding of the dynamics of membership and exclusion. Even where it is empirically weak, it retains practical importance. While it is a mistake to accord presumptive legitimacy to the state, it is necessary to recognise that:

> In a context in which local power dynamics are the source of so much violence, people have little choice but to look to the state – a state that holds so little promise, but to which there are few alternatives in a context in which rights are realised primarily through securing a link with a state. (Human Rights Watch 2009: 27)

International meanings, like those embedded in the UDHR, play an important role in granting power to the state. Attention to statelessness, by contrast, can highlight the limits of the state and state system in assigning to everyone an advocate or protector (Goodin 2008: 275). Indeed, struggles to establish certainty and loyalty remain substantial obstacles to individual status in the twenty-first century.

III SUMMARY

The first part of this book outlined my scepticism about the value of beginning a political theory with abstract individual rights. It also presented my concern with allowing the state to over-determine the scope and limits of inclusion in world politics. While it is probably not possible to fix the scope of ethical thinking, close attention to the wealth of meanings which constitute and constrain inclusion in specific cases will be vital to understanding the potential for incremental and contingent inclusion. The case of the Eastern Democratic Republic of Congo has, I hope, shown that there are good reasons for focusing on plurality, as well as good reasons for thinking through their implications for individuality.

Back in Chapter 1, I explored the difficulties of identifying neutral justifications for inclusion. As Arendt so famously argued, declarations about the inherent dignity of 'man' have never been sufficient as justifications for, or constraints on, state power. This can be seen as part of a wider flaw in declaratory arguments, which assume the presence of some objective criteria. The declaratory approach to statehood, for example, holds that statehood is independent of its recognition by other states (Sloane 2002: 115–116). There are various potential problems with this kind of approach. In this book, I have argued that the appeal to objective criteria is hopeless in light of the fallibility of human knowledge and that greater engagement with the ways in which personality is, in fact, constituted is needed. On the basis of a more constitutive view of personality, I have argued that identity is substantially relational. At the same time, I have tried to be aware of the risks of according foundational value to the contingent relationships of mutual recognition which we encounter today. The book has begun to develop the idea that there might be a way to avoid both empty declarations about individual rights to nationality and about the general necessity of the state.

Attempts to determine or verify claims to belonging are always really reliant on relationships of mutual recognition. This does not make it impossible to conceive of more inclusive ways of structuring recognition and, hence, membership. It does mean, however, that we should let go of any assumptions that we can objectively identify who belongs where:

> At the heart of this story is the question of the 'true' citizenship of this group of Congolese refugees at both a national and local level. There is no 'true' answer to this question, and certainly not one that can be answered only at a legal level, or that can be imposed from outside. The task of negotiating the return of this group of refugees to DRC is a multi-dimensional challenge that requires political compromise, imagination and courage by those in exile, by home communities and by those in positions of power. (International Refugee Rights Initiative 2011: 28)

In this chapter, I have tried to show why it is so tempting and, yet, so problematic to adequately determine who belongs where, in cases like that of the Eastern Democratic Republic of Congo. For the individual, the result is often radical insecurity. The difficulties of deriving universal guarantees from particularist entitlements are dramatically demonstrated by the extreme vulnerabilities of stateless individuals.

Chapter 7

CONTEMPORARY STATELESSNESS: THE ROHINGYA

Following on from the previous chapter, this chapter sets out to explore the individual implications of collective rights in the case of the stateless Rohingya, largely resident in Burma, Bangladesh, Malaysia and Thailand. The range of forces and practices which constitute the severe restrictions on the citizenship, documentation and freedom of movement of the Rohingya will be explored throughout this chapter. The chapter will focus, in particular, on the dynamics of repatriation and the scope and limits of documentation in the statelessness of the Rohingya.

I BELONGING AND EXCLUSION: THE ROHINGYA

According to a publication by the Equal Rights Trust in 2010: 'The Rohingya are one of the most vulnerable and abused stateless communities in the world' (Equal Rights Trust 2010: 148). The Rohingya, also sometimes referred to as the Arakanese Muslims, have primarily resided in the northern part of Arakan (Burma) that borders Bangladesh (Minorities at Risk Project 2006a). According to Minorities at Risk, there 'have been significant migrations by group members both within Burma and into neighboring Bangladesh due to threats of or actual attacks by state authorities' (Ibid.). Rohingya people have also migrated south to Thailand and onwards to Malaysia. There is a clear religious dimension to their persecution in Burma. While there is no official state religion in the country, the majority of the population is Buddhist, and the military regime has sought recently to elevate the status of Buddhism 'to the detriment of the country's religious minorities' (Ibid.). It is widely agreed, outside of Burma, that the Rohingya have a long history in Arakan, pre-dating its incorporation into Burmese sovereign territory in the eighteenth century, its subsequent colonisation by the British and eventual independence in 1948. For much of this history, the relationship between the Arakan Muslims and the Burmese has been tense. Today, the Rohingya 'face many demographic stresses such as deteriorating public health conditions, declining caloric intake, dispossession from their land, and internal resettlement as a result of government policies' (Ibid.). Cultural disputes and resource disputes are part of the dynamics of Rohingyan exclusion. It is reported that thousands have been evicted from lands they customarily used for agriculture. The Rohingya also experience serious restrictions on the practice of their religion and on their civil rights, including the right to marry.

Of particular interest to this book, with its international orientation, are the significant restrictions on freedom of movement that the Rohingya presently face. Within Burma, there is a longstanding requirement that they apply for documented permission to leave their own villages. No travel to the Arakan state capital is permitted. Where permission is granted, the national government effectively enforces homelessness by preventing return. Those who overstay their granted permission to visit another village routinely have their names deleted from the 'family lists', which are the only documentary proof of any right to residence. After being 'obliterated administratively', they are then 'compelled to leave Burma' (Lewa 2009: 12). Others who leave the country face the same fate: 'their names are struck off family lists and they face long-term imprisonment if captured upon re-entry' (Equal Rights Trust 2010: 5).

The local and international dynamics which impel their exit from Burma are vital to understanding their situation overall. As we will see, the statelessness of the Rohingya makes it almost impossible for them to secure documented legal residence in a new state. It also makes their return to Burma extremely problematic. One of the individual implications of the exclusionary dynamic at hand is frequent and prolonged detention. On crossing the border into Bangladesh, Rohingya individuals are often arrested on the charge of illegal entry. Given that there is nowhere to deport them to at the end of their sentences, many are kept in prolonged detention (Lewa 2009: 13). This corresponds to a general pattern, in that:

> Unnecessary imprisonment is one of the most pervasive and most difficult problems faced by stateless persons. According to

the UNHCR, when stateless persons are unable to return to their countries of habitual residence after having left them [. . .] the result is often prolonged detention outside of the country in which they habitually reside. (Weissbrodt and Collins 2006: 267)

Given that the majority of refugees who flee Arakan do so via the Arakan border with Bangladesh and that this has been a site of repeated waves of migration, this dimension of the plight of the Rohingya will be addressed first:

In 2009, Burma began constructing a concrete and barbed-wire fence along its border with Bangladesh. It said the fence was to prevent smuggling, but human rights groups argued that its true purpose was to prevent more than 200,000 Rohingya refugees from returning. (Ferrie 2010: 127)

Many thousands of Rohingya refugees are deprived of the ostensible right to return to their own country (United Nations 1948: Article 13) by what is assumed to be their own government. However, as we will see in due course, it can be equally problematic to assume that the option of return is, indeed, valuable in all cases. To the extent that we can talk meaningfully about the right to re-enter one's own country, we will need to think about its relationship to other rights and its implications, both for states and for individuals.

In the previous chapter, I briefly discussed some of the major criticisms of forced repatriation in the Great Lakes in the 1990s. In the same decade, UNHCR engaged in large-scale repatriations of Rohingya to Burma and these, too, have been the subject of substantial criticism. Voluntariness, long a criterion for repatriations, was said, in the case of repatriations to Burma in the 1990s, to have been pushed 'to its absolute limits, possibly beyond recognition' (Barnett and Finnemore 2004: 106). Others suggested that 'the principle of voluntary return became "a euphemism for 'no real alternative"' (Human Rights Watch 1996). This book is not interested in a discussion of the objective value of voluntariness or in assuming that there are situations in which the practical situation of the state excludes the possibility of alternatives. Nevertheless, an analysis of the wider implications of the repatriation efforts is essential for my purposes here.

Between 1991 and 1992, a large wave of Arakanese Muslims crossed the border into Bangladesh. UNHCR was involved quickly, and the agency played a lead role in two phases of repatriation. The first, effecting the return of approximately 50,000 people (Ibid.), took place between September 1992 and the end of 1993, with the second organised between 1994 and 1995, when progress in returning the Rohingya to Burma slowed.

The most authoritative reports on these two waves of repatriation come from NGOs, such as Human Rights Watch (HRW). In respect of the first wave, HRW makes various criticisms. In this large-scale 'forced' repatriation, it points, in a 1996 report, to the fact that UNHCR had no presence in Burma and no agreement with the Burmese government to provide any support to the returnees. More seriously, in the organisation's view, the refugee agency proved unable to prevent measures taken by the government of Bangladesh to provoke returns. These included 'beatings and the denial of food rations' (Ibid.). Mid-way through the repatriation, UNHCR temporarily withdrew in response to these abuses and began the process of negotiating a new agreement with the government of Bangladesh. Having done so, the agency resumed its interviews of refugees 'volunteering' to return home. It is not clear that this agreement had any effect in preventing the coercion of 'volunteers' (Ibid.). In its 1994 Oslo Declaration, UNHCR itself acknowledged that 'in some instances UNHCR has placed too much emphasis on early return to countries of origin which has resulted in return movements to less than favourable conditions' (cited by Human Rights Watch 1996).

The second repatriation effort 'took place after the UNHCR had established a limited field presence in Arakan state in 1994' (Ibid.). At this point, UNHCR began to argue that conditions in Arakan were 'conducive to return' (Ibid.). The agency's declaration to this effect suggests that an objective change had taken place. In doing so, it neglects the important relational dimension of recognition and individual status. In the same vein, the agency moved from a practice of offering individual interviews to refugees (Ibid.), to one which assumed again the objective value of state-citizen links. While refugees were still permitted to approach UNHCR to state their wish not to return, the assumption in favour of repatriation prevailed. While interviews carry their own risks in contexts characterised by violence and coercion, HRW also questioned the basis on which UNHCR even made its ostensibly objective assessments. Barnett and Finnemore also describe the way in which UNHCR officials allegedly 'bent standard procedures, ignored disconfirming evidence, and avoided troubling questions' (Barnett and Finnemore 2004: 106). It is argued that the Agency's access remained limited and that the exclusion of other civilian monitoring groups made UNHCR's assessments difficult to substantiate. Events here in the 1990s, therefore, make it difficult to affirm a universal right to leave any country, let alone to seek asylum. The importance of political will – of the state as well as a range of other actors – can hardly be underestimated.

Nevertheless, this second repatriation was reported more favourably by the Agency itself. HRW reports that, in various places, the second Rohingyan repatriation was reported as 'a vindication' of UNHCR's new commitment to voluntary repatriation (Human Rights Watch 1996). While accurate numbers are difficult to ascertain, the government of Bangladesh claims that about 150,000 refugees were repatriated in 1994, 'with another 100,000 scheduled to return' in 1995 (Agence France Press 1995, cited by Minorities at Risk Project 2006a). By the end of 1995, the Chinese Xinhua News Agency (1995, cited by Minorities at Risk Project 2006a) reported that approximately 195,000 refugees in total had returned home. This second repatriation began to grind to a halt in 1996, when between 5,500 and 10,000 were believed to have re-entered Bangladesh in the early part of the year (Minorities at Risk Project 2006a). While the government of Bangladesh maintained efforts to deport these new arrivals, agreeing with the government of Burma that all remaining refugees would be repatriated by March 1997 (Ibid.), few more repatriations were achieved by 1999. At the same time, new refugees continued to arrive from Arakan, in spite of attempts by UNHCR to discourage asylum seekers from leaving Burma. According to HRW, the agency was even involved in helping the government of Burma prevent people from leaving (HRW 1996).

The situation of the Rohingya demonstrates the practical mechanisms which such states can use to get rid of stateless persons, particularly those who the 'home' state wants back for punishment (Arendt 1973: 279). Other groups also testify to the disciplinary character of the Burmese government's policy of 'clearing' Rohingya for return (Médecins sans Frontières 2002: 24), indicating that other returnees will simply be refused proper recognition (Arendt 1973: 279). Repatriations can partly be understood as assertions of the unlawful character of denationalisation. Given, however, that denationalisation is at the same time 'valid' (Weis 1979: 242), it remains difficult to punish the state of origin. Rather, in many cases, the state of origin and the state of residence work towards agreements which enable more-or-less friendly relations and contain the potentially disruptive effects of statelessness on inter-state relations. UNHCR and the government of Bangladesh have found various ways, in the last twenty years, of minimising the burden of statelessness, preventing the exit of some, facilitating or enforcing the 'mere' return of others and refusing to recognise many of those remaining. No arrivals in Bangladesh have been registered since 1993 (IRIN 2010). Many of the others have been described by UNHCR as 'economic migrants', by which 'UNHCR gave carte blanche to Bangladesh to push them back' (HRW 1996).

A formal Memorandum of Understanding between the two countries in 1992 obligated Burma to accept the return of all those able to establish previous residence (Barnett and Finnemore 2004: 108). This might be understood as a vacuous obligation, in light of the fact that the means of proof of residence are routinely withheld from the Rohingya. As such, more informal mechanisms of repatriation have been constructed. Bangladesh and UNHCR both sought to encourage returns by warning returnees that further border crossing would result in arrests for illegal departure (Ibid. p. 112). This kind of policy seems to reflect an agreement by UNHCR and Bangladesh to turn a blind eye to on-going persecution in exchange for returns.

In the last decade, the situation of the Rohingya has remained basically the same. Of the 300,000 estimated to be resident in Bangladesh in 2011, only 28,700 are recognised by UNHCR to be refugees (UNHCR 2011c). Recognised refugees are eligible for a UNHCR letter outlining their status as asylum seekers (Shukla and Mailman 2006: 31). These documents are not as widely recognised as the documents provided for by the 1951 Refugee Convention, given that Bangladesh is not a signatory to the Convention. Given the narrower scope of recognition, the documents arguably provide for a more limited status. Nonetheless, those who are not recognised are not entitled to any international assistance. The general assumption is that they are, in many cases, illegal entrants, who should return to Burma. Recognition can therefore offer real, though limited, benefits to individuals. When it comes to statelessness, a recent comparative study affirmed these advantages. Field researchers tend to confirm the value of obtaining documents 'in the form of passports, civil identification documents, birth certificates, or even licenses', as those who lack documentation are, by contrast, often 'liable to abuse, including deportation' (Blitz and Lynch 2009: 102). Indeed, there are concerns about the effect of a new national ID card scheme in Bangladesh on its Rohingya residents, who will be excluded (IRIN 2011)

It is not, however, to be assumed that documentary recognition is an objective good in itself. A couple of examples might be helpful here. In August 1995, the UNHCR started a registration drive for the Rohingya in Bangladesh, as a precursor for the continuation of its repatriation exercise. Ostensibly, registration provided the refugees with the opportunity to 'volunteer' for repatriation. As we have already seen, however, there was limited assistance in place for the returnees. It was not, for example, clear that they would be re-added to the family lists, which provide for the minimal residence rights available to the Rohingya. There were, furthermore, questions about the way the repatriation lists were drafted. The UNHCR list had 8,903 people down as 'undecided'. However, HRW argued that the far longer list of those 'decided' to return included a larger group, which 'could expect reprisals or persecution in Burma' (HRW 1996). In highly unequal relationships of recognition, it is difficult to talk meaningfully of rights or protections. In this case, it was generally suspected that the refugees had been deliberately misinformed about their legal rights. In such cases, it becomes difficult to even talk about legal rights.

Even where formalised documented rights do tend to confer protection, this will often exacerbate the vulnerability of those who do not qualify for these rights. In Bangladesh, for example, the 2008 national elections have exacerbated the vulnerability of unregistered Rohingyas, thousands of whom were evicted from the villages in which they were resident during a drive to register voters (Refugees International 2011: 3). The drive was also accompanied by an 'intense campaign of arrests and violence', which effectively ghettoised the refugees (Ibid. p. 3). There are parallels here to the case of the Democratic Republic of Congo (considered in Chapter 6), in which the attempt at consolidating power and statehood by constructing a majority has had such devastating effects.

In Bangladesh, aggressive crackdowns by the government continue – in 2010, it was warned that such a policy was 'pushing humanitarian conditions to the brink at a makeshift camp', home to approximately 30,000 undocumented Rohingya (IRIN 2010). Some progress has, however, been made. In 2007, UNHCR worked with the government of Bangladesh for the relocation of some 9,000 unregistered Rohingya to a safer location in Bangladesh (IRIN 2008). The break in repatriations has also continued, with the Integrated Regional Information Networks of the UN Office for the Coordination of Humanitarian Affairs (IRIN) reporting that there have been no returns since 2006 (IRIN 2009). The organisation also quotes the head of UNHCR's sub-office in Cox's Bazar, Bangladesh, as saying that the refugees will only be able to go back 'when conditions inside Myanmar are conducive and when they themselves feel it is safe to do so' (cited by IRIN 2008). Even so, the government of Bangladesh remains committed to their repatriation. In 2011, it requested the assistance of the US in dealing with the Rohingya, estimated that year to number approximately 300,000 (Deutsche Press Agentur 2011). There therefore remain a very large number of people who have no advocate or protector (see Goodin 2008: 275). There have also, at various times, been proposals to phase out support for those refugees registered with UNHCR, in favour of a 'self-sufficiency plan' aimed at better integrating the Rohingya with the local Bangladeshi population (Shukla and Thompson 2005: 1). In light of the violence and hostility which has tended to characterise relations between the Rohingya and the government of Bangladesh, there is good reason to fear the individual implications of throwing the refugees on the mercy of that government's agents. It is also an approach which would leave in place their underlying statelessness and, hence, their underlying need for effective protection.

There are also demographic pressures which make local integration in Bangladesh difficult. The region in which the two official refugee camps (and their unofficial counterparts) are located is a poor and over-populated area, which has led to strained relationships between the refugees and local people. A perception, however problematic, that the refugees are receiving beneficial treatment has hampered integration (Refugees International 2008). Given the problems related to return and local integration, it might be thought that resettlement provides an option for the Rohingya. However, resettlement has proved the most problematic option of all. For a wide variety of reasons, governments are reluctant to provide for the large-scale resettlement of refugees. In the case of stateless persons, this general reluctance is complicated by the international importance of outlawing denationalisation (in accord-ance with states' sovereign rights). States are unwilling to countenance policies which might have the effect of validating denationalisations in ways which risk recognising statelessness. It is partly in this light that the emphasis on return should be understood. In the case of the Rohingya, we see a range of attempts to cajole Burma into re-accepting responsibility for their would-be nationals, with an additional burden placed on Bangladesh – its, perhaps unfortunate, neighbour. Given the way that important, ostensibly universal rights are constituted and constrained by state-based norms and practices, this should not be surprising. Indeed, it is difficult to imagine what more UNHCR – a state-based and state-funded agency – might realistically do. Within the organisation:

> The problem of statelessness is regarded as a very sensitive one touching directly upon the issues of sovereignty and identity. As a result, UNHCR has on some occasions been reluctant to intervene in this area, especially when it is considered that such an involve-ment will have an adverse effect on the organization's activities in relation to refugees, returnees and asylum seekers. It should also be noted that UNHCR's major donors have not generally pressed the organization to assume a more active global role in this area. (Obi and Engstrom 2001: 3)

Further constraints on UNHCR's role derive from its strictly humanitar-ian mandate, its need to acknowledge in certain cases that 'its mandate on statelessness' is not recognised (Ibid. p. 24), and the fact that in countries which are not signatories to the 1951 Refugee Convention, the agency itself often goes unrecognised. Thailand, a non-signatory, refuses to acknowledge the status of UNHCR and has therefore refused to allow the Agency access to Rohingya arrivals in the country (Yan Naing 2011).

The kinds of practices outlined in Chapter 5, which constrain UNHCR's activity, are highly relevant to understanding the situation of the Rohingya (and, indeed, other stateless groups). These norms and practices both give meaning to individual lives and constitute con-straints on the distribution of those individual meanings and values. For the Rohingya, they result in similar treatment, whether they remain in Burma, make it over the border to Bangladesh or make the longer journey to Thailand or Malaysia. In Thailand, many Rohingya arrivals have been subject to forcible repatriations (Sciortino 2009). In Malaysia, there are again widespread and credible reports of Rohingya facing deportations to Thailand, in the absence of the necessary documentation (Mun Ching 2002). Here, we can see that the legal ambiguity which characterises statelessness allows states to exercise unconstrained power over the lives of stateless persons. Many Rohingya – like other stateless persons – 'end up in the revolving door of "informal" deportations' (Lewa 2009: 13). Since Burma retains the strict legal right to refuse their re-entry, 'Thailand has occasionally deported Rohingya boat people unofficially into border areas of Burma controlled by insurgent groups', whereas 'Malaysia usually deports them over the border into Thailand' (Ibid. p. 13).

In the previous chapter, I outlined some of the problems with taking a declaratory approach to the verification of an individual's nationality status. And yet, we saw that the certainty which is generally required makes objective verification a seductive objective. When questioned by the press in 2003, the Malaysian Foreign Minister declared that the Rohingya are 'definitely from Myanmar [Burma] and they should be sent back to Myanmar' (cited by Mun Ching 2004). Of course, this belies the reality that international law still – strictly speaking – prohibits the expulsion of stateless persons. The underlying importance of the permanent state-citizen link has, however, made expulsions and returns practically possible.

We have also seen that the individual implications of the practices examined in Chapter 5 are far from universalised. In 2003, UNHCR representatives in Malaysia stopped processing individual asylum applications from the Rohingya (Mun Ching 2004). They are instead treated as a group, being issued certificates stating that they are 'registered as a Rohingya Muslim with the UNHCR' (Ibid.). While it is possible to understand this measure as a way of granting effective acknowledgement of their collective exclusion, it is a measure which seems to overlook the individual dimensions of recognition, which allow the person to exercise a range of rights. The situation of statelessness shows that collective entitlement remains a double-edged sword when it comes to understanding membership in world politics. Indeed, late in 2005, even the temporary protection conferred by UNHCR's collective acknowledgement of the Rohingya was withdrawn (Lewa 2008: 42), although it was resumed again in 2009 (Equal Rights Trust 2010: 7). According to the Equal Rights Trust, UNHCR registration affords a degree of 'informal protection against arrest and in case of detention'

(Ibid. p. 7). Unfortunately, it is not clear how effective 'informal' protection can be, in the face of increasingly strict legal regimes for dealing with so-called illegal immigration. In Malaysia, there is a 'well established legal and policy framework behind the caning, detention and deportation of Rohingya and others' (Ibid. p. 32).

II MEMBERSHIP IN BURMA: THE PROSPECTS FOR INCLUSION

The Burmese Citizenship Law of 1982 specifies that there are 135 'national groups' with permanent homes in state territories before 1823 (Burma Council of State 1982: chapter II). These groups constitute the country's permanent citizenship. The Rohingya are not one of these recognised groups (Lewa 2009: 32) and generally lack the documentation necessary to contest this exclusion. In any case, under the 1982 Citizenship Law, the Council of State reserves the right to 'decide whether any ethnic group is national or not' (Burma Council of State 1982: chapter II). The State Peace and Development Council's regime, in power since 1988, has seen the mistreatment of the Rohingya worsen. Indeed, treatment of all Burmese citizens remains harsh. In the 2011 Failed State Index, Burma ranks in 5th place when it comes to 'de-legitimization of the state' (Foreign Policy 2011). The Index places Burma in 18th place overall, with high rankings for 'human rights' and 'group grievance' factoring into this position (Foreign Policy 2011). In this context, there seems to be little hope of securing effective personality for Rohingya residents and returnees. The regime's attitude can be seen in a widely-quoted letter of 2009, in which the Burmese Consul-General in Hong Kong reportedly told his fellow heads of mission that:

> In reality, Rohingya are neither 'Myanmar People' nor Myanmar's ethnic group. You will see in the photos that their complexion is 'dark brown'. The complexion of Myanmar people is fair and soft, good-looking as well. They are ugly as ogres. (Ferrie 2010: 127)

It is clear that the government of Burma understands that it may use deprivation of citizenship as a 'key strategy to justify arbitrary treatment and discriminatory policies' (Lewa 2009: 12). Given the wider international context, it is difficult to argue with their conclusion. And yet, of course, one of the main aims of this book is to explore the potential for extending the individual benefits of membership to presently excluded persons. In spite of serious difficulties, UNHCR – with the diplomatic support of other governments (United Kingdom Border Agency 2007: 8) – has persisted in trying to secure individual documentation for Rohingya returnees to Burma. The agreement of the government of Burma in 1995 to issue Temporary Registration Certificates to Rohingya residents and returnees was greeted with cautious optimism by the humanitarian community, with Lewa calling it 'a first step towards citizenship' (Lewa 2009: 13) and the United Kingdom Border Agency (UKBA) claiming it as 'an important first step in terms of recognition by the Burmese authorities [. . . which] gives hope that some may achieve citizenship at a later stage' (United Kingdom Border Agency 2007: 8). According to UNHCR, the document is important in that it 'facilitates the enjoyment of a number of rights for which proof of identity is necessary', including the right to acquire a marriage licence and the right to travel authorisation (UNHCR 2010: 26). In practice, granting of these conditional rights seems to have been subject to the vagaries of state power. Following a crackdown in April 2011, an improvement was reported in July 2011 when 'Muslims in five principal townships in western Burma [. . . were] granted permission by the immigration department to travel freely, providing they carry ID cards' (Noreen 2011). At the very least, the document is individual in character, supplementing the family books from which individual names have been so easy to remove. Nevertheless, the Temporary Registration Certificates are inevitably limited in that they are recognised only in Burma. Indeed, their granting is dependent on the Rohingya remaining in, or returning to, Burma, in spite of considerable evidence of the wider risks of doing so. Human Rights Watch Asia notes several outstanding areas of ambiguity in respect of the documents, although the organisation does concede that their provision should 'be seen as a considerable breakthrough', owing 'much to the efforts of the UNHCR' (HRW 1996). In the end, though, the lack of meaningful and effective recognition of these documents seems to constitute an inevitable limit. Indeed, HRW concludes that the government of Burma has 'the power to rescind them at will, and continue to ignore Rohingyas claims to their rights as full citizens' (Ibid.).

Since 2007, UNHCR has been involved at a logistical level in issuing these certificates (UNHCR 2010: 26). Indeed, those in possession of such certificates were permitted to vote in 2008's constitutional referendum (Lewa 2009: 13). Even so, these certificates lack all of the basic attributes of national status, including nationality, the right to leave and re-enter one's own state and the right to recognition outside one's state as a person before the law. They were also only provided to those who 'agreed' to remain in, or return to, Burma, a point which undermines the ostensible right of non-refoulement provided to legal persons under customary international law. On that basis, Lewa herself finds that there 'is no political will for the Rohingya to be accepted as Burmese citizens in the foreseeable future' (Ibid. p. 13).

The UKBA also acknowledges that there are serious risks associated with the government of Burma's policy of imprisoning returnees who have illegally left the country. In such cases, it urges its own personnel to consider a grant of Humanitarian Protection in the UK for persons in fear of persecution on these grounds (United Kingdom Border Agency 2007: 10–16). The government of Bangladesh has not reached a similar conclusion about the need of the Rohingya, or indeed other Burmese refugees, for international protection. However, in light of the fact that these two countries share a border, Bangladesh's burden weighs far more heavily than that of the UK. Healthy Burma/Bangladesh relations are also arguably more important than Burma/UK relations. One means of attempting to normalise bilateral relations has been the targeted repression of the Rohingya exiles. One camp refugee articulated the understanding of the Rohingya that part of the purpose of crackdowns against them is to 'uphold the bilateral relationship with the Burmese government' (Radio Free Asia 2010). The evidence considered so far in this chapter tends to support this interpretation; in a context where more formal agreement is extraordinarily difficult to achieve, this is not really surprising. Nonetheless, there are two potentially encouraging developments to be considered.

In 2010, UNHCR's country representative in Burma was quoted as saying that the government of Burma 'is looking sympathetically at their legal position, and seeing how to improve it' (cited by IRIN 2010a). The 'possible shift in government policy' is said to reflect 'some political commitment to tackle the situation' (Ibid.). If these hopes develop into something more tangible, it will be interesting to consider the effect of international pressure and of international engagement with the government of Burma. On the ground, Rohingya in Bangladesh – though sometimes critical of UNHCR and others – have explained that in their view, 'the presence of international humanitarian agencies and their expatriate staff in northern Rakhine state is the chief protection they have against the Burmese authorities and border security force' (Shukla and Mailman 2006: 1). It is unlikely that purely unilateral solutions will achieve the kind of changes necessary and, therefore, any engagement with external partners will be important.

The Association of South East Asian Nations (ASEAN) has also put the situation of the Rohingya on the agenda in recent years. At the end of the 2009 summit, ASEAN members agreed to use the Bali process to try to find a solution to the Rohingya crisis. The Bali process 'brings participants together to work on practical measures to help combat people smuggling, trafficking in persons and related transnational crimes' in the region (Bali Process 2011). From the outset, the government of Burma again stated its agreement to accept all those Rohingya who could prove their citizenship (IRIN 2009a). Of course, this constitutes a negligible group. In the absence of more forthcoming commitments, other members of the Bali process were delegated the task of trying to verify the objective situation of the Rohingya. In addition to the general problems with the declaratory approach to status, critical recognition theorists like Rainer Forst have warned of the risks of permissive 'recognition' practices, which can, in practice, lead to 'cultural and social stigmatization, political powerlessness, and dependency' (Forst 2007: 218). The 'repressive and disciplinary effects' of such practices (Ibid. p. 220) are serious obstacles to the achievement of rights in contexts where individuals lack effective relationships with their own and other governments. It will therefore be important to monitor the individual implications of the present attempt to get to grips with the situation by collecting data on the Rohingya (IRIN 2009; 2009b)

More forceful measures have additionally been proposed as a way of dealing with the government of Burma's intransigence. HRW has suggested, for example, making Burma's full membership of ASEAN conditional on its implementation of human rights (HRW 1996). Refugees International has similarly acknowledged that only respect for the rights of the Rohingya in Burma will represent any lasting regional solution to the problem. As they have it, for as long as the Rohingya continue to be persecuted in Burma, they are going to 'continue to leave the country, regardless of their legal status elsewhere' (cited by IRIN 2009). In the opposite direction, the United States has moved from a diplomatic policy of isolation to a policy of greater engagement with the military regime (Ferrie 2010). In the final analysis, however, the Burmese regime has much to lose from loosening its control over citizenship and the electorate. As in the context of Congo, the requirements of democratisation and statehood, in countries with significant minority populations, seem to constitute an understandable – if not justifiable – logic of exclusion. The practical tension is encapsulated in Lynch's observation that, in general, 'statelessness and disputed nationality can only be addressed by the very governments that regularly breach protection and citizenship norms' (Lynch 2005: 1).

III SUMMARY

One of the most worrying lessons to emerge from study of the situation of the Rohingya is about the risks of containment. There seem to be very good reasons to be wary of proposed solutions which assume some objective content to the right of the Rohingya to return to Arakan. Ignoring the vital importance of active government recognition to both domestic and international status is a risky strategy, which has often tended to lead to imprisonment and other forms of effective detention (for example, strict restrictions on movement).

International norms and relationships are vital to understanding membership, including individuality, in the world today. And yet, international relationships of recognition can do harm as well as good. When, at various junctures, the government of Burma has acceded to demands to repatriate the Rohingya, this has had little to do with any new found respect for human rights. In the view of HRW, the decision to accept repatriation in the 1990s 'was a pragmatic move by the SLORC [State Law and Order Restoration Council] to secure membership in the Association of South East Asian Nations (ASEAN), not one made willingly' (HRW 1996). Particular care should therefore be taken in the use of housing grants and other financial incentives for repatriation (Shukla and Thompson 2005: 1), given the underlying importance of a functioning citizen-state relationship. As this book has so far attempted to show, much of what has developed to be of value to individuals about legal personality today entails, at best, a functioning relationship and, at least, the possibility of meaningful exit.

In the last couple of years, some have interpreted the regime's decision to hold elections as a sign that it is willing to take incremental steps toward allowing more political freedom (Ferrie 2010). The wariness of the 1990s still seems valid, however:

> In a country like Burma, which has an appalling human rights record and has shown itself to be remarkably impervious to international criticism, UNHCR is failing to live up to its own responsibilities and protective function by expecting the government to assume 'ultimate responsibility' for the safety of a persecuted minority. The government has shown twice in the past thirty years (1976 and 1991) that it does not want the Rohingyas and that it will only accept them as non-citizens. (HRW 1996)

It is therefore incredibly short-sighted to continue to cling to policies which overlook the legal validity of denationalisations and, hence, fail to recognise statelessness for what it is – an international problem. The EU position that 'the problem came from Myanmar', so 'any resolution should come from Myanmar' (BurmaNet News 2010) is beginning to look increasingly unsustainable.

IV TOWARDS A THEORY OF STATELESSNESS

In the last two chapters, I have wanted to show how attention to statelessness can help the theorist interested in understanding the impact of existing institutions of mutual recognition on individual lives. By looking, therefore, at the ways in which laws, practices and other institutions affect some of the practical membership-type claims that individuals can make, it was anticipated that Chapters 6 and 7 would provide critical insight into the relationship between sovereignty and individual personality. The two empirical chapters aimed also to remain critical in their approach to the conditional value of the state and state system when it comes to individuality.

Chapter 6 demonstrated some of the individual vulnerabilities which arise in the context of state weakness. The ineffectiveness, in particular, of the executive and judicial branches of government in Congo, raises the stakes of inter-group struggles for recognition. The ability of armed groups to gain effective control over practices of documentation and distribution that are generally accepted to be in the gift of the state has been a source of capability and vulnerability for individuals in the country. The narratives which give meaning (Jackson 2007: 495) to these struggles draw on divisive and exclusive conceptions of belonging, even where these have been linked to processes of democratisation. I have argued that this kind of rhetoric is closely connected to the underlying practices of membership, which demand objectivity and certainty about who belongs where. This certainty is always exclusive and never objective; there seems no way to 'fix' the scope of state membership in a way that guarantees meaningful inclusion. Indeed, this kind of approach assumes that there is a clearly identifiable pool of legitimate recipients. On the other hand, it is also problematic to begin with a foundational view of personhood, given the practical importance of recognition to individuality.

One of the main lessons I have taken from the reports of NGOs working on the ground in Eastern Congo and with the Rohingya is about the close practical links between the recognition of effective sovereignty claims and individual status. For the Banyarwanda in Congo and the Rohingya, the absence of group recognition is clearly linked to their statelessness. Their experiences also seem to back up my arguments about the risks of leaving solutions to the state and about the troubling way in which the state system facilitates exclusion. Truth claims seem to be part of the problem, rather than part of the solution, when it comes to statelessness.

Chapter 7 looked broadly at the difficulties of repatriating stateless persons. In particular, it considered the problems associated with looking for 'objective facts' on which repatriations can be based. As both chapters show, objective facts – like time of residence in a country – can easily be rendered practically meaningless. Similarly, documentation of entitlements – found, for example, in the 'family lists' used in Burma – remain subject to political manipulation. One could equally point to the CNDP's manipulation of returnee lists in Eastern Congo. One interesting difference between the two situations is the difference in 'empirical citizenship' (Jackson 2007: 483). In Arakan, Burma, there is no structure like the CNDP's parallel administration in place to provide for the Rohingya; the state remains the sole effective source of meaningful protection. Today, statelessness can be the situation in totalitarian regimes and in 'decaying and weak nation-states' (Benhabib 2002: 540). Engagement with states and statehood is vital in both cases.

As things stand more generally, there seem to be two interesting developments in the practical tension between sovereignty and individuality. First, there have been attempts to formalise the unlawful character of denationalisation. Second, there have been related attempts to formalise the illegality of international movements by stateless persons. The individual implications are varied. Using my framework emphasises the much degraded conception of nationality which is being constructed. The emphasis on illegality, or the refusal to recognise statelessness, works to emphasise nationality, while restricting key aspects of its general content. Without any effective individual right to leave or to recognition outside of one's 'own' state, the state is empowered to seriously mistreat its own nationals. Governments and aspiring governments, therefore, accurately understand that they may use deprivation of citizenship as a strategy for justifying discrimination and the exercise of arbitrary power (Lewa 2009: 12).

There remain, however, residues of validity in denationalisation and in stateless persons' refusal to remain in a state which denies them citizenship. Without recourse to a foundational view of personhood, it is possible to see that even stateless persons are persons. While they lack the attributes of effective personality constituted by state recognition, their undeniable ability to challenge and subvert repatriations demonstrates a claim for political alternatives which cannot be rejected out of hand. While the recent trend seems to have been towards the formalisation of the 'unlawful' character of stateless persons' attempt to exit and re-enter state territory, there remains a tension. UNHCR's acknowledgement of its repatriation mistakes and shift towards activities helping prevent refoulement (UNHCR 2010: 65), as well as the United Kingdom Border Agency's statement about the need for protection of those at risk of detention on the charge of illegal exit, provide some evidence of an opposing norm. While the right to asylum is now more heavily restricted than ever before, there are still arguments and arrangements which validate the right of even stateless individuals to be recognised outside of their state of origin. While there is nothing to be gained from merely asserting the importance of individual rights, there may be communicable ways of exploring the implications of existing tensions and of attempting to counter some of the conditional exclusions.

It has been quite common to use individual rights to argue against denials of membership. On such accounts, part of the unlawful character of denationalisation derives from its individual effects. However, as we have seen, one, probably unintended, consequence of refusing to recognise statelessness has been the restriction of individual recognition. The relationship between sovereignty and individuality is, therefore, far more complex than it first appears. Instead of trying to reconcile this tension, my hope is that we can begin to see as it as an unhelpful way of understanding membership in world politics. The kind of 'quasi-foundational' (Cochran 1999: 170) approach developed in this book might help us think more constructively about statelessness and membership, taking us beyond foundational claims about its invalidity or inevitability, as well as beyond the constraints of oppositional thinking more generally. By rejecting both types of argument, we might be set free to think more critically about the international politics of exclusion.

The practical tension between sovereignty and individuality outlined in Chapter 1 does, of course, still have tangible effects on the lives of millions of stateless people. For these people, neither universal declarations of human rights, nor promises of self-determination seem helpful. At the individual level, it is obvious that the collective basis of membership entitlement in the world today has constitutive limits. It would be easy, therefore, to come to the conclusion that statelessness is unavoidable and discussions of individuality pointless. I have wanted to take seriously the idea that we can avoid this ontological trap from closing down political theory.

The final task of the book is to offer some, inevitably fallible, discussion of the possibility of extending the protection and constitution of individuality in the world today. Guided by acknowledgement of the contingent importance of effective relationships of recognition, Chapter 8 will try to build on the lessons learnt so far about the challenges faced by UNHCR in offering meaningful status, the impossibility of objective determinations of status and the webs of meaning which can render strictly legal (Robinson 1955: 1) accounts of membership fictitious (Weis 1979: 241). The final chapter will need to ensure that it remains in keeping with the bounds of the background theory of membership offered in Chapter 5. In particular, it should aim for communicability in a way that neither defers to existing power, nor makes its own claims to objectivity. We will see in the last chapter what possibility there might be for new or extended relationships of recognition, based on the rather minimalist approach of the book, to membership in world politics.

Chapter 8

RETHEORISING STATELESSNESS

There is one task remaining for this book. In order to address its title, it needs to set out an approach to theorising statelessness. This chapter offers up some admittedly imperfect discussions of statelessness and of the possibility of extending the protection and constitution of individuality in the world today.

The attempt to retheorise statelessness rests on empirical foundations. As I acknowledged in Chapter 5, there is no way for the observer to separate him or herself from the content of his or her empirical observations. Neither is it possible to separate out political and social practices from the norms and narratives which give them meaning. The foundations on which the present theory of statelessness rests are, therefore, inescapably contentious. Nonetheless, they are – I hope – more-or-less acceptable, even if they cannot be upheld as 'settled norms' (Frost 1996: 9). I will offer a brief summary of my quasi-empirical observations here, before moving onto my theoretical reflections on these aspects of statelessness.

Chapters 6 and 7 outlined some of the individual vulnerabilities faced by stateless persons today. In particular, the chapters emphasised the difficulties stateless persons tend to face when trying to leave and/ or remain outside of their 'home' states and the general lack of recognition faced by the stateless. By contrast, Chapter 5 emphasised the centrality of the ostensible 'rights' to recognition, and to leaving and re-entering one's own state, to the international regime governing membership in international relations. I have, therefore, claimed, in the preceding chapters, that there is an important (though limited) constitutive relationship between sovereignty and individuality. The ability of states to identify non-members rests on states' mutual recognition of each other's presumed commitments to their own nationals. However, as we have seen, not all states are inclined, or able, to document the status of long-term stateless residents. There are also limited sanctions available to other states in such cases, although there has been a marked tendency for states to attempt to enforce state-citizen links in cases of statelessness. There is considerable evidence (see Chapters 6 and 7) that this tendency causes injury to individuals. Recognition in the state system is, therefore, constitutive of considerable vulnerability. This vulnerability is rendered problematic by the norms and meanings which are constitutive of individual status, including the widespread practical ability of individuals to leave their own states and, hence, to be recognised in other countries.

I RECOGNITION AND THE STATE

While there is probably no way to reconcile the tensions which remain at the heart of the state system of mutual recognition and which have particular effects on the individual scope of recognition, it is important to try to understand these practical tensions. A particular source of strain is the 'splicing' (O'Neill 2001: 185) of declaratory and constitutive understandings of individuality. Put another way, it is problematic for membership to be conferred or constituted by the state and, yet, based on states' identification of some pre-existing 'special characteristic' (Shachar 2009: 151). It is a contradictory framework and one in which state power to constitute individual status, in fact, dominates. As Krause notes, stateless persons 'induce us to grow fully aware [. . .] of the fact that, in the modern nation state, it is the state that constitutes the citizenry, and not the other way round' (Krause 2008: 338). As I have been arguing throughout this book, however, this does not necessarily require Arendtian pessimism. What it will require is some rethinking about statelessness. I will turn first to the implications for its analytical separation (outlined in Chapter 1) into the categories of *de facto* and *de jure*.

The *de facto/de jure* distinction aims, in part, to differentiate between 'the deprivation of a nationality previously held [. . . and] failure to acquire a given nationality for lack of determining the most effective link' (Batchelor 1998: 179). In practice, the two categories are often blurred. Changes to nationality law, for example, tend to have both retrospective and future-oriented effects. This means that statelessness is an inherited injury and also renders the *de jure/de facto* distinction rather unhelpful. As we have seen, the ability to determine the most effective link between an individual and a given state – that is, to assert a person's status – does not, by itself, confer meaningful status. While the international travel I discussed in Chapter 5 requires possession of a 'high truth-claim' document like a passport (Anderson 2004: 323), such documents are generally conditional on documents such as birth certificates, whose distribution is routinely politicised. The individual recognition which the passport verifies is never quite the embodiment of an objective link or the 'attestation of citizenship' (Ibid. p. 323) which it suggests.[1]

I have been suggesting throughout this book that there may sometimes be good reasons not to revert to pre-existing links. Individual recognition depends on the state, and in places like Congo, it depends on a weak state, whereas in Burma, it is conditional on a state of questionable legitimacy. In both cases and in countless others, the presumption of state legitimacy constitutes and constrains individuality in dangerous ways. The complexities are illustrated by the Palestinian case. While many agree that statehood will be a necessary condition of meaningful status for the Palestinian people, it has recently been argued that it might, in this case, also be problematic to presume statehood of a collective entity which falls 'short of meeting the internationally agreed criteria of statehood' (Goodwin-Gill 2011: 3). The case studies already explored in this book vividly demonstrate the potential risks.

While there are internationally agreed criteria of statehood, this does not make recognition of statehood a straightforward process. If we dig a little deeper, it becomes clear that state recognition itself rests on a practice which makes personality conditional on a confused combination of law and politics, of ostensibly objective criteria and actual recognition. A state's inclusion in the international society of states is argued, in different places, to be conditional on satisfaction of criteria ranging from a permanent population (League of Nations 1933: Article 1) to democratic legitimacy (Sloane 2002: 124). The actual weight of these benchmarks depends, however, on the extent of agreement at any given time and on the concrete recognition of others. For the state, as for the individual, inclusion both depends on, and constitutes, personality or 'statehood':

> Just as some states are not properly so-called despite fulfilling the conventional criteria for statehood, some governments appraised

by contemporary international norms of legitimacy are not properly so-called despite the existence of a state they purport to
govern and the effective control they exercise – often by virtue of
the military – over that state's population. (Ibid. pp. 119–20)

Some states, then, are assumed to have the special trait of statehood as
competence, even where they lack statehood as legitimacy or popular
support (Ibid. p. 124). A very minimum baseline of capability, therefore,
often underlies states' mutual recognition. It is, indeed, widely accepted
that in international relations, the state has a longer and firmer history
of personality than the individual (for example, Brown 2002: 115). In
international law, the declaratory view of statehood, which claims for
the state a pre-political existence, remains 'the predominant view [. . .]
among international law scholars, officials and courts today' (Roth
1999, cited by Sloane 2002: 117). However, given the enormous vari-
ation in states' actual capacities, we cannot escape the conclusion that
recognition has political dimensions (Sloane 2002: 118). State practice
in acknowledging statehood is underpinned by recognition; some
states are granted recognition on what seem like very thin premises,
whereas others are denied inclusion, in spite of meeting normative
criteria of legitimacy.

Those states which are recognised to be competent members of
international society are, of course, assumed – rightly or wrongly – to
exercise some degree of responsibility for their own citizens. The presumptive legitimacy of the state remains a limiting factor when it comes
to individual membership. In the case of the proposal (under consideration at the time of writing) to recognise the statehood of Palestine,
refugee expert Goodwin-Gill has outlined a valid and important
concern with the 'implications for Palestinians at large' (Goodwin-Gill
2011: 3). As Chapters 6 and 7 demonstrated, recognition of statehood
is not a sufficient condition for the achievement of individual personality. One of the risks Goodwin-Gill identifies is that affording greater
recognition to a state without agreed borders would risk voiding the
present acknowledgement that Palestinian refugees are in need of
international protection (Ibid. p. 3). He also questions the legitimacy, in
terms of self-determination and democracy, of the proto-state – whose
recognition is being discussed by the UN at the time of writing (Ibid.
p. 6) – identifying the risks of non-representative states and, hence, the
importance of the 'link between the State [. . .] and the people it claims

to represent' (Ibid. p. 5). International recognition could, ironically, exacerbate existing exclusions and generate new patterns of exclusion. In the light of these observations, it is important to avoid theories which overestimate the scope of norms like self-determination and go on, thereby, to offer unwarranted justifications of a state system in which political forms of recognition, and the basic competencies they require, are constitutive of powers so fundamental to individuality. By overlooking the individual implications of particularism, theorists like Frost and Walzer can end up making presumptions about collective entitlement, which exacerbate the practical exclusions which often result.

These observations also make it necessary to rethink Frost's account of the relationship between individuality, the state and state system and international society. Frost's theory is extremely helpful in its observational starting point that 'we are constituted as the actors we are within social practices' (Frost 2002: 112). Central to his constitutive theory is the claim that, first, the state system and then international society have been constitutive of real reductions in the tensions of recognition and, hence, of real improvements in individual status (Frost 1996: 158). Making this point is necessary for Frost to accept his own background theory as a satisfactory one (Ibid. p. 112): 'It must be shown that it is not the case that the set of citizenship rights created in democratic states undermines or eradicates the rights enjoyed by civilians within civil society' (Ibid. p. 114). I am not sure this can ever be satisfactorily demonstrated. All I aim to do here is throw some light on the contrary tendencies. By letting go of the aim of reconciling different social practices, I have instead claimed that there are situations in which the norms of international society lead to downward spirals of treatment. In today's membership practices, international society piles exclusion upon that which results from the denial of state membership. It does so, in part, because of the immense value it accords to state membership. When international norms sanction deportation and return, they can be seen as trumping the interests of individual states. However, there is no guarantee that those same international norms constitute any improvement in the status of the 'repatriated' individual. In fact, there are countless examples of persons whose status has been considerably degraded by international challenges to state power. This is not really surprising if we take into account the fact that states remain the primary parties to international recognition.

I have been trying to demonstrate, in this book as a whole, that the duty of a state to receive its nationals back is often, in practice, separate from the individual right of residence. While political theory has not always engaged productively with this tension, at least one specialist on statelessness clearly identified what was at stake back in the 1940s. Imagining a body with universal jurisdiction over state membership, Weis argued that:

> It must be realised [. . .] that the decision of an International Court would not, in all cases, give complete redress to the person violated in his rights. A State upon which a person is forced by such a decision whom it does not wish to retain as its national may well seek other means to deprive him of his rights. It is for this reason also that the general prohibition of denationalisation cannot, for the present, be considered as a sufficient means for safeguarding the rights of the individual. (Weis 1944: 23)

As Chapter 2 noted, the idea of facilitating peoples' actual links to states has been quite widely explored within political theory. Walzer, for example, argues that it is morally impermissible to restrict citizenship to a privileged sub-section of residents (for example, Walzer 1982: 61). It can, however, be argued that all attempts to offer pragmatic grounds for the entitlements of resident non-members are 'hopelessly circular' or even contradictory (Shachar 2009: 151), insofar as they are conditional on members' (or, often, governments') identification of precisely that 'special characteristic' which defines and limits inclusion. Shachar wants to argue that it is incoherent to argue that inclusion is both dependent on, and generative of, this special status.

Some theorists, like Shachar, have tried to argue that rights could be (or even should be) based on the ostensibly neutral facts of people's existing connections to given states. The idea of an 'ascending citizenship matrix' (Ibid. p. 171) is one such theory of connection-based entitlement. The 'genuine-connection principle of membership allocation' which Shachar defends (Ibid. p. 171) is, nevertheless, incompatible with the background theory of membership outlined in Chapter 5. It is antagonistic to that background theory, because it imputes objective value to one's connections to a given state. In the vast majority of cases, this may be valid. There are, however, many examples which demonstrate the value of, instead, recognising statelessness. Statelessness today is no longer a condition in which the individual can take refuge (Arendt 1973: 278). Stateless persons have not for a long time found it possible to 'remain where they are and avoid being deported to a "homeland" where they would be strangers' (Ibid. p. 278). However, many stateless persons have understandable reasons for being 'unwilling to return to their countries where they have enjoyed indescribable hardship, where their brothers and sisters have been persecuted and murdered. They have severed the spiritual links with their homeland and have dissociated themselves from it' (Weis 1944: 24). It is therefore still possible to 'exaggerate the conception of nationality as based on a link' (Lauterpacht 1952, cited by Weis 1979: 201). Indeed, as the European Council on Refugees and Exiles claims:

> Although documents provided by UNHCR, such as 'protection letters' or 'persons of concern' letters may establish that a person is in need of protection, they will not suffice to establish that an individual has access to protection that is effective. (Buscher, Lester and Coelho 2005: 35)

The European Council on Refugees and Exile makes an important point here, in respect of the theory/practice gap which limits the effect of unilateral statements about individual needs and interests (or, indeed, other 'fundamental' characteristics of individual personhood). The act of articulating such a contingent need might still, however, be an important step in working towards the implementation of appropriate forms of recognition and, hence, status. Of course, state recognition will be central to this endeavour. As Arendt warned long ago, 'non-national' guarantees of status are weak, when compared to citizenship (Arendt 1973: 292). While there are certain functions which remain the privilege of states as things are organised today, there are others which may be more easily assigned to other actors (see O'Neill 2001). Even so, there is – as we have seen – something fundamental about the kinds of capability constituted by international membership practices.

Indeed, the tension, in practice, between claims to inherent status and the practice of recognition has been shown to make justifications of 'mere' residency rights difficult to argue. Benhabib suggests that we can look to isolate the entitlement to civil rights as itself 'a human right' (Benhabib 2004: 140). She further argues that we can push this agenda, without relying on any foundational claim to truth (Ibid. p. 143).

Instead, we can work on the basis that the human right to member-ship is today 'increasingly incorporated into existing rights regimes through various practices and institutions' (Benhabib 2004: 142). On that basis, she claims that 'the sovereign privilege of naturalization appears increasingly as a relic from a bygone era of statist supremacy' (Ibid. p. 142).

As I mentioned in Chapter 1, Benhabib has been one of those theo-rists concerned with the 'constitutive tension' between sovereignty and individual rights (Benhabib 2004: 365) and with the related question of how we might 'create a network of obligations and imbrications around sovereignty' (Ibid. p. 67). She acknowledges that this must be done – if at all – outside of the context of sovereign authority (Benhabib 2001: 369). This is a social context which, I have argued, includes substantial shared meanings, but excludes recourse to truth. I cannot, therefore, argue, as she does, that 'the sovereign discretion of the democratic community is circumscribed' (Benhabib 2004: 140) and much less that the sovereign discretion of all community is limited. As the reader will by now be aware, I am rather less convinced than Benhabib about the developed scope of a human right to membership, even though it is not desirable to grant states the theoretical power over 'human subjectivity itself' (Heter 2006: 24).

The idea of isolating and emphasising political rights is, nevertheless, a very interesting one, which acknowledges the practical implications of political disenfranchisement. Benhabib's attention to political rights seems, then, to fit well with Arendt's theory of statelessness, which holds that neither:

> physical safety – being fed by some state or private welfare agency – nor freedom of opinion changes in the least their fundamental situation of rightlessness. The prolongation of their lives is due to charity and not to right, for no law exists which could force the nations to feed them; their freedom of movement, if they have it all, gives them no right to residence, which even the jailed crimi-nal enjoys as a matter of course; and their freedom of opinion is a fool's freedom for nothing they think matters anyhow. (Arendt 1973: 296)

In the next section, I aim to show that while Benhabib's emphasis on political rights captures something important about the vulnerability of non-membership, the continuing tension between sovereignty and individuality requires a more international theory. Benhabib wants to argue that political rights or 'the privileges of membership' could – given their importance – be given special emphasis in the attempt to counter exclusion (Benhabib 2001: 379). I do not intend to give full consideration to her argument here, which presumes a distribution influenced by international norms, but implemented within the confines of a (liberal democratic) sovereign state. I will just note that the extension of political rights to non-citizen residents in Congo and Burma is currently extremely unlikely. This is related to a wider difficulty in deriving universal guarantees from particularist sources of entitlement.

Of greater interest in the context of my own framework is Benhabib's discussion of an empirical trend towards the 'disaggregation' of citizenship (Benhabib 2004: 48). The possibilities of disaggregation have also been discussed by O'Neill, who, as we saw in Chapter 4, has suggested that it might make sense to consider 'functional rather than territorial divisions of the tasks of government' (O'Neill 1994: 72). Legal experts on nationality have also recently come to the conclusion that even international law 'would be better served by atomizing the concept by its distinct functions and regulating (or not regulating) nationality at the international level commensurately' (Sloane 2009: 59). If I am right that statelessness is not equivalent to expulsion from humanity altogether, then membership is not best thought of as a zero-sum condition of individuality. State-membership is, as we have seen, neither strictly 'necessary', nor sufficient as a condition of individuality, in spite of the close practical connection between the two. In that case, disaggregation is feasible, at least conceptually.

II GENUINE AND EFFECTIVE LINKS: A CONSTRUCTIVE APPROACH

Benhabib's argument about civil rights, outlined above, relies on an assumption about the scope of rights-claims as effective challenges to state power. This can be seen as part of the wider debate about the power of individuals' 'genuine and effective links' (Weissbrodt and Collins 2006: 276) as a source of rights-claims. Gibney provides an interesting example of when this narrative has been used to protect an individual threatened with deportation to a nominal 'home' state with which he had no meaningful connection (Gibney 2009: 51). In essence, the doctrine holds that 'a person's legal right to citizenship should be operative in the country in which the person is most deeply embedded' (Goris et al. 2009: 6). Within international law, the doctrine of individual, genuine and effective links has, in fact, been used more often as a way of challenging 'bad faith' attempts to invoke the protection of a nominal second nationality (see International Court of Justice 1955; see also, Sloane 2009). Nonetheless, the idea of rights in bad faith – that Sloane outlines in some depth – is an interesting one, which I consider further here. Given my interest in the ways in which laws, practices and institutions construct and deconstruct 'the individual person as a subject' (Douzinas 2007: 7) within the limits which my foundations acknowledge, I want specifically to consider the possibility of extending the idea of 'bad faith' to deconstruct demands that states give stateless persons back their right to residence.

When it comes to the situation of the Banyarwanda in Congo, the Rohingya or of many other stateless persons, repatriation is often a condition of vulnerability. A state which acquiesces in the return of a group deemed to be its ultimate responsibility cannot always be equated with meaningful governmental recognition of that group. Talk, therefore, of 'the right to return' must therefore be careful to avoid bad-faith accounts of the individual implications of international recognition. If one were to take the path outlined by O'Neill, it would be necessary – in the strong sense – for all actors engaged with stateless persons to include them in the scope of ethical consideration (see Chapter 4). In O'Neill's view, to do otherwise is 'ethically disreputable' and manipulative (O'Neill 1996: 107). In my more contingent appropriation of O'Neill, it would only be possible to make a much weaker claim; nonetheless, the more-or-less cosmopolitan scope of international membership norms might – I want to argue – enable us to work towards an implementation of some relations that extend the individual value of membership.

There is, as I have mentioned, at least some legal precedent for the rejection of disingenuous exercises of states' rights. Sloane draws upon jurisprudence to demonstrate the evolving limits on the state's right to naturalise non-members. He demonstrates that it is possible to evaluate a state's exercise of its sovereign right on the basis of its conformity with the protection of a legitimate interest (Sloane 2009: 19). Sloane argues that there can be meaningful grounds for challenging state abuses of rights. A state may abuse a right when it exercises it for a different purpose than that intended by the right's creation (Sloane 2009: 19–20). Of course, there may be no clear agreement on what is to count as a legitimate interest, nor any objective grounds for identifying such interests. Neither can we clearly ascribe intentionality to rights. However, as I have been arguing throughout this book, there are substantive international meanings which include individuals.

While to date, there is no obvious international mechanism which might effectively challenge states' increasing recourse to deportation and repatriation, such acts might, in some cases, be seen as bad-faith invocations of 'the duty of a State to grant its nationals a right of residence and to receive them back in its territory' (Hudson 1953: 10). As we have seen, in many cases, the attempt, therefore, to invalidate statelessness has led to individual injury. At least part of what is at stake in this state right is the individual value of residence, which includes international attributes. It is therefore unhelpful to paint state power over the content of membership out of the picture. And yet, on the other hand, it also seems risky in the absence of internationally guaranteed human rights to seek recognition of statelessness by straightforwardly acknowledging the right of the state to withdraw nationality. There remains a practical tension between these two rights (Hudson 1953: 10; see also, Kuhn 1936: 496; Weissbrodt and Collins 2006: 249). On that basis, it is incredibly important to engage with both, rather than acting on the misguided assumption that the importance of sovereignty (and, hence, of membership) has been eroded. A good faith analysis of contemporary membership, such as that attempted by this book, demonstrates that the network of inter-state rights and recognition as a whole is constitutive of individual benefits and vulnerabilities. Without the ability to build from the ground up, we are left with the more limited task of examining how the plurality which underpins recognition might be amended to provide for alternatives for the excluded.

As this book has demonstrated, the limits of the legal doctrine of 'genuine and effective links' are its possible use to return individuals to 'homes' which are dangerous outright and the residual difficulties of overriding sovereign disavowals of these apparently objective links. For the idea of genuine and effective links to confer tangible benefits on individual stateless persons, there would need to be some effective provision for their ability to leave the state of origin and, hence, for their effective recognition by other states. UNHCR itself now emphasises the importance of these rights, stating that the agency endeavours to 'advocate against the expulsion and detention of stateless people' (UNHCR 2010a: 43) and stating that:

> When an immediate solution for stateless persons may not be possible, it is imperative that a secure status is granted, documentation issued, and human rights are respected. Establishing fair protection and documentation processes is therefore a strategic priority and one of the best means of protecting stateless persons. (Ibid. p. 42)

It is these practical rights which might, I will argue, be disaggregated from the bewildering array of rights often attached to state membership. Of course, my choice here is inescapably arbitrary. Nonetheless, it is based on a reading of contemporary membership practice, which shows why the possibility of alternative residence and of recognition are important and which aims to counter an alternative and much degraded image of membership, which has often been used to legitimise the repatriation of stateless persons to insecure 'homes'.

The book has been discussing the way in which international relations facilitate the exercise of state rights, based on a limited understanding of the meaning of those rights. Specifically, we have seen that states continue to act in ways that void the individual value of recognition practices. State actions in response to statelessness often assume and facilitate a much degraded individual version of nationality. On that basis, it is difficult to see international society as an improvement on other forms of recognition. The background theory of membership offered in this book accepts that there is no way of making any objective judgement about the individual meaning of state recognition or therefore asserting the 'bad faith' character of laws, practices and institutions. However, it retains some scope for contingent theorising and for the discussion of the individual implications of existing frameworks and narratives.

Any concrete moves towards better recognition of statelessness as one of the practical individual consequences of existing membership practice will necessarily involve political negotiation and recognition, as well as legal codification. A 'strictly legal definition of stateless persons which [. . .] is not one of content and quality but simply one of fact' (Batchelor 1998: 173) has been shown to be illusory. A great many stateless persons today are not victims of persecution (Ibid. p. 173), however, as we have seen, manipulations of citizenship are often highly discriminatory. Protection – both from return and from arbitrary and/or discriminatory treatment in the state of residence – remains an important concern for many stateless persons. It is probable, therefore, that protection will take different forms in different cases. In all cases, however, the legal aspect will need to be constructed, rather than asserted or discovered. International practice, in relation to membership, already obtains of widely shared meanings, although these remain underdeveloped when it comes to the construction of individuality. In the absence of any latent authority for the distribution of membership or the identification of any persuasive individual characteristic, these shared international meanings – uneven and open to criticism as they are – may be the best we have to work with.

Any suggestion for how the right to recognition and the right to leave one's country of origin might be extended more fully will also need to take into account the unrealistic burdens placed on weak states and on states bordering illegitimate and oppressive regimes. It will, furthermore, need to avoid over-extending itself. In the chapters leading up to this one, I have begun to suggest that there is contingent, if limited, available knowledge about the present needs of strangers and about the existing value of membership practice which might help us begin this task. The contextual approach that I am required to observe is, of course, intended to avoid at least some of the pitfalls of generalisation. Indeed, it is clear from Chapters 6 and 7 that people can 'share rightlessness despite immense differences in material living conditions, which also depend on the available social networks, and on the degree of regulation in a given society' (Krause 2008: 334).

The last part of this chapter identifies some of the tools which I think will be helpful in conceiving of greater inclusion for stateless persons, in the light of the constraints on theorising acknowledged in the rest of the book. In it, I suggest that we already have means at our disposal which can challenge the partial, limited and, if you like, 'bad faith' accounts of 'genuine and effective' links, without assuming the existence of latent conditions of individuality or providing a justification for the continuation of the state right to withdraw membership.

III TOWARDS RECOGNITION?

As we have seen, the parameters of recognition are not fixed. This implies a degree of flexibility, which makes claims about the objectivity of recognition suspect. The scope for more flexible recognition practice is necessarily limited. However, there is some evidence of the potential for greater inclusion. In a wide-ranging empirical study (Blitz and Lynch 2009), two experts on statelessness provide a range of examples of stateless groups whose exclusion has been mitigated by improved recognition. There is further evidence that denials of recognition can, in fact, motivate struggles for recognition. Again, by avoiding a zero-sum conception of personality, it is possible to conceive of a degree of political agency, in spite of the obvious power granted to the contemporary state. It has been claimed that 'unjustly denied claim[s] to legal recognition' can often animate 'civil recognition' (Sloane 2002: 110). Going back to Chapter 1, the evidence outlined by Blitz and Lynch provides substance to the claims of people like Rancière – that rights are held by those able to 'do something with them to construct a dissensus against the denial of rights they suffer' (Rancière 2004: 305–6).

Obviously, any effective claim to the international recognition which is my focus here will need to work towards 'the provision and recognition of official documentation' (Blitz and Lynch 2009: 102). Mechanisms like the use of local pacification committees (LPCs) in Congo represent an attempt to secure such recognition, which is in keeping with the realities of inclusion in that country. Outside of the domestic context, we can point to UNHCR's acknowledgement of past mistakes and the (limited) willingness of third party states to offer protection to stateless persons. While the legal formalisation of recognition claims is not an infallible safeguard, it is a necessary, but insufficient, condition of the possibility of claiming alternative residence and recognition outside of one's 'own' state. Other attempts to provide documentation, such as the Temporary Registration Certificates provided to the Rohingya, have been much more problematic. I have argued, furthermore, that the possibilities of protection and of alternatives are often explicitly closed off by a range of laws, practices and institutions aimed at the invalidation and non-recognition of statelessness.

Today, as things stand, recognition of statelessness is very limited. In 2004, UNHCR published the findings of an international survey conducted in 2003 (UNHCR 2004a). A 'notable' finding (UNHCR 2004a: 4) was that only 54.1 per cent of states surveyed had measures to identify and protect stateless persons in place. The fact that many states have no mechanisms in place means that 'the actual magnitude of the problem remains unknown' (Ibid. p. 5). The report also finds that some states 'may have avoided problems of statelessness precisely because of the approaches and mechanisms they had in place' (Ibid. p. 4). Various reports point to progress in recognition within the European Union. However, as we might well imagine, given what I have been arguing about recognition, it is important to consider the implications of these practices critically. In Belgium, for example:

> Recognition of statelessness does not have an automatic consequence on the residence status of the stateless person. No particular or privileged residence status is attached to the recognition of statelessness. A stateless person must thus follow the common rules of the Aliens Act. (European Migration Network 2009: 50)

According to the European Migration Network, the result for the individual is that his or her fundamental rights are undermined 'in a discriminatory manner', as a consequence of a lack 'in Belgian legislation which foresees a right of residence to stateless persons' (Ibid. p. 50). Spain, France and Italy are among the EU countries which also have procedures for the recognition of statelessness (Batchelor 2005: 39). In Batchelor's view, the Spanish procedure is favourable, by virtue of its legislative regulation (Ibid. p. 39). Without a clear pathway to residence, any moves towards recognition of statelessness will be unable to provide the kind of meaningful alternatives necessary to improve the individual status of stateless persons. Within the EU, at least, Batchelor notes that the key questions of admission and legal status are generally connected to discussions about the recognition of statelessness (Ibid. p. 42). Outside of Europe, Mexico is also an interesting case study, in terms of the wide recognition of statelessness provided for by a domestic Administrative Order of 2007 (see Equal Rights Trust 2010a: 203).

Batchelor also outlines a range of legal safeguards aimed at ensuring that the individual applicant for residency and, hence, protection from expulsion is treated fairly (Batchelor 2005: 42). These safeguards are linked to the existing rule of law in EU states and would be likely to provide for increased access to documented recognition and the wider international recognition which it underpins. Given the on-going difficulties of constructing international relations of recognition in cases of statelessness (Ibid. p. 40), there are very good reasons to focus on 'normalising' the situation of stateless persons in states where the relevant processes include legal protections against arbitrariness and discrimination. The gaps in Canadian provision for the recognition of stateless persons have also been identified and challenged. Andrew Brouwer – an expert on the rights of non-citizens – has argued that recognition of statelessness in the Canadian context ought to be linked to 'protection of stateless persons' as a category of permanent residency status (Brouwer 2003: 29). His claims here take in to account the 'special hardships faced by stateless persons' (Ibid. p. 29), which are, of course, closely related to international membership norms. Any improvements of this kind will necessarily be piecemeal and limited in scope. They will also confront deeper difficulties in recognising statelessness, which include the considerable difficulties of proving it, especially in the light of states' mutual interest in the exclusion of stateless persons. In many EU countries, it remains the case that 'the burden of proof in establishing statelessness rests on the stateless individual' (Batchelor 2005: 40; see also, Batchelor 1995: 257–8). It is also worth noting that the developed states which are major donors to UNHCR have been reluctant to countenance resettlement, since at least the 1990s (UNHCR 2007: 40).

The need for regional solutions is therefore particularly pressing in those parts of the world most affected by statelessness. UNHCR's role in South-East Asia, for example, is substantially determined by the context on the ground. In Malaysia, for example, the agency is focused on registration, determining refugee status, the provision of documentation and intervention in cases where stateless persons are arrested. However, 'without prospects for return or local integration, UNHCR will boost resettlement as the only available solution for many' (UNHCR 2010c: 51). Advocating for resettlement in the current international climate is not an easy task. And yet, the practical value to individuals of alternative and secure countries of residence cannot be underestimated. As such, any attempt to extend the constitution of individuality today will have to engage with the construction of alternative residence. Within Burma, the agency attests to the difficulty of offering recognition or protection by outlining an alternative focus on development objectives (Ibid. p. 51). Insofar as the repatriation of stateless Rohingya to Burma is seen as a solution, it is one which assumes not only effective state-citizen links, but also, thereby, undercuts the space for international protection and intervention. Linking protection and return is therefore a bad-faith representation of the real individual implications of the framework, which favours return.

In South-East Asia as a whole, UNHCR clearly acknowledges the central role that states play in recognition: 'The cornerstone of the protection strategy is to initiate and promote activities that will lead to increased government ownership of refugee protection, particularly in the areas of access to protection and basic services and registration' (UNHCR 2010c: 52). Statelessness has proved particularly intractable in the Asia-Pacific region, which incorporates Burma (Obi and Engstrom 2001: 13), for reasons partially explored in Chapter 7. In Burma, Bangladesh, Malaysia and Thailand, the prospects for access to protected residence differ from those in the EU. In part, this is because of the far lighter burden on EU states. It will only be through international agreements that this burden, which has devastating individual implications, will be shared. If the difficulties of recognising stateless persons could be overcome, there would be clear benefits for states. Formalising stateless persons' ability to leave their country of residence would enable them to pursue opportunities without being 'warehoused' in camps (Smith 2004: 53). In the view of one expert on refugees, there is, therefore, 'no logical reason why their protection should be limited to countries that happen to border their own' (Ibid. p. 53). If we are, as I urge, to take seriously the idea that statelessness should be recognised, this kind of thinking will need to be extended to the specific cases of stateless persons.

Continuing international oversight will almost certainly be necessary if a commitment to protection – for example, against expulsion and detention – is to be maintained. The Equal Rights Trust is a strong advocate for the importance of this kind of protection. It notes that while states have (often reluctantly) acknowledged a norm against returning refugees to countries where they face threats to life or freedom, 'they have not always taken the next step of recognising the individual as having ineffective nationality – and the need to protect on this basis' (Equal Rights Trust 2010: xv). Where repatriation is likely to degrade the ability of the individual to exercise the basic rights of international personality outlined in Chapter 5, it will be clear that part of what these 'strangers' lack is precisely those capacities which are central to the membership experience of the majority. Neither will it make much sense (or, in the language of Chapter 4, be communicable) for practices of detention to be justified as appropriate responses to the impossibility of deportation (Equal Rights Trust 2010a: 235).

Of course, 'empirical developments alone' cannot 'resolve the normative dilemmas of membership rights' (Benhabib 2004: 143). There also clearly remain significant obstacles to the development of empirical improvements. However, there are some grounds for the hope that international encounters might lead to improvements in the recognition and protection of stateless persons. Even without any recourse to foundational vocabulary, we are able to talk meaningfully about the general need of stateless persons for protection and recognition; for today, the international practice of mutual recognition is such that the denial of protection and recognition constitute serious limits on individuality. We can, as O'Neill suggested, know something about how the lives of distant others would be improved (O'Neill 1996: 115). The attempt to implement any improvement will need to pay attention to the particular situation of the stateless person or group, to the international dimensions of individuality and to the ways in which these sometimes work to limit individual recognition and protection. No political theory which is closed off to the scope of international understandings will be very helpful in understanding contemporary membership or statelessness. As most experts on statelessness agree, 'the involvement of the international community is a necessity', in spite (or because) of the reality that 'most of the international instruments currently addressing issues relative to citizenship or to the denial of citizenship are not effectively binding on States' (Sokoloff 2005: 34). The practical tension first discussed at the very beginning of this book remains problematic to the attempt to theorise greater inclusion. And yet, it need not be a tension which leads us to give up the attempt.

Note

1 Interestingly, the political character of the passport and its documentary prerequisites can be a pathway to inclusion, as much as exclusion (Sadiq 2009: 16).

BIBLIOGRAPHY

Acharya, Jagat M., Manjita Gurung and Ranabir Samaddar (2003), *Chronicles of a No-Where People on the Indo-Bangladesh Border*, New Delhi: South Asia Forum for Human Rights.

Agamben, Giorgio (1998), *Homo Sacer: Sovereign Power and Bare Life*, Stanford, CA: Stanford University Press.

Aleinikoff, T. Alexander (1992), 'State-centred refugee law: from resettlement to containment', *Michigan Journal of International Law*, 14: 1, 120–38.

Amnesty International (2008), *Democratic Republic of Congo: Crisis in North Kivu*, London: Amnesty International.

Amnesty International (2011), *Annual Report 2011 – Rwanda*, London: Amnesty International.

Anderson, Benedict (2004), 'Exodus', *Critical Inquiry*, 20: 2, 314–27.

Arendt, Hannah (1973), *Origins of Totalitarianism*, 5th edition, New York, NY: Harcourt Brace Jovanovich.

Bafilemba, Fidel (2010), *North Kivu: Controversy as Refugee Returns Exacerbate Land Conflicts*, Washington, DC: Enough.

Bafilemba, Fidel and Heaton, Laura (2010), *Saber-Rattling in the Kivus: Rwandan Troops in Walikale*, Washington, DC: Enough.

Bali Process (2011), 'Welcome to the Bali Process', webpage, accessed 23 August 2011. www.baliprocess.net

Balibar, Etienne (1994), *Masses, Classes, Ideas*, Cambridge: Polity.

Barnett, Michael and Finnemore, Martha (2004), *Rules for the World: International Organizations in Global Politics*, Ithaca, NY: Cornell University Press.

Batchelor, Carol A. (1995), 'Stateless persons – some gaps in international protection', *International Journal of Refugee Law*, 7: 2, 232–59.

Batchelor, Carol A. (1998), 'Statelessness and the problem of resolving nationality status', *International Journal of Refugee Law*, 10: 1–2, 156–83.

Batchelor, Carol A. (2005), 'The 1954 Convention relating to the Status of

Stateless Persons: implementation within the European Union member states and recommendations for harmonisation', *Refuge*, 22: 2, 31–58.

Benhabib, Seyla (2001), 'Of guests, aliens, and citizens', in William Rehg (ed.), *Pluralism and the Pragmatic Turn: The Transformation of Critical Theory – Essays in Honour of Thomas McCarthy*, Cambridge, MA: The MIT Press, pp. 361–87.

Benhabib, Seyla (2002), 'Political geographies in a global world: Arendtian reflections', *Social Research*, 69: 2, 539–66.

Benhabib, Seyla (2004), *The Rights of Others: Aliens, Residents and Citizens*, Cambridge: Cambridge University Press.

Bentwich, Norman (1962), 'Human rights and the reduction of statelessness', *Contemporary Review*, 201: 1153, 57–60.

Besch, Thomas M. (2009), 'Kantian constructivism, the issue of scope, and perfectionism: O'Neill on ethical standing', *European Journal of Philosophy*, 19: 1, 1–20.

Bhabha, Jacqueline (2002), 'Internationalist gatekeepers?: the tension between asylum advocacy and human rights', *Harvard Human Rights Journal*, 15, 155–82.

Blitz, Brad and Lynch, Maureen (2009), *Statelessness and the Benefits of Citizenship*, Geneva: Geneva Academy of International Humanitarian Law and Human Rights.

Bloch, Alice and Schuster, Liza (2005), 'At the extremes of exclusion: deportation, detention and dispersal', *Ethnic and Racial Studies*, 28: 3, 491–512.

Borger, Julian (2010), 'Britain expels Mossad agent over forged passport plot', online article, 23 March 2010, accessed 23 August 2011. www.guardian.co.uk/politics/2010/mar/23/israel-mossad-agent-expelled-passport

Bourdieu, Pierre (1990), *In Other Words: Essays Towards a Reflexive Sociology*, Cambridge: Polity.

Brookings Institution (2008), *Index of State Weakness in the Developing World*, Washington, DC: Brookings Institution.

Brouwer, Andrew (2003), *Statelessness in Canadian Context*, Geneva: UNHCR.

Brown, Chris (2002), *Sovereignty, Rights and Justice: International Political Theory Today*, Cambridge: Polity.

Burma Council of State (1982), 'Pyithu Hluttaw Law No. 4 of 1982', *Working Peoples' Daily*, 16 October 1982, Rangoon: Myanmar. www.unhcr.org/refworld/docid/3ae6b4f71b.html.

BurmaNet News (2010), 'EU wants Burma to resolve refugee crisis in Bangladesh', online article, 10 May 2010, accessed 23 August 2011. www.burmanet.org/news/2010/05/10/new-age-bangladesh-eu-wants-burma-to-resolve-refugee-crisis-in-bangladesh/

Burrows, Jo (1990), 'Conversational politics', in Alan Malachowski (ed.), *Reading Rorty*, Oxford: Blackwell, pp. 322–38.

Buscher, Dale, Lester, Eve and Coelho, Patricia (2005), *Guarding Refugee Protection Standards in Regions of Origin*, Brussels: European Council on Refugees and Exiles.

Calder, Gideon (2007), *Rorty's Politics of Redescription*, Cardiff: University of Wales Press.

Chimni, B.S. (2004), 'From resettlement to involuntary repatriation: towards a critical history of durable solutions to refugee problems', *Refugee Survey Quarterly*, 23: 3, 56–73.

Church, Laura Jacqueline (2010), 'The data centre for IDPS in North Kivu', *Forced Migration Review*, 36, 36.

Cochran, Molly (1999), *Normative Theory in International Relations*, Cambridge: Cambridge University Press.

Conway, Daniel (2001), 'Irony, state and utopia', in Matthew Festenstein and Simon Thompson (eds), *Richard Rorty: Critical Dialogues*, Oxford: Blackwell, pp. 55–88.

Cover, Robert (1983), 'The Supreme Court 1982 term foreword: nomos and narrative', *Harvard Law Review*, 97: 1, 4–68.

Deutsche Presse Agentur (2011), 'Bangladesh asks for US help in repatriation of Rohingya Refugees', online article, accessed 23 August 2011. www.burmanet.org/news/2011/06/08/deutsche-presse-agentur-bangladesh-asks-for-us-help-in-repatriation-of-rohingya-refugees/

Donnelly, Jack (2003), *Universal Human Rights in Theory and Practice*, Ithaca, NY: Cornell University Press.

Douzinas, Costas (2000), *The End of Human Rights: Critical Legal Thought at the Turn of the Century*, Oxford: Hart.

Douzinas, Costas (2007), *Human Rights and Empire: The Political Philosophy of Cosmopolitanism*, London: Routledge.

Duffy, Aoife (2008), 'Expulsion to face torture? Non-refoulement in international law', *International Journal of Refugee Law*, 20: 3, 373–90.

Dworkin, Ronald (1981), *Taking Rights Seriously*, London: Gerald Duckworth and Co. Ltd.

Equal Rights Trust (2010), *Unravelling Anomaly: Detention, Discrimination and the Protection Needs of Stateless Persons*, London: Equal Rights Trust.

Equal Rights Trust (2010a), *Trapped in a Cycle of Flight: Stateless Rohingya in Malaysia*, London: Equal Rights Trust.

European Migration Network (2009), *EU and Non-EU Harmonised Protection Statuses in Belgium*, Brussels: European Migration Network, Belgian National Contact Point.

Fern Haber, Honi (1994), *Beyond Postmodern Politics: Selves, Community and the Politics of Difference*, London: Routledge.

Ferrie, Jared (2010) 'South-East Asia', in Preti Taneja (ed.), *State of the World's Minorities and Indigenous Peoples 2010*, London: Minority Rights Group International, pp. 123–37.

Foreign Policy (2011), *The 2011 Failed States Index*, Washington, DC: Foreign Policy.

Forst, Rainer (2007), 'To tolerate means to insult: toleration, recognition, and emancipation', in Bert van den Brink and David Owen (eds), *Recognition and Power: Axel Honneth and the Tradition of Critical Social Theory*, Cambridge: Cambridge University Press, pp. 215–37.

Forsythe, David P. (2001), 'Humanitarian protection: the international committee of the Red Cross and the United Nations High Commissioner for refugees', *International Review of the Red Cross*, 83: 843, 675–98.

Forsythe, David P. (2006), *Human Rights in International Relations*, Cambridge: Cambridge University Press.

Foucault, Michel (2008), *The Birth of Biopolitics: Lectures at the Collège de France, 1978–1979*, Basingstoke: Palgrave Macmillan.

Frost, Mervyn (1986), *Towards a Normative Theory of International Relations*, Cambridge: Cambridge University Press.

Frost, Mervyn (1996), *Ethics in International Relations: A Constitutive Theory*, Cambridge: Cambridge University Press.

Frost, Mervyn (2002), *Constituting Human Rights: Global Civil Society and the Society of Democratic States*, London: Routledge.

Frost, Mervyn (2009), *Global Ethics: Anarchy, Freedom and International Relations*, London: Routledge.

Gearty, Conor (2007), *Essays on Human Rights and Terrorism*, London: Cameron May.

Geschiere, Peter and Stephen Jackson (2006), 'Autochthony and the crisis of citizenship: democratization, decentralization, and the politics of belonging', *African Studies Review*, 49: 2, 1–14.

Gibney, Matthew (2009), 'Statelessness and the right to citizenship', *Forced Migration Review* 39, 50–1.

Goodin, Robert E. (2008), 'What is so special about our fellow countrymen?', in Thom Brooks (ed.), *The Global Justice Reader*, Oxford: Wiley-Blackwell, pp. 263–83.

Goodwin-Gill, Guy S. (2008), 'The politics of refugee protection', *Refugee Survey Quarterly*, 27: 1, 8–23.

Goodwin-Gill, Guy S. (2011), *Opinion Re The Palestine Liberation Organization, the future State of Palestine, and the Question of Popular Representation*, online opinion, accessed 20 September 2011. http://www.jadaliyya.com/pages/index/2530/guy-s.-goodwin-gill-legal-opinion-on-palestinian-s

Goris, Indira, Harrington, Julia and Köhn, Sebastian (2009), 'Statelessness: what it is and why it matters', *Forced Migration Review* 32, 4–6.

Habermas, Jürgen (2000), 'Richard Rorty's Pragmatic Turn', in Robert R. Brandom (ed.), *Rorty and His Critics*, Oxford: Blackwell, pp. 31–55.

Haddad, Emma (2003), 'Refugee protection: a clash of values', *The International Journal of Human Rights*, 7: 3, 1–26.

Harrington, Julia (2005), 'Voiding human rights: citizenship and discrimination in Africa', in Open Society Justice Initiative (ed.), *Human Rights and Justice Sector Reform in Africa: Contemporary Issues and Responses*, New York, NY: Open Society Justice Initiative, pp. 23–8.

Hathaway, James C. (2005), *The Rights of Refugees Under International Law*, Cambridge: Cambridge University Press.

Hege, Steve (2010), 'Of tripartites, peace and returns', *Forced Migration Review*, 36, 51–3.

Heter, T. Storm (2006), 'Authenticity and others: Sartre's ethics of recognition', *Sartre Studies International*, 12 (2), 17–43.

Higgins, Rosalyn (1985), 'The abuse of diplomatic privileges and immunities: recent United Kingdom experience', *The American Journal of International Law*, 79: 3, 641–51.

Honneth, Axel (1996), *The Struggle for Recognition: The Moral Grammar of Social Conflicts*, Cambridge, MA: The MIT Press.

Hovil, Lucy (2008), *The Inter-Relationship Between Violence, Displacement and the Transition to Stability in the Great Lakes Region*, Johannesburg: Centre for the Study of Violence and Reconciliation.

Hudson, Manley O. (1953), *Nationality, Including Statelessness*, New York, NY: United Nations.

Human Rights Watch (HRW) (1996), *Burma: The Rohingya Muslims: Ending a Cycle of Exodus?* Washington, DC: HRW.

Human Rights Watch (HRW) (2009), *Democratic Republic of Congo: "You Will Be Punished": Attacks on Civilians in Eastern Congo*, New York, NY: Human Rights Watch.

Human Rights Watch (HRW) (2009a), *Perilous Plight: Burma's Rohingyas Take to the Seas*, Washington, DC: HRW.

Human Rights Watch (HRW) (2010), *World Report 2009: Democratic Republic of Congo*, Washington, DC: Human Rights Watch.

Hutchings, Kimberly (1999), *International Political Theory: Rethinking Ethics in a Global Era*, London: Sage.

Ikäheimo, Heikki and Arto Laitinen (2007), 'Analyzing recognition: identification, acknowledgement, and recognitive attitudes towards persons', in Bert van den Brink and David Owen (eds), *Recognition and Power: Axel Honneth and the Tradition of Critical Social Theory*, Cambridge: Cambridge University Press, pp. 33–56.

Immigration and Refugee Board of Canada (2008), *Rwanda/Democratic Republic of Congo: Process by which Congolese Nationals of Rwandan Origin can Obtain*

Entitlement to Rwandan Nationality, Ottawa: Immigration and Refugee Board of Canada.

Integrated Regional Information Networks (IRIN) (2008), *Bangladesh-Myanmar: Bleak Prospects for the Rohingya*, Cox's Bazar: UN Office for the Coordination of Humanitarian Affairs.

Integrated Regional Information Networks (IRIN) (2009), *Bangladesh: Some 1,000 Rohingyas Evicted from Makeshift Huts*, Dhaka: UN Office for the Coordination of Humanitarian Affairs.

Integrated Regional Information Networks (IRIN) (2009a), *Asia: Regional Approach to Rohingya Boat People*, Hua Hin: UN Office for the Coordination of Humanitarian Affairs.

Integrated Regional Information Networks (IRIN) (2009b), *Myanmar: Key Asian Meeting Fails to Resolve Rohingya Issue*, Bangkok: UN Office for the Coordination of Humanitarian Affairs.

Integrated Regional Information Networks (IRIN) (2010), *Bangladesh: Rohingya Humanitarian Crisis Looms*, Kutupalong: UN Office for the Coordination of Humanitarian Affairs.

Integrated Regional Information Networks (IRIN) (2010a), *Myanmar: Tentative Steps Towards Rohingya Rehabilitation*, Rangoon: UN Office for the Coordination of Humanitarian Affairs.

Integrated Regional Information Networks (IRIN) (2011), *Bangladesh: New ID Card Policy Could Hit Rohingya Asylum-Seekers*, Dhaka: UN Office for the Coordination of Humanitarian Affairs.

International Conference of American States (1933), *The Montevideo Convention on the Rights and Duties of States*, Montevideo: International Conference of American States.

International Court of Justice (1955), *Nottebohm Case (Liechtenstein v. Guatemala), Second Phase*, The Hague: International Court of Justice.

International Crisis Group (2010), *DR Congo: Why is There Still a Kivu Problem?* Brussels: International Crisis Group.

International Crisis Group (2010a), *Congo: No Stability in Kivu despite Rapprochement with Rwanda*, Brussels: International Crisis Group.

International Refugee Rights Initiative (2010), *Who Belongs Where? Conflict, Displacement, Land and Identity in North Kivu, Democratic Republic of Congo*, New York, NY: International Refugee Rights Initiative.

International Refugee Rights Initiative (2011), *Shadows of Return: The Dilemmas of Congolese Refugees in Rwanda*, New York, NY: International Refugee Rights Initiative.

Jackson, Stephen (2006), 'Sons of which soil? The language and politics of autochthony in Eastern D. R. Congo', *African Studies Review*, 49: 2, 95–123.

Jackson, Stephen (2007), 'Of "doubtful nationality": political manipulation of citizenship in the D. R. Congo', *Citizenship Studies*, 11: 5, 481–500.

Jacquemot, Pierre (2010), 'The dynamics of instability in eastern DRC', *Forced Migration Review*, 36, 6–7.

Keohane, Robert O. (1986), 'Reciprocity in international relations', *International Organization*, 40: 1, 1–27.

Krause, Monika (2008), 'Undocumented migrants: an Arendtian perspective', *European Journal of Political Theory*, 7: 3, 331–48.

Kuhn, Arthur K. (1936), 'International measures for the relief of stateless persons', *The American Journal of International Law*, 30: 3, 495–99.

Lange, Maria (2010), 'Refugee return and root causes of conflict', *Forced Migration Review*, 36, 48–9.

Lattimer, Mark (2011), 'Reference section including peoples under threat 2011', in Joanna

Hoare (ed.), *State of the World's Minorities and Indigenous Peoples 2011*, London: Minority Rights Group International, pp. 231–60.

League of Nations (1933), *Montevideo Convention on the Rights and Duties of States*, New York, NY: United Nations.

Lewa, Chris (2008), 'Asia's new boat people', *Forced Migration Review*, 30, 140–2.

Lewa, Chris (2009), 'North Arakan: an open prison for the Rohingya in Burma', *Forced Migration Review*, 32, 11–13.

Lynch, Maureen (2005), *Lives on Hold: The Human Cost of Statelessness*, Washington, DC: Refugees International.

Malkki, Liisa H. (1996), 'Speechless emissaries: refugees, humanitarianism, and dehistoricization', *Cultural Anthropology*, 1: 3, 377–404.

Mamdani, Mahmood (1998), *Understanding the Crisis in Kivu: Report of the CODESRIA Mission to the Democratic Republic of Congo*, Cape Town: Centre for African Studies.

Mamdani, Mahmood (2002), 'African states, citizenship and war: a case-study', *International Affairs*, 78: 3, 1493–506.

Manby, Bronwen (2009), *Struggles for Citizenship in Africa*, London: Zed Books.

McCarthy, Thomas (1990), 'Ironist theory as a vocation: a response to Rorty's reply', *Critical Inquiry*, 16: 3, 644–55.

McGreal, Chris (2008), 'The roots of war in Eastern Congo', online article, accessed 23 August 2011. www.guardian.co.uk/world/2008/may/16/congo

Médecins Sans Frontières (2002), *10 Years for the Rohingya Refugees in Bangladesh: Past, Present and Future*, Amsterdam: Médecins sans Frontières.

Minorities at Risk Project (2006), *Assessment for Tutsis in the Democratic Republic of Congo*, College Park, MD: University of Maryland.

Minorities at Risk Project (2006a), *Assessment for Rohingya (Arakanese), in Burma*, College Park, MD: University of Maryland.

Morris, Nicholas (2007), 'Prisons of the stateless: a response to New Left Review', New Issues in Refugee Research, 141 (March), 1–7.

Mun Ching, Yap (2002), 'No Asylum: Burmese in Malaysia', online article, accessed 23 August 2011. www.irrawaddy.org/article.php?art_id=2650&page=1

Mun Ching, Yap (2004), 'Rohingya discontent troubles Malaysia', online article, accessed 23 August 2011. www.irrawaddy.org/opinion_story.php?art_id=3828&page=1

Noreen, Naw (2011), *Travel Restrictions for Muslims Loosened*, Oslo: Democratic Voice of Burma.

Nyers, Peter (2006), *Rethinking Refugees: Beyond States of Emergency*, New York, NY: Routledge.

Nzongola-Ntalaja, Georges (2004), 'Citizenship, political violence, and democratization in Africa', *Global Governance*, 10: 4, 403–9.

Obi, Naoko and Engstrom, Marcus (2001), *Evaluation of UNHCR's Role and Activities in Relation to Statelessness*, Geneva: UNHCR Evaluation and Policy Analysis Unit.

Office of the High Commissioner for Human Rights (OHCHR) (2006), *The Rights of Non-Citizens*, New York, Geneva: OHCHR.

O'Neill, Onora (1979), *Faces of Hunger: An Essay on Poverty, Justice and Development*, Oxford: Oxford University Press.

O'Neill, Onora (1988), 'Ethical reasoning and ideological pluralism', *Ethics*, 98: 4, 705–22.

O'Neill, Onora (1989), *Constructions of Reason: Explorations of Kant's Practical Philosophy*, Cambridge: Cambridge University Press.

O'Neill, Onora (1993), 'Duties and virtues', *Royal Institute of Philosophy Supplement*, 35, 107–20.

O'Neill, Onora (1994), 'Justice and boundaries', in Chris Brown (ed.), *Political Restructuring in Europe: Ethical Perspectives*, London: Routledge, pp. 69–88.

O'Neill, Onora (1996), *Towards Justice and Virtue: A Constructive Account of Practical Reasoning*, Cambridge: Cambridge University Press.

O'Neill, Onora (2000), *Bounds of Justice*, Cambridge: Cambridge University Press.

O'Neill, Onora (2000a), 'Bounded and cosmopolitan justice', *Review of International Studies Special Issue*, 26: Special Issue, 45–60.

O'Neill, Onora (2001), 'Agents of justice (international justice)', *Metaphilosophy*, 32: 1–2, 180–95.

O'Neill, Onora (2001a), 'Practical principles and practical judgment', *The Hastings Centre Report*, 31: 4, 15–23.

O'Neill, Onora (2003), 'Autonomy: the emperor's new clothes', *Aristotelian Society Supplementary Volume*, 77: 1, 1–21.

Open Society Justice Initiative (2004), *Racial Discrimination and the Rights of Non-Citizens*, New York, NY: Open Society Justice Initiative.

Open Society Justice Initiative (2007), *More Primitive than Torture: Statelessness and Arbitrary Denial of Citizenship in Africa - A Call to Action*, Kampala: Open Society Justice Initiative.

Orend, Brian (2000), *Michael Walzer on War and Justice*, Cardiff: University of Wales Press.

Pin-Fat, Véronique (2009), *Universality, Ethics and International Relations*, London: Routledge.

Radio Free Asia (2010), *Bangladesh: Rohingya Beaten, Deported*, Bangkok: Radio Free Asia.

Rancière, Jacques (2004), 'Who is the subject of the rights of man?', *The South Atlantic Quarterly*, 103: 2/3, 297–310.

Raymond, Baptiste (2010), 'Land, IDPs and mediation', *Forced Migration Review*, 36, 20–1.

Refugees International (2008), *Rohingya: Burma's Forgotten Minority*, Washington, DC: Refugees International.

Refugees International (2010), *DR Congo: Unstable Areas Endanger Returns*, Washington, DC: Refugees International.

Refugees International (2011), *Bangladesh: The Silent Crisis*, Washington, DC: Refugees International.

Rice, Susan E. and Patrick, Stewart (eds) (2008) *Index of State Weakness in the Developing World*, Washington, DC: Brookings Institution.

Robinson, Nehemiah (1955), *Convention Relating to the Status of Stateless Persons: Its History and Interpretation*, New York, NY: World Jewish Congress.

Rorty, Richard (1982), *Consequences of Pragmatism: Essays, 1972–1980*, Minneapolis, MN: University of Minnesota Press.

Rorty, Richard (1983), 'Postmodernist bourgeois liberalism', *The Journal of Philosophy*, 80: 10, 583–9.

Rorty, Richard (1987), 'The priority of democracy to philosophy', in Merrill D. Peterson and Robert C. Vaughan (eds), *The Virginia Statute of Religious Freedom: Its Evolution and Consequences in American History*, Cambridge: Cambridge University Press, pp. 257–82.

Rorty, Richard (1989), *Contingency, Irony and Solidarity*, Cambridge: Cambridge University Press.

Rorty, Richard (1990), 'The priority of democracy to philosophy', in Alan R. Malachowski (ed.), *Reading Rorty: Critical Responses to Philosophy and The Mirror of Nature and Beyond*, Oxford: Blackwell, pp. 279–302.

Rorty, Richard (1992), *Contingency, Irony and Solidarity*, New York, NY: Basic Books.

Rorty, Richard (ed.) (1998), 'Human rights, rationality, and sentimentality', in *Truth and Progress: Philosophical Papers Volume 3*, Cambridge: Cambridge University Press, pp. 167–85.

Rorty, Richard (1999), *Philosophy and Social Hope*, London: Penguin.

Rorty, Richard (2000), 'Universality and truth', in Robert R. Brandom (ed.), *Rorty and His Critics*, Oxford: Wiley-Blackwell, pp. 1–30.

Rorty, Richard (2002), 'Religion in the public sphere', *Journal of Religious Ethics*, 31: 1, 141–9.

Rubinstein, J. L. (1936), 'The refugee problem', *International Affairs*, 15: 5, 716–34.

Sadiq, Kamal (2009), *Paper Citizens: How Illegal Immigrants Acquire Citizenship in Developing Countries*, Oxford: Oxford University Press.

Salter, Mark B. (2004), 'Passports, mobility, and security: how smart can the border be?', *International Studies Perspectives*, 5: 1, 71–91.

Schaap, Andrew (2011), 'Enacting the right to have rights: Jacque Rancière's critique of Hannah Arendt', *European Journal of Political Theory* 10: 1, 22–45.

Sciortino, Rosalia (2009), 'Rohingya status needs careful definition', online opinion, 26 January 2009, accessed 23 August 2011. www.irrawaddy.org/opinion_story.php?art_id=14991&page=1

Shachar, Ayelet (2009), *The Birthright Lottery: Citizenship and Global Inequality*, Cambridge, MA: Harvard University Press.

Shukla, Kavita and Nicole Mailman (2006), *The Rohingya: Discrimination in Burma and Denial of Rights in Bangladesh*, Washington, DC: Refugees International.

Shukla, Kavita and Larry Thompson (2005), *Bangladesh: Burmese Rohingya Refugees Virtual Hostages*, Washington, DC: Refugees International.

Sloane, Robert D. (2002), 'The changing face of recognition in international law: a case study of Tibet', *Emory International Law Review*, 16: 1, 107–86.

Sloane, Robert D. (2009), 'Breaking the genuine link: the contemporary international legal regulation of nationality', *Harvard International Law Journal*, 50: 1, 1–60.

Smith, Merrill (2004), 'Warehousing refugees: a denial of rights, a waste of humanity', in UNHCR (ed.), *World Refugee Survey*, Geneva: UNHCR, pp. 38–56.

Smith, Nicholas H. (2005), 'Rorty on religion and hope', *Inquiry*, 48: 1, 76–98.

Sokoloff, Constantin (2005), *Denial of Citizenship: A Challenge to Human Security*, New York, NY: United Nations Advisory Board on Human Security.

Stevens, Jacob (2006), 'Prisons of the stateless: the derelictions of UNHCR', *New Left Review*, 42: 276, 53–67.

Sutch, Peter (2006), *Ethics, Justice and International Relations*, London: Routledge.

UNHCR (1995), *Note on UNHCR and Stateless Persons*, Geneva: UNHCR.

UNHCR (2004), *Resettlement Handbook*, Geneva: UNHCR.

UNHCR (2004a), *Final Report Concerning the Questionnaire on Statelessness Pursuant to the Agenda for Protection*, Geneva: UNHCR.

UNHCR (2007), *Statistical Yearbook 2006*, Geneva: UNHCR.

UNHCR, (2009), *Statelessness: An Analytical Framework for Prevention, Reduction and Protection*, Geneva: UNHCR.

UNHCR (2010), *Global Trends 2010*, Geneva: UNHCR.

UNHCR (2010a), 'Introduction: addressing statelessness', in *Global Appeal 2010–11*, Geneva: UNHCR, pp. 40–3.

UNHCR (2010b), 'Central Africa and the Great Lakes: subregional overview', in *Global Appeal 2010–11*, Geneva: UNHCR, pp. 2–5.

UNHCR (2010c), 'South-East Asia: subregional overview', in *Global Appeal 2010–11*, Geneva: UNHCR, pp. 50–3.

UNHCR (2011), 'Annex: populations of concern', in *Global Appeal 2010–2011*, Geneva: UNHCR, pp. 112–13.

UNHCR (2011a), 'Introduction: addressing statelessness', in *Global Appeal 2011 Update*, Geneva: UNHCR, pp. 44–7.

UNHCR (2011b), 'Stateless people: searching for citizenship', online webpage, accessed 2 September 2011. www.unhcr.org/pages/49c3646c155.html

UNHCR (2011c), 'Country operations profile – bangladesh', *UNHCR*, online webpage, accessed 23 August 2011. www.unhcr.org/cgi-bin/texis/vtx/page?page=49e4875463.

United Kingdom Border Agency (2007), *Operational Guidance Note: Burma*, London: United Kingdom Border Agency.

United Kingdom Border Agency (2008), *Operational Guidance Note: Democratic Republic of Congo*, London: United Kingdom Border Agency.

United Nations (1948), *Universal Declaration of Human Rights*, New York, NY: United Nations.

United Nations (1949), *A Study of Statelessness*, Lake Success, NY: United Nations.

United Nations (1954), *Convention Relating to the Status of Stateless Persons*, New York, NY: United Nations.

United Nations (1961), *International Covenant on Civil and Political Rights*, New York, NY: United Nations.

United Nations (1965), *International Convention on the Elimination of all Forms of Racial Discrimination*, New York, NY: United Nations.

United Nations (1966), *International Covenant on Civil and Political Rights*, New York, NY: United Nations.

United Nations (1979), *Convention on the Elimination of All Forms of Discrimination Against Women*, New York, NY: United Nations.

United Nations (1989), *Convention on the Rights of the Child*, New York, NY: United Nations.

United Nations (1999), *ICCPR General Comment No. 27: Freedom of Movement (Article 12)*, New York, NY: United Nations.

US Department Of State (2009), *2009 Human Rights Report: Democratic Republic of Congo*, Washington, DC: US Department of State.

US Department Of State (2010), *Reciprocity by Country*, Washington, DC: US Department of State.

US Department of State (2011), 'Visas: reciprocity by country', online webpage, accessed 23 August 2011. www.travel.state.gov/visa/fees/fees_3272.html

United States Supreme Court (1958), *Judgment of the Court: Trop v. Dulles*, Washington, DC: US Supreme Court.

Van Gunsteren, Herman Robert (1988), 'Admission to citizenship', *Ethics*, 98: 4, 731–41.

Vlassenroot, Koen (2002), 'Citizenship, identity formation & conflict in South Kivu', *Review of African Political Economy*, 29: 93/94, 499–515.

Walker, Dorothy Jean (1981), 'Statelessness: violation or conduit for violation of human rights?', *Human Rights Quarterly*, 3: 1, 106–23.

Walker, R. J. B. (1993), *Inside/Outside: International Relations as Political Theory*, Cambridge: Cambridge University Press.

Walzer, Michael (1970), *Obligations: Essays on Disobedience, War and Citizenship*, Cambridge, MA: Harvard University Press.

Walzer, Michael (1977), *Just and Unjust Wars: A Moral Argument with Historical Illustrations*, New York, NY: Basic Books.

Walzer, Michael (1980), 'The moral standing of states: a response to four critics', *Philosophy and Public Affairs*, 9: 3, 209–29.

Walzer, Michael (1982), *Spheres of Justice: A Defense of Pluralism and Equality*, Oxford: Oxford University Press.

Walzer, Michael (1984), 'Liberalism and the art of separation', *Political Theory*, 12: 3, 315–30.

Walzer, Michael (1985), Interpretation and Social Criticism, in *The Tanner Lectures on Human Values*, Cambridge, MA: Harvard University, pp. 4–80.

Walzer, Michael (1986), 'The reform of the international system', in Øyvind Østerud (ed.), *Studies of War and Peace*, Oslo: Norwegian University Press, pp. 227–40.

Walzer, Michael (1989), 'Nation and universe', in *The Tanner Lectures on Human Values*, Oxford: Brasenose College, Oxford University, pp. 509–56.

Walzer, Michael (1990), 'The communitarian critique of liberalism', *Political Theory*, 18: 1, 6–23.

Walzer, Michael (1993), 'Objectivity and social meaning', in Martha Nussbaum (ed.), *The Quality of Life*, Oxford: Clarendon Press, pp. 165–77.

Walzer, Michael (1994), *Thick and Thin: Moral Argument at Home and Abroad*, Notre Dame, IN: Notre Dame University Press.

Walzer, Michael (1995), 'Response', in Michael Walzer and David Miller (eds), *Pluralism, Justice and Equality*, New York, NY: Oxford University Press, pp. 281–97.

Walzer, Michael (1997), *On Toleration: The Castle Lectures in Ethics, Politics and Economics*, New Haven, CT: Yale University Press.

Walzer, Michael (2004), *Arguing about War*, New Haven, CT: Yale University Press.

Weis, Paul (1944), *Statelessness as a Legal-Political Problem*, London: World Jewish Congress, British Section.

Weis, Paul (1961), 'The Convention relating to the Status of Stateless Persons', *The International and Comparative Law Quarterly*, 10: 2, 255–64.

Weis, Paul (1979), *Nationality and Statelessness in International Law*, 2nd edition, Alphen aan denj Rijn: Sijthoof and Noordhoff.

Weissbrodt, David P. (2008), *The Human Rights of Non-Citizens*, Oxford: Oxford University Press.

Weissbrodt, David P. and Clay Collins (2006), 'The human rights of stateless persons', *Human Rights Quarterly*, 28: 1, 245–76.

Yan Naing, Saw (2011), 'Thailand ignores calls for UN access to Rohingyas', online article, accessed 23 August 2011. www.irrawaddy.org/article.php?art_id=20664

Zetter, Roger (2007), 'More labels, fewer refugees: remaking the refugee label in an era of globalization', *Journal of Refugee Studies*, 20: 2, 172–92.

INDEX